Get the eBooks FREE!

(PDF, ePub, Kindle, and liveBook all included)

We believe that once you buy a book from us, you should be able to read it in any format we have available. To get electronic versions of this book at no additional cost to you, purchase and then register this book at the Manning website.

Go to https://www.manning.com/freebook and follow the instructions to complete your pBook registration.

That's it!
Thanks from Manning!

Reactive Application Development

DUNCAN DEVORE
SEAN WALSH
BRIAN HANAFEE

MANNING
SHELTER ISLAND

For online information and ordering of this and other Manning books, please visit
www.manning.com. The publisher offers discounts on this book when ordered in quantity.
For more information, please contact

Special Sales Department
Manning Publications Co.
20 Baldwin Road
PO Box 761
Shelter Island, NY 11964
Email: orders@manning.com

Manning Publications Co.
20 Baldwin Road
PO Box 761
Shelter Island, NY 11964

Development editor:	Susanna Kline
Review editor:	Aleksandar Dragosavljević
Technical development editor:	Mark Elston
Project editor:	David Novak
Copyeditor:	Kathy Simpson
Proofreader:	Alyson Brener
Technical proofreader:	William Wheeler
Typesetter:	Marija Tudor
Cover designer:	Leslie Haimes

ISBN 9781617292460
Printed in the United States of America
1 2 3 4 5 6 7 8 9 10 – DP – 23 22 21 20 19 18

To my wife, Patty
— Brian

To my family,
Duncan, Jordan, Noah, Mckenna, and William
— Duncan

To particularly difficult client challenges
that encouraged thinking outside the box
— Sean

contents

v

foreword

In the past five years, we have seen reactive progress from a virtually unacknowledged technique used only by fringe projects within a select few corporations to part of the overall platform strategy of numerous big players in many fields, including middleware, financial services, retail, social media, and betting/gaming. Its use has moved beyond early adopters and distributed-systems experts; today, it's the foundation of some of the most interesting emerging technologies, including cloud computing, microservices, streaming/fast data, and the Internet of Things.

The Reactive Manifesto—which I helped co-author in 2013—defines reactive as a set of architectural design principles that are geared to meeting the demands that systems face today and tomorrow. These principles aren't new but can be traced back to the 1970s and 1980s and to the groundbreaking work by Jim Gray and Pat Helland on the Tandem System and by Joe Armstrong and Robert Virding on Erlang. These pioneers were ahead of their time, however; it wasn't until the past 5 to 10 years that the technology industry at large was forced to rethink current best practices for enterprise system development and to apply the hard-won knowledge of reactive principles to today's world of distributed systems and multicore architectures.

I think that this learning experience—running into the limitations and constraints of traditional system design; being forced to challenge, rethink, and relearn current practices; and eventually reaping the benefits of a reactive design—is probably how Duncan, Sean, and Brian would describe their journey. I met Duncan and Sean in 2012, when they were working at a startup in Philadelphia and building a product in the smart energy space, allowing customers to reduce their energy costs by interacting proactively with the electric grid. They were about a year into development of the platform, which they had built on Akka, following the principles of reactive systems, and were in the middle of building out their persistence story by using Event Sourcing and CQRS. I remember how enthusiastic they were, and their passion was contagious. Later, Sean and Duncan joined Lightbend, where they've helped many customers around the world build highly concurrent, resilient, and elastic systems by using reactive design principles.

This book makes it clear that the authors have been there, getting their hands dirty, learning by doing. The book is packed with hard-won wisdom and practical advice that will set you on the path toward effective reactive application development. Along the way, you learn how bounded contexts, domain events, futures, actors, streaming, and Event Sourcing/CQRS compose into highly responsive, scalable, and available systems while keeping complexity under control. The book is a working book, and you have a lot of work in front of you. If you put in the hours, you'll be rewarded in spades.

I hope you'll enjoy the ride. I know I did.

—JONAS BONÉR
FOUNDER AND CHIEF TECHNOLOGY OFFICER
OF LIGHTBEND, CREATOR OF AKKA

preface

Duncan and Sean had various Internet of Things (IoT) problems back in 2011 and realized that the typical application architectures weren't going to work for them. They needed to look into other options, which led them to discovering Akka, as well as embracing concepts of domain-driven design, Command Query Responsibility Segregation (CQRS), and Event Sourcing. In embracing these concepts, they were able to concentrate on their challenging business problems and enjoyed an architecture that worked as well for 1,000 transactions a day as it did for 1 billion.

After enjoying some early successes, they quickly realized that reactive Akka applications would be the wave of the future and that scale and IoT would grow proportionately over time. Sean had already been in contact with Manning and had been working on book reviews for the company. With this relationship already in place, Duncan thought that he and Sean should write this book. Reactive architectures did become hot—so much so that Duncan and Sean became very busy and stayed that way. Sean founded Reactibility and quickly took on Weight Watchers' digital transformation as chief architect of the effort. Duncan, realized his dream of joining Lightbend (then named Typesafe). Finding time to write was a challenge, and they were lucky that Brian joined them to get the book finished.

The world of reactive evolved while this book was being written, but we think that the ideas are still sound; they're being embraced by many Fortune 500 companies, including IBM, which has made a large investment in Akka technologies as well as in Lightbend. We were able to include newer subjects such as streaming and Lightbend's Lagom microservice framework to keep the book fresh.

The book covers everything that a developer needs to understand to build, deploy, and test a reactive application. Akka is the backbone of the programming model, and we prefer the Scala language for its conciseness and functional beauty, but Akka works just as well with Java. In fact, most new programmers who are discovering Akka these days are using Java.

acknowledgments

The authors gratefully acknowledge the help of technical proofreader William Wheeler and technical development editor Mark Elston, along with the staff at Manning, who did an outstanding job pushing this project to completion. We'd also like to thank the many reviewers who gave their time and expertise to make this book better: Adrian Bilauca, Amr Gawish, Arun Noronha, Christian Bach, Hugo Sereno Ferreira, Jean-François Morin, John Schwitz, Jürgen De Commer, Shabesh Balan, Subhasis Ghosh, Sven Loesekann, Thomas Lockney, and William E. Wheeler.

Brian thanks his wife, Patty, for supporting and encouraging him through the long and arduous process of writing a second book. He also thanks his children for understanding the time that went into this project. Finally, he thanks the many speakers and organizers who make the San Francisco Bay Area a vibrant and educational community for developers and the curious.

Duncan thanks his children for understanding the long process of being an author. In addition, he thanks the many folks at Lightbend—specifically, Jonas, Roland, and Viktor—for being such an important part of his career.

about this book

This book is intended to introduce experienced developers to reactive applications using the actor model. Readers should be familiar with traditional model-view-controller (MVC) design and have some understanding of its strengths as well its weaknesses. Ideally, readers have seen what happens as traditional MVC design is stretched to its performance and reliability limits and begins to fail.

Who should read this book

If you've come to realize that building a distributed system that runs reliably in the real world is vastly more difficult than drawing one on a whiteboard, *Reactive Application Development* is for you. Reactive applications use actors to scale smoothly and handle failure gracefully. Read this book to get started with the actor model, and learn how to work with concurrency by using messages instead of fighting it with threads and locks.

To get the most out of this book, you should have some knowledge of Scala or Java. The examples are written in Scala, with some of the most difficult concepts being explained along the way. Some experience with concurrency concepts such as synchronized methods and multiple threads will be helpful, as will some experience making remote calls to REST services.

How this book is organized: a road map

This book is written in two parts. The first part consists of three chapters that delve into factors that can prevent your application from taking advantage of the power offered by modern high-performance servers:

- Chapter 1 breaks down a traditional application and shows why more servers sometimes make performance worse. It describes the properties of an application that avoids these limits.
- Chapter 2 is a fast-paced introduction to the Akka toolkit. It starts with a simple example that runs in a single process; with a few small changes, the example transforms into a flexible architecture that spans multiple servers.
- Chapter 3 examines the workings of the toolkit and addresses handling failure gracefully.

The second part steps you through the process of building a reactive application, interweaving the practical aspects of Akka, reactive streaming and production readiness, and the theoretical, such as domain-driven design and Command Query Responsibility Segregation:

- Chapter 4 illustrates domain-driven design by mapping a domain onto an actor model, including translating some features to behavior of the toolkit rather than things you have to write yourself.
- Chapter 5 solidifies your understanding of domain-driven design by formalizing key concepts and useful patterns.
- Chapter 6 turns to a more concrete programming example, using remote actors to demonstrate how working with asynchronous peers is different from traditional service call-and-response.
- Chapter 7 discusses streams and the role of backpressure, and examines the Reactive Streams API for interoperability among reactive implementations.
- Chapter 8 addresses the difficult topic of working with persistent data, as well as the roles of commands and events in your design using the CQRS pattern.
- Chapter 9 covers alternatives for exposing your reactive services so that they can be consumed by external clients.
- Chapter 10 puts you on the path to production-readiness with brief discussions of testing patterns, application security, logging, tracing, monitoring, configuration, and packaging.

You should read the first part to understand why reactive design is important, examine a simple reactive application with real code, and get an overview of the actor model and how it's implemented by Akka. Read chapters 4 and 5 together to see how to map a domain-driven design onto the actor model. The remaining chapters may be read in any order.

About the code

This book contains many examples of source code, both in numbered listings and inline with normal text. In both cases, source code is formatted in a `fixed-width font like this` to separate it from ordinary text. Sometimes, code is also **in bold** to highlight code that has changed from previous steps in the chapter, such as when a new feature is added to an existing line of code.

In many cases, the original source code has been reformatted; we've added line breaks and reworked indentation to accommodate the available page space in the book. In rare cases, even this space wasn't enough, so some listings include line-continuation markers (➡). Additionally, many comments in the source code have been removed from the listings when the code is described in the text. Code annotations accompany many listings, highlighting important concepts.

Source code for chapters 2, 4, 5, 6, 7, and 8 is available for download from GitHub at https://github.com/ironfish/reactive-application-development-scala and from the publisher's website at https://www.manning.com/books/reactive-application-development.

Most of the samples are written in Scala and use sbt for the build definition; please refer to https://www.scala-sbt.org for detailed documentation. The online source uses Scala version 2.12.3 and Akka version 2.5.4, and is built with sbt 1.0.0. A Java development kit supporting Java 8 or Java 9 is required to build and run the samples.

Book forum

Purchase of *Reactive Application Development* includes free access to a private web forum run by Manning Publications, where you can make comments about the book, ask technical questions, and receive help from the authors and from other users. To access the forum, go to https://forums.manning.com/forums/reactive-application-development. You can learn more about Manning's forums and their rules of conduct at https://forums.manning.com/forums/about.

Manning's commitment to readers is to provide a venue where a meaningful dialogue among individual readers and among readers and authors can take place. It's not a commitment to any specific amount of participation on the part of authors, whose contribution to the forum remains voluntary (and unpaid). We suggest that you try asking authors some challenging questions, lest their interest stray! The forum and the archives of previous discussions will be accessible from the publisher's website as long as the book is in print.

about the authors

 **SEAN WALSH** has been in the technology industry for more than 20 years. During that time, he progressed from programming in Microsoft languages and frameworks to becoming an early adopter of Java in the mid-1990s. Sean consulted for a large number of startups and enterprises in many verticals, particularly financial, energy, and retail. He has been the chief technology officer and co-founder of a successful medium-size consulting company in Manhattan, vice president of services for SOA Software, and the owner of a lucrative software consulting company since 1996.

After the sale of his last company and taking some time off, Sean decided that it was time for a rebirth and again began hands-on consulting in the energy industry, first using Java and Spring, but after seeing their limitations, embracing Akka and Scala. He has accumulated years of experience in building distributed applications by using the Lightbend open source stack, including the digital transformation of Weight Watchers.

Sean is now field CTO of Lightbend, helping Lightbend's clients realize reactive architectures.

 **DUNCAN DEVORE** is a principal systems engineer at Lightbend and has been a staunch advocate of Scala, Akka, and reactive applications for several years, producing one of the first reactive applications in production. He is also a committer on the original event-sourced project by Martin Krasser that became Akka persistence and maintains the Akka Persistence Mongo Journal.

 **BRIAN HANAFEE'S** first foray into authoring was serving as a collaborator on *Reactive Design Patterns* (Manning Press, 2017). He is a principal systems architect at Wells Fargo Bank, where he's responsible for a wide range of development activity, as well as a consistent advocate of raising the technology bar. Previously, he was with Oracle, working on new and emerging products and systems for interactive television and for text processing. He sent his first email from a moving vehicle in 1994. Before that, Brian was an associate at Booz, Allen & Hamilton and at Advanced Decision Systems, where he applied artificial intelligence techniques to military planning systems. He also wrote software for one of the first ejection-safe helmet-mounted display systems.

Brian received his BS in Electrical Engineering and Computer Science from the University of California–Berkeley.

Part 1

Fundamentals

The words *react*, *reactive*, and *streams* are popular today. You may think that they're the newest trends in programming, but though they *are* trendy, they're hardly new. Reactive programming techniques, especially the actor model, are decades old. What has changed is that internet-scale applications are no longer limited to a few giant companies. Your application may have to grow from toy to powerhouse in far less time than you'd need to rewrite it.

Services such as Amazon Web Services (AWS) make adding servers easy, but that capability does you no good if your application isn't designed to be scalable. The first part of this book delves into factors that can prevent your application from taking advantage of the additional power. Chapter 1 breaks down a traditional application and shows why more servers sometimes make performance even worse. It describes properties of an application that avoid these limits. Chapter 2 is a fast-paced introduction to the Akka toolkit. You start with a simple example that runs in a single process, and with a few small changes, you transform it into a flexible architecture that spans multiple servers. Chapter 3 examines the workings of the toolkit and addresses a problem that you probably didn't encounter in chapter 2: handling failure gracefully. With this foundation, you'll understand why reactive applications can withstand often-unpredictable challenges.

What is a reactive application?

This chapter covers

- The changing world of technology
- Applications with massive user bases
- Traditional versus reactive: modeling complex, distributed software
- The Reactive Manifesto

One of the most fascinating things in nature is the ability of a species to adapt to its changing environment. The canonical example is Great Britain's peppered moth. When newly industrialized Great Britain became polluted in the 19th century, slow-growing, light-colored lichens that covered trees died, resulting in a blackening of the trees' bark. The impact was quite profound: light-colored peppered moths, which historically were well-camouflaged and in the majority, now found themselves the obvious targets of many a hungry bird. Their rare dark-colored siblings, which had been conspicuous before, now blended into the recently polluted eco-system. As the birds changed from eating dark-colored to light-colored moths, the previously common light-colored moth became the minority, and the dynamics of Britain's moth population changed.

What do moths have to do with programming? Moths in and of themselves aren't particularly interesting in this regard, but how the population adapted to its environment is. The peppered moth survived because a genetic variation allowed it to react to its changing environment. Likewise, a reactive application reacts to its changing environment by design. It's constructed from the beginning to react to load, react to failure, and react to users. This is achieved by the underlying notion of reacting to messages; more on that later.

With the ever-growing complexities of modern computing, you must be able to build applications that display this trait. As user expectations of split-second performance, spikes in application load, demands to run on multicore hardware for parallelism, and data needs expand into the petabytes, modern applications must embrace these changes by incorporating this behavior into their DNA. A reactive application embraces these challenges, as it's designed from the ground up to meet them head on.

Although the peppered moth achieved adaptation by way of a genetic selection, reactive applications achieve it through a set of well-founded principles, patterns, and programming techniques. The key for the peppered moth was DNA that included the basic building blocks for selection. The same is true of reactive applications.

Sound programming principles such as message-driven, elastic, resilient, and responsive must be embedded in a reactive application's DNA from the beginning. The following list defines these principles, which are contained in the Reactive Manifesto[1] (a blueprint for building reactive applications):

- *Message-driven*—Based on asynchronous communication in which the designs of sender and recipient aren't affected by the means of message propagation, which means that you can design your system in isolation without worrying about how the messages are transmitted. Message-driven communication leads to a loosely coupled design that provides scalability, resilience, and responsiveness.
- *Elastic*—Reacting to load. The system stays responsive under varying workloads. Reactive applications can actively scale up or scale down based on use or other metrics employed by system designers, saving money on unused computing power, but (most importantly) ensuring the servicing of a growing or spiking user base.
- *Resilient*—Reacting to failure. The system stays responsive in the face of failure. Failure is expected and embraced, and because many systems exist in isolation, a single point of failure remains just that. The system responds appropriately with strategies for restarting or reprovisioning, seamless to the overall systems.

---

[1] We go into more detail on the Reactive Manifesto throughout the book. Jonas Bonér, Dave Farley, Roland Kuhn, and Martin Thompson contributed to this blueprint for building reactive applications, which you can find at http://www.reactivemanifesto.org/.

- *Responsive*—Reacting to users. The system responds in a timely manner if at all possible. Responsiveness is the cornerstone of usability and utility; more than that, it also means that problems may be detected quickly and dealt with effectively.

Reactive applications aren't boilerplate applications; they're challenging to build. They're designed to react to changes in their surrounding environment without new code, which is a hefty task. Additionally, they're based on principles and techniques that aren't new but are only now becoming mainstream.

Many current applications on the Java virtual machine (JVM) favor frameworks such as Spring and Hibernate, whereas reactive applications tend to favor toolkits such as Akka, which is both a toolkit and a runtime for building highly concurrent, distributed, resilient, message-driven applications.

Don't let this new paradigm, with its use of robust toolkits such as Akka, give you pause. This book teaches you a very different way of building applications, embracing the traits listed earlier in this section. This book enables you to solve the complex problems associated with distributed systems, concurrent programming, fault tolerance, and more. This chapter introduces you to the key principles of reactive applications that we explore in the rest of the book.

1.1 Why do I need a reactive application?

Arguably, one of the greatest inventions of mankind in the past 50 years is the internet. The internet dates back to the 1960s, when the U.S. government commissioned research to build a robust, fault-tolerant computer network. This process began with a series of memos written by J.C.R. Licklider of the Massachusetts Institute of Technology in August 1962 and was known as the Galactic Network concept. Licklider envisioned a globally interconnected network of computers that allowed users to access data and programs from anywhere in the world. Licklider was director of the Information Processing Techniques Office within the Advanced Research Projects Agency, which we know today as the Defense Advanced Research Projects Agency (DARPA).

In 1964, MIT professor Leonard Kleinrock published the first book on packet switching theory. Kleinrock persuaded Licklider's successor, Lawrence G. Roberts, that the theory of communicating via packets rather than circuits was the next major step for networking computers. To explore this theory, Thomas Merrill and Lawrence Roberts connected two computers—a TX-2 computer in Massachusetts and a Q-32 computer in California—via a low-speed dial-up line. This significant event represented the first wide-area network and allowed time-sharing-based computers to interchange data and run programs on a remote machine. This effort led in 1968 to a DARPA-funded RFQ known as ARPANET. The RFQ focused on the development of a key component: an interface for packet switches called Interface Message Protocol. In December 1968, Frank Heart of Bolt Beranek and Newman won the RFQ, working with the University of California-Los Angeles to bring the first computer node online in September 1969.

1.1.1 Distributed computing

The result of this work in the 1960s and 1970s in the United States, as well as some additional work in Great Britain and France, paved the way for what we know as the internet. This work also resulted in a new computer model, known as distributed systems, that represented a shift in the computing paradigm. Before distributed systems, the foundational computer model was large, expensive mainframe systems affectionately referred to as Big Iron.

Mainframes historically represent a centralized computing model that focuses on efficiency, local scalability, and reliability. Although this model is effective, it's also expensive beyond the reach of many companies, with the cost of memory, storage units, processing cores, and the like running into millions of dollars. Distributed systems are a less expensive way to achieve and even exceed the raw computing power that typical mainframe configurations represent.

That being said, however, distributed systems don't preclude mainframes. A distributed system might consist of mainframes, minicomputers, and personal computers. The goal of a distributed system is to network a group of computers to work as a single system. We cover distributed systems throughout the book, with special focus in chapters 3 and 4.

1.1.2 Cloud computing

The advent of distributed systems and continual progress toward more powerful, less expensive computing hardware paved the way for cloud computing. Cloud computing represents another significant paradigm shift in the way that computer applications are written and managed.

Whereas distributed systems focus on the technical details of interconnected independent computer systems, cloud computing focuses on economics. It represents a departure from the norm of managing, operating, and developing IT systems that provides substantial economic savings as well as greater agility and flexibility, and this trend is here to stay.

In January 2008, Amazon announced that Amazon Web Services (AWS) consumed more bandwidth than its entire global network of retail services. This new landscape of distributed cloud computing represents a dramatic change for the modern programmer, much as the Industrial Revolution of the nineteenth century did for the peppered moth. Recent hardware enhancements such as multicore central processing units (CPUs) and multisocket servers provide computing capabilities that didn't exist even five years ago.

The decrease in the cost of storage, CPU cycles, and bandwidth coupled with an increase in network nodes means that cloud computing is shaping up to be a competitive environment.[2] The reactive paradigm is designed for this environment, providing ready distribution across this vast ocean of processing power while maintaining resilience and responsiveness.

The best way to understand the advantages of a reactive architecture over other approaches is to view a comparison example. Our example uses a construct that everyone is familiar with: a web shopping cart. We provide a simple example of a customer browsing online inventory, choosing items, and checking out, in both monolithic (applications in which all layers are mutually dependent) and reactive architectures, and we explore how each type of architecture solves the complexities we've just explored, to show the stark differences between the two approaches and the notable advantages of a reactive solution.

1.2　Web shopping cart: complexity beneath the surface

Before you dig into the comparison, you need to know a few things about the example shopping cart. On the surface, it seems to be a simple use case, but a lot more is going on than meets the eye. On the internet, the customer is king. As a result, modern retailers have to fight for customers; they need to have an edge that draws the customer base back. To facilitate this, online sites craft a scenario in which the shopper is browsing a catalog blithely and tossing items into a cart; meanwhile, in the background, the application is busy checking inventory, pulling up reviews, finding images to display, and perhaps enticing the customer with a discount.

Each of these activities requires interaction with other systems, managing responses and handling failure while the shopper is none the wiser. In a traditional monolithic application, these interactions may be slow or fail entirely, because they're only as strong as their weakest link. The reactive design paradigm deals with these challenges in an isolating, succinct manner, maximizing overall performance and dependability.

1.2.1　Monolithic architecture: difficult to distribute

Since the dawn of web development, most web applications have been based on a monolithic architecture. A *monolithic* architecture is one in which functionally discernible aspects of the system aren't architecturally separate. Figure 1.1 shows the example shopping cart as it might look in a monolithic architecture.

---

[2]　Setting the stage: http://radar.oreilly.com/2011/08/building-data-startups.html

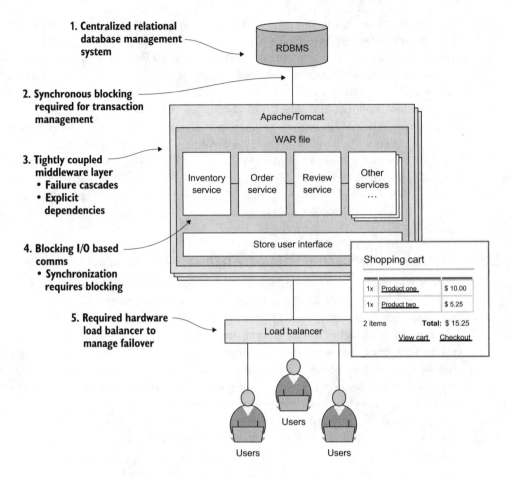

1. **Centralized relational database management system**

2. **Synchronous blocking required for transaction management**

3. **Tightly coupled middleware layer**
   - **Failure cascades**
   - **Explicit dependencies**

4. **Blocking I/O based comms**
   - **Synchronization requires blocking**

5. **Required hardware load balancer to manage failover**

Figure 1.1   Shopping cart modeled in typical monolithic architecture style

As the figure shows, components such as data access, error handling, and user interface are tightly coupled. Blocking I/O is the norm, and for fault tolerance, a hardware component is usually required.

CENTRALIZED RELATIONAL DATABASE MANAGEMENT SYSTEM

Looking at the monolithic architecture from the top down, you can that it centers on a centralized relational database management system. As a result, you encounter the first of many challenges with this model.

The majority of relational databases today use synchronous blocking drivers for transaction management. This kills scalability because all the components must run in the same application space, such as a single JVM process. They typically share a connection pool and often become a single point of failure. Optimization is commonly made over time by means of queueing technologies and enterprise service buses

(ESBs) to orchestrate processes and allow system-to-system communication. Admittedly, this technique is an improvement, because blocking at service level is better than a blocked database transaction, but it's not enough, because any blocking is bad blocking and always results in diminishing returns (if not reduced returns), as more hardware is thrown at the problem.

TIGHTLY COUPLED MIDDLEWARE

Next is a tightly coupled middleware layer comprised of several services that typically rely on blocking synchronous I/O-based communication. This tight coupling and blocking I/O compromise scalability; even worse, they make it difficult to version an application programming interface (API). You can't update only part of an API, because of the interdependencies. More often than not, you have to reason about the entire system as a whole because of the rippling effect of tight coupling. The blocking nature of these communications can become a substantial bottleneck. You can imagine calls being made to the other service components to retrieve daily deals, reviews by other customers, images, and so on. To create the final composite view, you must wait until all associated data is retrieved, which can result in a delay.

To solve some of these problems, more often than not you enter the dark world of concurrent programming. You attempt to spawn threads, write synchronized blocks, lock on a mutable state, use atomic variables, and use the other tools provided in a threaded environment. Although threaded programming provides a useful abstraction for concurrent or parallel execution, the price becomes unsustainable. You begin to experience significant problems in understanding your code, let alone predicting or determining what it's supposed to do, and as a result, your code becomes widely nondeterministic.

Edward A. Lee sums up this situation nicely:

> *Although threads seem to be a small step from sequential computation, in fact, they represent a* **huge step***. They discard the most essential and appealing properties of sequential computation:* **understandability, predictability***, and* **determinism***. Threads, as a model of computation, are wildly non-deterministic, and the job of the programmer becomes one of* **pruning** *that* **non-determinism***.*[3]

These services, in a monolithic application, share a domain model, usually built on top of an object relational mapping (ORM) abstraction layer, that implements a create, read, update, and delete (CRUD) process to manage the domain's current state. As you'll see shortly, this CRUD pattern can significantly diminish the value of your data. Traditionally, these services are designed with strict dependencies on one another and rely on blocking I/O for communication.

LOAD BALANCER

Finally, to support fault tolerance and load spikes, you must implement a load balancer, as shown at the bottom of figure 1.1. Although load balancers mitigate load

---

[3] The Problem with Threads, Edward A. Lee, Berkeley 2006

spikes to some degree, they don't address the underlying problem, in that they fail/ retry at the entire operation level rather than only the failing part. For the architecture to be truly fault-tolerant, load balancers must be resilient, by accepting failure and healing themselves at runtime. This notion of resilience needs to be baked into the architecture from the beginning; it can't be bolted on as an afterthought. Another technique that's commonly used is server clustering. The challenges with this approach are that it's extremely costly and that it can open the door to an ominous cascading failure scenario that brings down the entire cluster.

All this IO blocking at all levels has proved to be a bad thing that must be avoided at all costs, as dictated by Gunther's and Amdahl's laws, which we explain in the next section.

UNIVERSAL SCALABILITY LAW

Blocking of any kind anywhere in the system has been proved to measurably affect scale due to the following:

- *Contention*—the wait for queues or shared resources
- *Coherency*—the delay for data to become consistent

Originally, this effect was shown by computer architect Gene Amdahl, who theorized that blocking causes diminishing returns with regard to scaling. His theory became known as *Amdahl's Law.* Neil J. Gunther, a computer systems researcher, further proved that blocking reduces concurrency as a system is scaled. This theory holds true today and is called *Gunther's Law,* but is widely known as *The Universal Scalability Law.* The reason is that the cost of coherency as the system grows becomes a drag on the overall system and causes a loss over overall scale, as figure 1.2 shows.

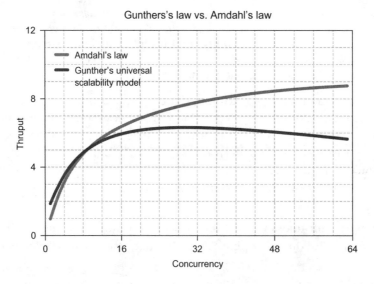

Figure 1.2   Gunther's and Amdahl's laws (http://cmg.org/publications/measureit/2007)

The figure overlays Gunther's and Amdahl's laws, clearly showing that whereas Amdahl *theorized* diminishing returns, Gunther proved that concurrency—and, therefore, scale—drop off after a point. This law means that no matter how much hardware you throw at a problem, you make a blocking system *worse*.

Consistency is another topic often taken for granted by designers of traditional monolithic systems, as tightly coupled services are connected to a centralized database. These systems default to strong consistency, because access to data (in terms of reads and writes) is guaranteed to be *consistently ordered*, which means that every read must follow the last write, and vice versa. This consistency model is great for always having single-point access to the latest data, but it has a high cost in terms of distribution, as identified by the CAP theorem.

CONSISTENCY AND CAP THEOREM

In theoretical computer science, the *CAP Theorem* (also known as *Brewer's Theorem*) states that it's impossible for distributed systems to simultaneously provide all three of the following guarantees:

- *Consistency*—All nodes see the same data at the same time.
- *Availability*—Every request is guaranteed to receive a response about whether it was successful.
- *Partition tolerance*—The system continues to function regardless of message failure or partial system failure.

Figure 1.3 shows a Venn diagram of these guarantees.

As the figure shows, in distributed computing it's not possible to have all your cake and eat it too. By design, distributed systems are asynchronous and loosely coupled,

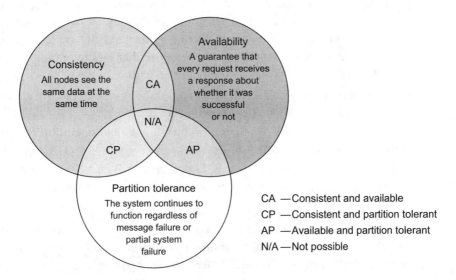

Figure 1.3   The CAP Theorem Venn diagram

relying on patterns such as atomic shared memory systems, distributed data stores, and consistency models to achieve availability and partition tolerance. A properly designed system must have partition tolerance, so you must decide whether to have higher availability or greater consistency.

CONSISTENCY MODEL

In distributed computing, a system supports a given consistency model if operations follow specific rules identified by the model. The model specifies a contractual agreement between the programmer and the system, wherein the system guarantees that if the rules are followed, data will be consistent and the results will be predictable:

- *Strong consistency* or *linearizability* is the strongest method of consistency, guaranteeing that data reads reflect the latest writes across all processes. Strong consistency is incredibly expensive in terms of scale; therefore, you must avoid it at all costs in building reactive applications.

- *Eventual consistency* is a consistency model used in distributed computing. This model informally guarantees that if no new updates are made to a given data item, all accesses to that item *eventually* return the last updated value. Eventual consistency is a pillar of modern distributed systems, often under the moniker of optimistic replication, and has origins in early mobile computing projects. A system that has achieved eventual consistency is often said to have converged or achieved replica convergence. Eventually consistent services are often classified as Basically Available, Soft state, Eventual consistency (BASE) semantics, as opposed to more traditional Atomicity, Consistency, Isolation, and Durability (ACID) guarantees—a key point and one of the key factors that allow distribution.

- *Causal consistency* is a stronger consistency model that ensures that operations are processed in the expected order. Causal consistency is the strongest method of consistency achievable while retaining availability. More precisely, partial order over operations is enforced through metadata. If operation A occurs before operation B, for example, any data store that sees operation B must see operation A first. Three rules define potential causality:
  - *Thread of execution*—If A and B are two operations in a single thread of execution, A → B if operation A happens before B.
  - *Reads from*—If A is a write operation and B is a read operation that returns the value written by A, A → B.
  - *Transitivity*—For operations A, B, and C, if A → B and B → C, then A → C. Thus, the causal relationship among operations is the transitive closure of the first two rules.

Causal consistency is stronger than eventual consistency because it ensures that these operations appear in order. Causal consistency is difficult to achieve in a distributed system because any transaction has multiple distributed parties.

Even Akka (as you see in the reactive architecture model of the shopping cart in the next section) doesn't have an out-of-the-box implementation of causal consistency, so the burden is on the programmer to implement it. The most common way to implement causal consistency in an Akka-based actor model is through Become/Unbecome, via the Process Manager pattern.

Why Akka?

If you look at building a system in terms of building a house, you clearly see that the tools are of utmost importance in guaranteeing success. A craftsman builder accumulates tools over the years, always getting more and better tools that prove to get the job done. Craftsman software programmers do the same thing, in that we learn constantly and gain access to new technologies for building software. Akka is an important item in a programmer's toolkit because it's a runtime and software library for building highly concurrent, distributed, resilient, message-driven applications on the JVM. Akka is by nature reactive. At its heart, Akka relies on a mathematical model of concurrent computation, known as the actor model. In this model, the actor provides a lightweight programming construct that sends and receives messages, makes local decisions, and creates new actors—all asynchronously, without locks.

Akka's value proposition

Akka is a single, unified programming model that provides the following:

- *Simpler concurrency*—Code written with the illusion of single-threadedness, without locks or synchronized or atomic variables
- *Simpler distribution*—Code distributed by default, remote, or local configuration
- *Simpler fault tolerance*—Communication decoupled from failure through supervision

---

As a result of the challenges of concurrency, nondeterminism, consistency guarantees, and other rapid technology changes (such as multicore processors and pay-as-you-go cloud services), monolithic architectures don't translate well to the modern world of distributed computing. Problems with concurrency, transaction management, scalability, and fault tolerance are rampant.

In the next section, we look at reactive architectures and show how they fare against these challenges.

1.2.2 *Reactive architecture: distributable by default*

Reactive applications adopt a radically different approach from monolithic ones. Rather than build an architecture based on a nondistributed environment and then try to retrofit it with locks for concurrency, load balancers, and so on, reactive applications assume a distributed environment.

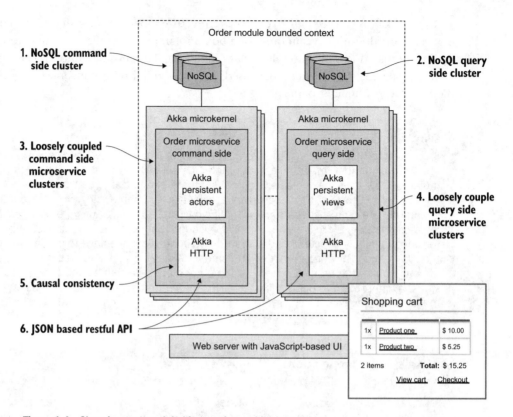

Figure 1.4   Shopping cart modeled in reactive architecture style

From the ground up, reactive applications bake in the four key traits explained earlier in this chapter: message-driven, elastic, resilient, and responsive. Figure 1.4 shows the example shopping cart in a reactive application.

If this architecture seems to be more complicated than the monolithic one, that's because it is. Distributed applications aren't easy to build, but with the advent of Akka, the task is a bit easier than it once was. For brevity's sake, we're showing only the order microservice; structurally, the inventory, review, and other services would be identical.

Looking at the figure from the top down, you see the following:

- *Order service*—The first thing you notice is that the top of the figure doesn't have a single centralized data store, like the monolithic example in figure 1.1. The order service is split into two sides: a command side and a query side, each supported by a clustered NoSQL data store and sitting atop its own JVM. This pattern is commonly referred to as Command Query Responsibility Segregation (CQRS). We break this pattern into its key parts (C, Q, R, and S) in chapter 8.

Each side of the order service is micro in nature and sits on top of a clustered Akka instance. The concept you should focus on for now is designing your application as a suite of small services, each running its own process, loosely coupled and communicating with a lightweight, message-driven process—in this case, Akka. These services are wrapped by the Akka microkernel, which offers a bundling mechanism and is distributable as a single payload. You don't need a Java application server or a startup script.

- *Loosely coupled command-side microservice clusters*—The command side uses Akka persistence as its storage mechanism and Akka HTTP to process commands from the user interface (UI). Akka persistence provides durability to your application by persisting the internal state of each actor, allowing for recovery when the actor is started, restarted after a JVM crash or by a supervisor, or migrated in a cluster. Akka persistence is the foundation of resilience in the Reactive Manifesto.

  Akka HTTP provides an actor-based, asynchronous, lightweight, fast REST/HTTP layer for your application. We explore the command construct in detail in chapter 5.

- *Loosely coupled query-side microservice clusters*—The query side uses Akka persistent views to project data from the data store and Akka HTTP to deliver the projected data to the UI.

- *Consistency models*—Finally, the two sides are synchronized via a *consistency model*, a common technique used in distributed computing to keep isolated systems synchronized. We discussed this model in relation to the CAP theorem earlier in this chapter. Consistency models can be *eventual* (eventually, all accesses to that item return the last updated value) or *causal* (the operations are processed in the expected order).

  We talk more about the importance of consistency models in chapters 5 and 8, but for the time being, you can think of consistency as being the logical glue that holds the command and query sides together. Consistency is essentially a contractual agreement that says that whatever happens on the command side makes its way to the query side, bound by some metrics such as content and time. We explore the query construct in detail in chapter 8.

In the next section, we look in depth at the principles of the Reactive Manifesto, which we introduced at the beginning of this chapter, and show how the reactive architecture is based on these principles.

1.2.3 Understanding the reactive architecture

The authoritative guide for reactive architectures is the Reactive Manifesto. Like many of us, Jonas Bonér, chief technology officer of Typesafe, grew increasingly frustrated with the way that modern applications were architected; he felt the need for a clear, concise way to articulate the philosophies of good distributed design. As a result, the Reactive Manifesto was released on September 23, 2013 (V1); it was updated on September 16, 2014 (V2).

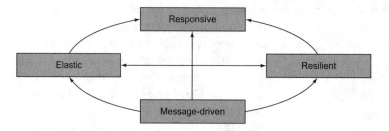

Figure 1.5   Traits of the Reactive Manifesto
(www.reactivemanifesto.org/images/reactive-traits.svg)

The manifesto centers on four attributes that lay the foundation for reactive applications, as shown in figure 1.5.

We discussed the four traits shown in the figure earlier in the chapter. In the following sections, we explore their implications for reactive design.

MESSAGE-DRIVEN

Message-driven architectures are loosely coupled, asynchronous, and nonblocking. Before we go any further, we'll define what these terms mean, as they're paramount to the concept:

- *Loosely coupled*—A system whose components depend on one another by the least amount practical
- *Asynchronous*—Capable of executing a task without waiting for it to complete (nonblocking)
- *Nonblocking*—Never waiting for a task to complete

This pattern results in no concrete dependencies and allows the use of a distributed domain model, which is crucial for scalability and which leads to lower latency and higher throughput. As a result, reactive architectures are naturally scalable, capable of elastically scaling in and out. This type of architecture mitigates financial risk, allowing for on-demand use of hardware and services such as those made popular by Amazon. When load is low, you spin down services, and when load spikes, you spin services back up. Because you're paying only for what you use, you save money. We cover the details of distributed domain modeling in chapter 4.

ELASTIC

Elastic architectures are key for distributed computing. They're expected to expand and contract as load demands change through *elasticity*—the ability to add or remove nodes on the fly. This unique feature allows these architectures to scale in and out and up and down, without the need for the application to be redesigned or rewritten. Elasticity also mitigates risk in that hardware can be used on demand, which eliminates the need to keep a bank of unused servers waiting for a load spike to occur. The technique that allows for this elastic behavior is *location transparency*, which uses logical names to find network resources, removing the need to know the physical locations of the users and the resource. We cover elasticity in detail in chapters 2 and 3, which explore the Akka actor model.

RESILIENT

Reactive applications don't use traditional fault-tolerance techniques. Instead, they embrace the notion of resilience. Merriam-Webster defines resilience as

- the ability of a substance or object to spring back into shape
- the capacity to recover quickly from difficulties

Resilience is achieved by accepting failure and making it a first-class citizen in the programming model, managed through isolation and recovery techniques such as the bulkhead pattern, which allow the application to self-heal. An example might be the shopping cart.

Imagine a scenario in which the shipping module fails temporarily. In a reactive system, the user can still interface with the shopping cart, adding and deleting items, while the shipping module (in the background) identifies failure and repairs itself. We discuss resilience in chapters 3, 4, and 5, where we deal with the distributed domain model and other error-recovery concepts.

RESPONSIVE

Finally, reactive applications are responsive. Users aren't interested in what your application does under the covers; they expect it to work the same way in high-load and low-load situations and in failover and nonfailover modes. Today's applications are expected to be real-time, engaging, and collaborative, capable of responding to a user's actions without hesitation. If the shipping module fails, for example, the application continues to respond. Reactive applications use stateful clients, streaming, and observable models, among other things, to provide a rich, collaborative environment for the user. We cover these concepts in great detail in chapters 7 and 8.

We've introduced a large number of concepts in this section. Most important, we showed you how to use asynchronous message passing and share-nothing designs. Don't worry; we cover all these concepts in detail throughout the book. For now, all that matters is that you understand the general concepts of a reactive architecture.

In the next section, we dig a little deeper into the specifics of implementing these two architectures in the shopping cart example. We look at the details of placing an online order in both monolithic and reactive shopping carts, showing the distinct advantage of the reactive paradigm and the message-driven trait of reactive applications, which is distinctly different from the monolithic approach.

1.2.4 *Monolithic shopping cart: creating an order*

As we note earlier in this chapter, the architectural problems of concurrency, scalability, and fault tolerance are significant in monolithic applications, but other challenges arise as well. One such challenge is the value of the data that a monolithic application persists. Typically, monolithic applications store domain information in current state form as opposed to behavioral form. As a result, much of the intent of the data stored is lost. To understand this problem, take a close look at a customer adding items to the example shopping cart in monolithic and reactive designs.

In a monolithic architecture, you typically build your shopping cart application in a client-server fashion, using CRUD to manage the current state of your domain model. A customer browses available inventory, chooses four items, adds shipping information, and then checks out. Meanwhile, many other things are happening in the background. Images are being fetched, reviews are being loaded, daily deals are being presented, and so on. The application needs to deal with all these activities. To keep the example simple, we focus in this section on the problem of data persistence in monolithic applications.

This order is most likely wrapped in a single transaction via an ORM implementation that inserts the values into three tables: order, order_item, and shipping_information. The information stored represents the current state of the shopping cart order, as shown in figure 1.6.

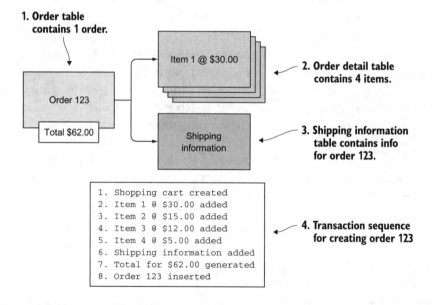

Figure 1.6   CRUD shopping cart current state after create

At some point in the future, before the order is shipped, the customer decides that he no longer wants one of the items he ordered. He logs back into the shopping cart application, fetches his order, and deletes the unwanted item. At that point, the order consists of three items that cost a total $47 (figure 1.7). The notion that item 2 was deleted is lost.

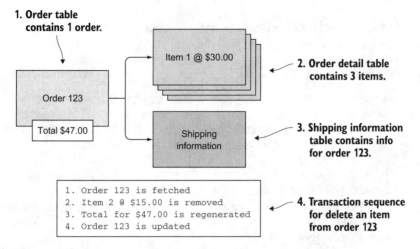

Figure 1.7 CRUD shopping cart current state after customer deletes an item

Concerned about the decrease in revenue from deleted items, the manager who oversees the shopping cart application asks the development team to generate a report for all items removed by customers before orders ship. Therein lies the rub!

THE PROBLEM: USER INTENT NOT CAPTURED

Because the domain model by way of CRUD stores only current state, the deleted data is lost. The development team has to add this task to a future sprint and implement an audit log that tracks deleted items. Even worse, after the log is implemented, the team can track only deletions from that point forward, which has substantial implications for the value of the data.

You should look to capture the intent of your users because, from a business perspective, customer behavior is paramount. Rather than model your domain as a current state model, you should look at it in the form of user behavior as a sequence of recorded transactions or events. The CRUD model of persisting current state, which you're so familiar with, does capture behavior, but the behavior that it captures is system behavior in the form of creating, reading, updating, and deleting, which doesn't tell you much about your users and compromises the value of your data. Most systems today rely on this model primarily because of the general acceptance of the relational database management system (RDBMS) as the center of web architecture. Fortunately, this way to view persistence isn't the only way.

Event Sourcing, or persisting a sequence of events (behaviors)—not to be confused with message-driven, which means reacting to a message—provides a means by which you can capture the real intent of your users. In an Event Sourcing system, all data operations are viewed as a sequence of events that are recorded to an append-only store. In this section, we provide two examples that best showcase the capabilities of Event Sourcing: the canonical example of a bank account register and the CRUD shopping cart redone as a reactive shopping cart.

What's the difference between messages, commands, and events?

The distinction between messages, commands, and events is important, and one that we need to make before going too far into our architecture discussion. Messages can come in two flavors: abstract and concrete. Following are two simple examples:

- You can think of an *abstract message* as being a blank sheet of paper—a structure to capture a conversation between two parties. The paper in and of itself isn't a conversation until something is written on it. To start the discussion, suppose that we write on the paper a request to borrow a book from you. The abstract message becomes (has been implemented as) a command—a request to do something. In response, you write back that you've mailed the book. At this point, the abstract message has become (has been implemented as) an event—a notification that something has occurred. In this example, the command and event are forms of messages. In computing lingo, they implement the message interface.

- A *concrete message* is like an envelope—a container that has a payload. That payload can be anything. In the preceding example, the payload is either a command or an event. The distinction is that a message is concrete, like a command and an event.

1.2.5   *Event Sourcing: a banking example*

In a mature business model, the notion of tracking behavior is quite common. Consider the bank accounting system shown in figure 1.8. This system allows customers to make deposits, write checks, make withdrawals, transfer money to another account, and so on.

The figure shows see a typical bank account register in

Date	Comment	Change	Balance
7/1/2014	Deposit from 3300	+ 10,000.00	10,000.00
7/3/2014	Check 001	−4,000.00	6,000.00
7/4/2014	ATM withdrawal	−3.00	5,997.00
7/11/2014	Check 002	−5.00	5,992.00
7/12/2014	Deposit from 3301	+ 2,000.00	7,992.00

Figure 1.8   **Bank account register transaction log with five transactions**

which the account holder deposits $10,000, writes a check for $4,000, makes an ATM withdrawal, writes another check, and makes another deposit.

The system stores a record of each transaction as an independent event. To calculate the balance, the delta (change caused by the current transaction) is applied to the last known value (the sum of all previous transactions). As a result, the system provides a verifiable audit log that can be reconciled to ensure validity. The balance at any point can be derived by replaying all the transactions up to that point. Additionally, the system captures the real intent of how the account holder manages her finances.

Suppose that the bank persisted only current state for the account. When the account holder tries to reconcile her account, she notices a discrepancy. She double-checks her reconciliation and concludes that the bank made a mistake. She quickly calls the bank and states her case, and the bank officer promptly replies, "I'm sorry; we have no record of that transaction. We only store the last update to your balance."

That scenario is ludicrous. Although it's an extreme example of losing the user's intent—changes in the balance—unfortunately, this situation happens in a CRUD-based monolithic application.

1.2.6 Reactive shopping cart: creating an order with Event Sourcing

Another way to look at events (which you might think of as transactions) is to look at them as notifications that something has happened. Events are indicative or evidential in mood, as they state recorded facts. We discuss in depth details such as these for Event Sourcing, especially in relation to CQRS and commands in general, in chapters 5 and 6.

For now, we dig back into the shopping cart example by modeling it in an Event Sourcing fashion, as shown in figure 1.9.

As you can see, the workflow addresses the same concerns as the earlier CRUD example, with crucial differences:

- No total is generated.
- Each item is a distinct delta that persists in sequential order.
- The entire construct as a stream of deltas is written to an append-only store.

As figure 1.9 shows, the reactive shopping cart has no current state of the order or line items that persist. Instead, it stores in order a sequence of deltas that capture user behavior. Note the indicative tense of an event, such as item added or shipping information added. Events are things that have happened, which is an important distinction compared with commands. You can reject a command because it's a request to do

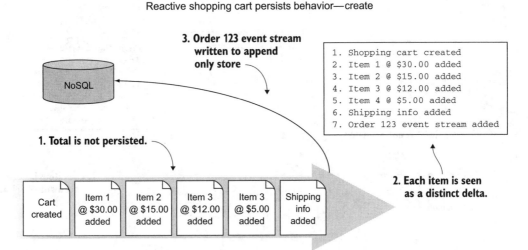

Figure 1.9 A reactive shopping cart stores events.

something, whereas you can't reject an event, because it represents something that has already occurred.

To wrap up the discussion of the differences between monolithic and reactive applications, figure 1.10 illustrates creating an order in shopping carts using both types of applications.

Monolithic shopping cart persists current state—create

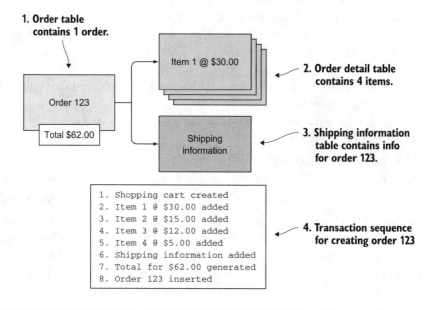

1. Order table contains 1 order.

Item 1 @ $30.00

2. Order detail table contains 4 items.

Order 123

Total $62.00

Shipping information

3. Shipping information table contains info for order 123.

```
1.  Shopping cart created
2.  Item 1 @ $30.00 added
3.  Item 2 @ $15.00 added
4.  Item 3 @ $12.00 added
5.  Item 4 @ $5.00 added
6.  Shipping information added
7.  Total for $62.00 generated
8.  Order 123 inserted
```

4. Transaction sequence for creating order 123

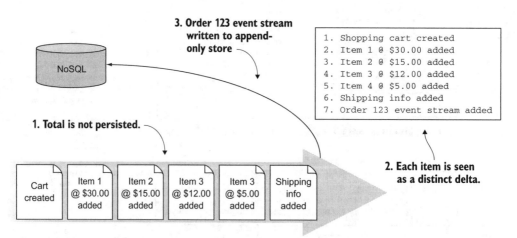

Reactive shopping cart persists behavior—create

3. Order 123 event stream written to append-only store

NoSQL

```
1.  Shopping cart created
2.  Item 1 @ $30.00 added
3.  Item 2 @ $15.00 added
4.  Item 3 @ $12.00 added
5.  Item 4 @ $5.00 added
6.  Shipping info added
7.  Order 123 event stream added
```

1. Total is not persisted.

| Cart created | Item 1 @ $30.00 added | Item 2 @ $15.00 added | Item 3 @ $12.00 added | Item 3 @ $5.00 added | Shipping info added |

2. Each item is seen as a distinct delta.

Figure 1.10   A CRUD shopping cart creates current state; a reactive shopping cart persists behavior.

The rest of this section shows what happens when at some point in the future, before the order is shipped, the customer decides that he no longer wants one of the items he ordered.

The customer logs back into the shopping cart application, fetches his order, and deletes the unwanted item, as shown in figure 1.11.

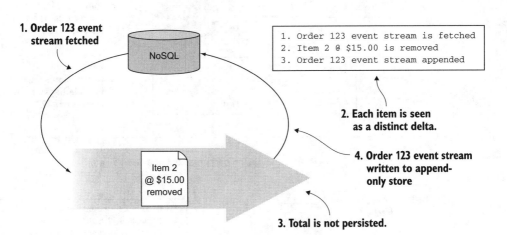

Reactive shopping cart persists behavior—delete

1. Order 123 event stream fetched

NoSQL

```
1. Order 123 event stream is fetched
2. Item 2 @ $15.00 is removed
3. Order 123 event stream appended
```

2. Each item is seen as a distinct delta.

Item 2 @ $15.00 removed

4. Order 123 event stream written to append-only store

3. Total is not persisted.

Figure 1.11   A reactive shopping cart appends a delete event.

Again, the workflow is similar to the CRUD example, with subtle but crucial differences:

- No total is generated.
- The delete is a distinct delta that persists at the end of the event stream.

As with the CRUD shopping cart, the manager who oversees the shopping cart application asks the development team to generate a report for all items removed by customers before orders ship. From a data perspective, this situation is one in which a reactive application shines:

- You have everything you need to craft the report, because you capture the intent of the user in the form of events, rather than the current state of the model.
- Deletes aren't updates to current state, as with a CRUD solution; they're simply events captured in a user's behavior workflow.
- In a reactive system, deletes are explicit and verifiable, whereas in a CRUD solution, they're implicit and require tracking.

Monolithic shopping cart persists current state—delete

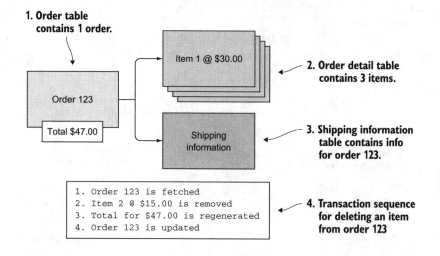

**1. Order table
contains 1 order.**

Order 123

Total $47.00

Item 1 @ $30.00

**2. Order detail table
contains 3 items.**

Shipping
information

**3. Shipping information
table contains info
for order 123.**

```
1. Order 123 is fetched
2. Item 2 @ $15.00 is removed
3. Total for $47.00 is regenerated
4. Order 123 is updated
```

**4. Transaction sequence
for deleting an item
from order 123**

Reactive shopping cart persists behavior—delete

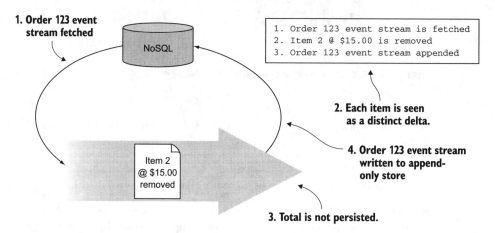

**1. Order 123 event
stream fetched**

NoSQL

```
1. Order 123 event stream is fetched
2. Item 2 @ $15.00 is removed
3. Order 123 event stream appended
```

Item 2
@ $15.00
removed

**2. Each item is seen
as a distinct delta.**

**4. Order 123 event stream
written to append-
only store**

3. Total is not persisted.

**Figure 1.12   A CRUD shopping cart deletes overwrites of state; a reactive shopping cart appends a
delete event.**

Figure 1.12 compares monolithic and reactive carts dealing with a deleted item.

So far, we've shown you how a reactive architecture solves several issues in reacting
to events and transactions: the first characteristic of reactive applications as defined by
the Reactive Manifesto. In the next section, we show you what else reactive applications can react to.

1.3 What are reactive applications reacting to?

A coming tidal wave will have a significant effect on application design. This tidal wave is the Internet of Things (IoT). Some theorists believe that by 2020, the internet will be comprised of 30 billion interconnected devices, as shown in figure 1.13.[4]

Figure 1.13 Logical view of IoT

Consider the impact of 30 billion devices. Currently, approximately 12 billion devices are interconnected, and you can already see the result: slow websites, longer down time than expected, email interruptions every couple of months. The effect of tripling the number of devices in seven years will be staggering. To make matters worse, an estimated 99 percent of the physical objects (homes, cars, buildings, wearables, and so on) that may someday join the internet are still unconnected.[5]

The IoT will have a dramatic effect on application failure rate as a result of load spikes and will compromise the application's ability to respond to its user base. Mono-

---

4   ABI Research, https://www.abiresearch.com/press/more-than-30-billion-devices-will-wirelessly-conne/
5   Forbes Magazine: https://www.forbes.com/forbes/welcome/?toURL=https://www.forbes.com/sites/quora/2013/01/07/how-many-things-are-currently-connected-to-the-internet-of-things-iot/&refURL=&referrer=

lithic applications will crumble under these conditions, in turn affecting every company's bottom line.

If modern programmers are going to be successful (not succumb to the fate of the light-colored peppered moth during the Industrial Revolution), they must learn new tools and techniques designed for this new environment, which embrace distributed systems and cloud computing. This is exactly what reactive applications are all about.

1.4   What you will learn in this book

We believe that the reactive paradigm is here to stay and will influence and shape the world of computing for years to come. To facilitate that process, we present a variety of philosophies, patterns, and technologies that you may not be familiar with. Don't let that fact give you pause. The purpose of this book is to walk you step by step through that process, and at the end, you'll be equipped to meet that goal.

Following are those philosophies, patterns, and technologies broken down by the traits of the Reactive Manifesto to give you a better sense of where we're heading in the following chapters. Strap in; you're in for a great ride.

1.4.1   Asynchronous communication with loosely coupled design

- *Akka*—A toolkit and runtime for building highly concurrent, distributed, and resilient message-driven applications on the JVM
- *Akka actors*—Lightweight concurrent entities that process messages asynchronously using a message-driven mailbox pattern (chapters 2 and 3)
- *Akka HTTP*—Embeddable HTTP stack built entirely on Akka actors
- *CQRS-ES*—A set of patterns communicating via event messages (chapter 8)

1.4.2   Elastic

Elastic means being capable of expansion and upgrade on demand:

- *Akka clustering*—Fault-tolerant, decentralized, peer-to-peer-based cluster membership service with no single point of failure or single point of bottleneck
- *Akka sharding*—Actors with an identifier automatically distributed across multiple nodes in the cluster
- *Akka Streams*—A streaming model that protects each consumer of data from being overwhelmed by its producer by propagating backpressure
- *CQRS*—An approach in which models used for commands (write) are different from models used to query (read)
- *Distributed domain-driven design (DDDD)*—A distributed approach to software development for complex needs that connects the implementation to an evolving model
- *Elasticity*—The expansion or contraction of the system according to load
- *Event Sourcing*—Persisting a sequence of behaviors

1.4.3 Resilient

More than fault tolerance, *resilience* is the ability to self-heal:

- *Akka clustering*—Fault-tolerant, decentralized, peer-to-peer-based cluster membership service with no single point of failure or single point of bottleneck
- *Akka persistence*—Enabling stateful actors to persist their internal state so that it can be recovered when an actor is started, restarted after a JVM crash or by a supervisor, or migrated in a cluster
- *Akka sharding*—Actors with an identifier automatically distributed across multiple nodes in the cluster
- *Akka Streams*—A streaming model that protects each consumer of data from being overwhelmed by its producer by propagating backpressure
- *Failure detection*—Responsible for detection of node failures or crashes in a distributed system
- *Modular/microservice architecture*—A way of designing software applications as suites of independently deployable services

1.4.4 Responsive

Responsiveness is the ability to respond regardless of circumstances:

- *CQRS*—Models used for commands (write) are different from the models used to query (read)
- *Futures*—A data structure used to retrieve the result of some concurrent operation
- *Akka HTTP*—An embeddable HTTP stack entirely built on Akka actors
- *Akka Streams*—A streaming model that protects each consumer of data from being overwhelmed by its producer by propagating backpressure

1.4.5 Testing

- *Test-driven development (TDD)*—A software development process that relies on the repetition of a short development cycle: first the developer writes an (initially failing) automated test case that defines a desired improvement or new function, then produces the minimum amount of code to pass that test, and finally refactors the new code to acceptable standards.
- *Behavioral-driven development (BDD)*—A software development process that combines the general techniques and principles of TDD with ideas from domain-driven design and object-oriented analysis and design to give software development and management teams shared tools and a shared process for collaborating on software development.
- *Test kit*—A test kit that provides all the means necessary to test actors asynchronously, mimicking how they behave in the real world at runtime.
- *Multi-JVM testing*—A process that supports running applications (objects with main methods) and ScalaTest tests in multiple JVMs at the same time; useful for integration testing in which multiple systems communicate.

Summary

- The Reactive Manifesto is
  - Message-driven
  - Elastic, expanding and contracting with load
  - Resilient in the face of failure
  - Responsive to users
- Traditional, monolithic architecture has pitfalls and limitations.
- Blocking limits concurrency, and, therefore, distribution and scale.
- Reactive design solves the distributed programming problems existing today.

Getting started with Akka

2

> **This chapter covers**
> - Building an actor system
> - Distributing and scaling horizontally
> - Applying reactive principles

You understand from chapter 1 the tenets of reactive design, but haven't yet seen them in practice. This chapter changes that situation. In this chapter, you build a simple reactive system by using the *actor* model that was introduced in chapter 1. The actor model is one of the most common reactive patterns. Actors can send and receive messages, make local decisions, create new actors, and do all that asynchronously and without locks. You build the example in this chapter with the Akka toolkit, which you also saw previously. Akka is a powerful system for creating and running actors. It's written in the Scala language, and the examples in this chapter are also written in Scala. Chapters 3 and 4 explain Akka in more depth.

The system you build consists of two actors passing messages to each other; you can use the same skills to create much larger applications. Next, you'll learn to scale the system horizontally by adding more copies of one of the actors. Finally, you'll see how this approach produces a system that's both message-driven and elastic—two of the four reactive properties from the Reactive Manifesto.

2.1   *Understanding messages and actors*

Reactive systems are message-driven, so it comes as no surprise that messages play a key role. Actors and messages are the building blocks of an actor system. An actor receives a message and does something in response to it. That something might include performing a computation, updating internal state, sending more messages, or perhaps initiating some I/O.

Much the same could be said of an ordinary function call. To understand what an actor is, it's useful first to consider some of the problems that can arise from an ordinary function call. A function accepts some input parameters, performs some processing, and returns a value. The processing may be quick or could take a long time. However long the processing takes, the caller is blocked while waiting for the return value.

2.1.1   *Moving from functions to actors*

If a function includes an I/O operation, control of the processor core most likely is handed off to another thread while the caller is waiting for a response. The caller won't be able to continue processing until the I/O operation is complete and the scheduler hands control back to the original processing thread, as shown in figure 2.1. The scheduling maintains the illusion for the caller that it made a simple synchronous call. What happened was that any number of other threads may have been running in the background, potentially even changing data structures referenced by the original input parameters.

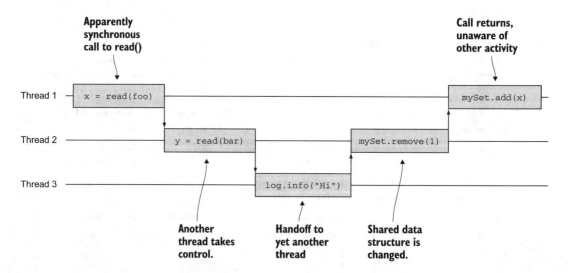

Figure 2.1   The illusion of a synchronous call can be the source of unexpected behavior.

The developer may know that the function is liable to take a long time and may design the system to accommodate thread safety and timing. Sometimes, however, the developer can't predict the amount of time that the function requires. If the function has a cache of recently used data in memory but must go to a database if the data isn't in the cache, for example, the amount of time that the function requires may vary by many orders of magnitude from one call to the next. Ensuring that the caller and callee have the correct synchronization and thread safety without deadlocks can be extremely difficult. If the application programming interface (API) is properly encapsulated, the entire implementation may be replaced by one that has different characteristics. An excellent design around the original characteristics could become an inappropriate design with respect to the replacement.

The result is often complex code littered with exception handlers, callbacks, synchronized blocks, thread pools, timeouts, mysterious tuning parameters, and bugs that developers never seem to be able to replicate in the test environment. What all these things have in common is that they have nothing to do with the business domain. Rather, they're aspects of the computing domain imposing themselves on the application.

The actor model pushes these concerns out of the business domain and into the actor system.

ACTORS ARE ASYNCHRONOUS MESSAGE HANDLERS

The simplified view of an actor shown in figure 2.2 is a receive function that accepts a message and produces no return value; it processes each message as each message is received from the actor system. The actor system manages a mailbox of messages addressed to the actor, ensuring that the actor has to process only one message at a time. An important consequence of this design is that the sender never calls the actor directly. Instead, the sender addresses a message to the actor and hands it to the actor system for delivery.

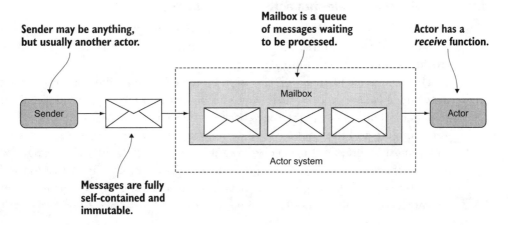

Figure 2.2   The sender obtains a *reference* to address messages to the actor through the actor system.

Actors remove many of the problems of function calls by abandoning the illusion that everything is synchronous. Instead, actors take the approach that everything is one-way and asynchronous. The underlying system takes responsibility for delivering the message to the receiving actor, immediately or some time later. An actor receives a new message only when it's ready to process that message. Until then, the actor system holds on to the message. The sender may proceed immediately to other tasks rather than wait for a response that may come some time later or perhaps not at all. If the receiving actor has a response for the sender, that response is handled with another asynchronous message.

> **TIP** Senders never call actors directly. All interactions between senders and actors are mediated by the actor system.

MESSAGES ARE SELF-CONTAINED AND IMMUTABLE

As messages are passed among actors, they may move to an actor system on a different server. Messages must be designed so that they can be copied from one system to another, which means that all the information has to be contained within the message itself. Messages can't include references to data outside the message. Sometimes, a message doesn't make it to the destination and must be sent again. In chapter 4, you learn that the same message may be broadcast to more than one actor.

For this process to work, a message must be *immutable*. When it's sent, it's read-only and can't be allowed to change. If the message did change after being sent, there'd be no way to know whether the change happened before or after it was received, or perhaps while it was being processed by another actor. If the message happened to have been sent to an actor on another server, the change may have been made before or after it was transmitted, and there'd be no way to know. Worse, if the message had to be sent more than once, some copies of the message may include the change, and some may not. Immutable messages make all those worries go away.

2.1.2   *Modeling the domain with actors and messages*

Actors should correspond to real things in the domain model. The example in this chapter consists of a tourist who has an inquiry about a country and a guidebook that provides guidance to the tourist.

The example actor system is shown in figure 2.3. The system contains two actors: a *tourist* and a *guidebook*. The tourist sends an *inquiry* message to the guidebook, and the guidebook sends *guidance* messages back to the tourist. Messages are one-way affairs, so the inquiry and the guidance are defined as separate messages. As in real life, the tourist must be prepared to receive no guidance, a single guidance message, or even multiple guidance messages in response to a single inquiry. (The tourist in the example can receive multiple guidance messages, but deciding what to believe would be the subject of a different book.)

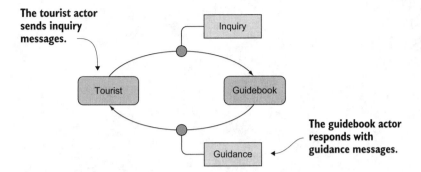

Figure 2.3 The tourist actor sends inquiry messages to the guidebook. The guidebook actor responds with guidance messages returned to the tourist actor.

2.1.3 *Defining the messages*

You know already that messages are self-contained and immutable, and now you've identified some messages that are needed for the example. In Scala, case classes provide an easy way to implement messages. The example messages, shown in listing 2.1, define a case class for each message. The definitions follow the convention that messages are defined in the companion object to the actor that receives the message. The Guidebook actor receives Inquiry messages that include a String for the country code that's being inquired about. The Tourist actor receives Guidance messages, which contain the original country code and a description of the country. The original country code is included in the guidance so that the information in the message is fully self-contained. Otherwise, there'd be no way to correlate which guidance goes with which inquiry. Finally, the Start message is used later to tell the Tourist actor to start sending inquiries.

> ### Scala case classes
>
> For readers who aren't familiar with Scala, a case class is defined by a class name and some parameters. By default, instances of a case class are immutable. Each parameter corresponds to a read-only value that's passed to the constructor. The compiler takes care of generating the rest of the boilerplate for you. The concise Scala definition
>
> ```
> case class Inquiry(code: String)
> ```
>
> produces a class equivalent in Java:
>
> ```
> public class Inquiry {
>     private final String code;
> ```

(continued)

```
    public Inquiry(String code) {
        this.code = code;
    }

    public String getCode() {
        return this.code;
    }

    // ...more methods are generated automatically
}
```

Case classes generate more than the getters. They automatically include correct equality, hash codes, a human-friendly `toString`, a `copy` method, a companion object, support for pattern matching, and additional methods that are useful for more advanced functional programming techniques.

Listing 2.1   Message definitions

```
object Guidebook {
  case class Inquiry(code: String)                                    ◁──┐  The Inquiry and
}                                                                          │  Guidance messages are
object Tourist {                                                           │  simple case classes.
  case class Guidance(code: String, description: String)   ◁──────────────┘
  case class Start(codes: Seq[String])                     ◁──┐  The Start message starts
}                                                               │  the tourist sending inquiries.
```

Now that the messages are defined, it's time to move on to the actors.

2.1.4   *Defining the actors*

The example requires a `Tourist` actor and a `Guidebook` actor. Most of the behavior of an actor is provided by extending the `akka.actor.Actor` trait. One thing that can't be built into the actor trait is what to do when a message is received, because that behavior is specific to the application. You provide that behavior by implementing the abstract `receive` method.

THE TOURIST ACTOR

As shown in listing 2.2, the `receive` method on the `Tourist` defines cases to handle the two types of message expected by the `Tourist`. In response to a `Start` message, it extracts codes and sends an `Inquiry` message to the `Guidebook` actor for each one it finds. It also receives `Guidance` messages, which it handles by printing the code and description to the console.

The `Tourist` needs to address messages to the `Guidebook`, but actors never keep direct references to other actors. Notice that the `Guidebook` is passed to the constructor as an `ActorRef`, not an `Actor`. An `ActorRef` is a *reference* to an actor. Because an actor may be on a different server, having a direct reference isn't always possible. In addition, actor instances may come and go over the lifetime of the actor system. The reference provides a level of isolation that allows the actor system to manage those events and prevents actors from directly changing the state of other actors. All communication between actors must occur through messages.

Listing 2.2 Tourist actor

```
import akka.actor.{Actor, ActorRef}

import Guidebook.Inquiry
import Tourist.{Guidance, Start}

class Tourist(guidebook: ActorRef) extends Actor {

  override def receive = {
    case Start(codes) =>
      codes.foreach(guidebook ! Inquiry(_))
    case Guidance(code, description) =>
      println(s"$code: $description")
  }
}
```

Extracts the codes from the message

For each code, send an inquiry message to the guidebook by using the ! operator.

Prints the guidance to the console

The ! operator

The use of the ! operator to send messages from one actor to another may be confusing the first few times you encounter it. The method is defined by the `ActorRef` trait. Writing

```
ref ! Message(x)
```

is equivalent to writing

```
ref.!(Message(x))(self)
```

Both methods use the `self` value, which is an `ActorRef` provided by the `Actor` trait as a reference to itself. The ! operator takes advantage of Scala infix notation and the fact that `self` is declared as an implicit value.

THE GUIDEBOOK ACTOR

The Guidebook in listing 2.3 is similar to the Tourist from listing 2.2. It processes one message: an Inquiry. When it receives an inquiry, the Guidebook uses a few classes built into the java.util package to generate a rudimentary description suitable for the example. Then it produces a Guidance message to send back to the tourist.

The Guidebook needs to address messages back to the tourist that sent the inquiry. An important difference between the Guidebook and the Tourist is how each actor acquires a reference to the other. In the Tourist, a fixed reference to the Guidebook is provided as a parameter to the constructor. Because many Tourists could be consulting the same Guidebook, that approach doesn't work here. It wouldn't make sense to tell a Guidebook in advance about every Tourist who might use it. Instead, the `Guidebook` sends the guidance message back to the same actor that sent the inquiry. The `sender` inherited from the `Actor` trait provides a reference back to the actor that sent the message. This reference can be used for simple request-reply messaging.

> **NOTE** Knowing that Akka is used for concurrent applications, you might expect the `sender` reference to be synchronized to prevent the receive processing for one message from inadvertently responding to the sender of another message. As you'll learn in chapters 3 and 4, the Akka design prevents this situation from happening. For now, rest assured that you don't need to worry about it.

Listing 2.3   Guidebook actor

```
import akka.actor.Actor

import Guidebook.Inquiry
import Tourist.Guidance

import java.util.{Currency, Locale}

class Guidebook extends Actor {
  def describe(locale: Locale) =
    s"""In ${locale.getDisplayCountry},
      ${locale.getDisplayLanguage} is spoken and the currency
      is the ${Currency.getInstance(locale).getDisplayName}"""

  override def receive = {
    case Inquiry(code) =>
println(s"Actor ${self.path.name}
 responding to inquiry about $code")
      Locale.getAvailableLocales.
      filter(_.getCountry == code).
      foreach { locale =>
        sender ! Guidance(code, describe(locale))
      }
  }
}
```

- Uses Java built-in packages to produce a rather basic description
- Prints a log message to the console
- Finds every locale with a matching country code. This implementation is rather inefficient.
- Sends the guidance back to the sender

Now that you have two complete actors and some messages to pass between them, you'll want to try it yourself. First set up your development environment to build and run an actor system.

2.2   *Setting up the example project*

The examples in this book are built with *sbt*, which is a build tool commonly used for Scala projects. The home page for the tool is www.scala-sbt.org; there, you can find instructions to install the tool for your operating system. The example code is available online. You can retrieve a copy of the complete example by using the command

```
git clone https://github.com/ironfish/reactive-application-development-scala
```

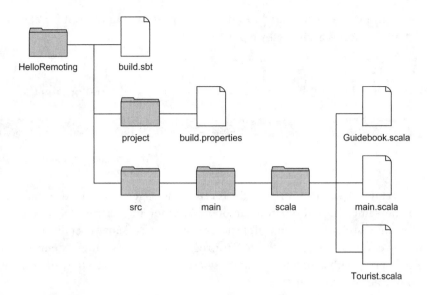

Figure 2.4   The layout of the sbt project follows the pattern used by other build systems, such as Maven and Gradle.

The source code is in the chapter2_001_guidebook_demo directory. The layout of the project is shown in figure 2.4 and is similar to that used by other build tools, such as Maven and Gradle. The project includes source code and the following files:

- *build.sbt*—Contains the build instructions
- *build.properties*—Tells sbt which version of sbt to use

As with other modern tools, sbt prefers convention to configuration. The build.sbt file shown in the following listing contains a project name and version, Scala version, repository URL, and a dependency on `akka-actor`.

Listing 2.4   build.sbt

```
name := "Guidebook"

version := "1.0"

scalaVersion := "2.12.3"          ◁── The example
                                        was tested with
                                        Scala 2.12.3.

val akkaVersion = "2.5.4"

resolvers += "Lightbend Repository" at
➥ http://repo.typesafe.com/typesafe/releases/   ◁──

libraryDependencies ++= Seq(
  "com.typesafe.akka" %% "akka-actor" % akkaVersion   ◁──
)
```

Typesafe is now known as Lightbend, but the repository at typesafe.com is still supported.

The example was tested with Akka 2.4.8. The %% tells sbt to use a version of the library that was compiled for the version of Scala defined above.

The build.properties file allows sbt to use a different version of itself for each project. The default version is available by typing

```
sbt about
```

at the console. The complete one-line file is shown in the following listing.

Listing 2.5   build.properties

```
sbt.version=0.13.12
```
◁——┐ **The example was tested
     with sbt 0.13.12.**

You've already seen the source code for the messages and the two actors, which remain the same throughout this chapter. Whether the example actors are in one actor system or spread across multiple actor systems across many servers is determined entirely by configuration and the `Main` programs that drive the system. In the next section, you run both actors in one actor system. Then you learn to scale the system by using multiple actor systems.

2.3   *Starting the actor system*

Akka doesn't require much to get started. You create the actor system and add some actors; the Akka library does the rest. Sometimes, as shown in figure 2.5, it's useful to

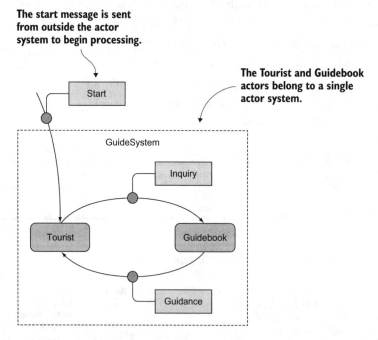

Figure 2.5   Both the `Tourist` **and** `Guidebook` **actors are deployed into the same actor system. The start message is sent from outside the actor system.**

get things moving by sending a first message to the system. In chapters 3 and 4, you learn a bit more about what Akka is doing behind the scenes. To learn even more about the internals, see *Akka in Action*, by Raymond Roestenburg, Rob Bakker, and Rob Williams (Manning, 2016).

2.3.1 *Creating the driver*

The driver program shown in listing 2.6 does as expected: creates an actor system, defines the actors, and sends the `Start` message. The definition of the actors is interesting. Actor instances may come and go over the life of the actor system. The actor system takes responsibility for creating new instances, so it needs enough information to construct a new instance. That information is passed via `Props`. The steps are

1 Create a `Props` object that contains the class of the actor and the constructor parameters, if any.
2 Pass the `Props` to the `actorOf` method to create a new actor and assign it a name. This method is defined by the `ActorRefFactory` trait. That trait is extended by several classes, including `ActorSystem`, which is used in the example.
3 Record the `ActorRef` returned by `actorOf`. Callers don't receive a direct reference to the new actor.

> **Listing 2.6 The `Main` driver application**

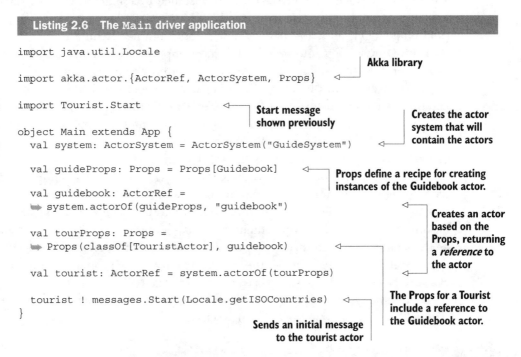

```
import java.util.Locale

import akka.actor.{ActorRef, ActorSystem, Props}          ◁── Akka library

import Tourist.Start          ◁── Start message shown previously

object Main extends App {
  val system: ActorSystem = ActorSystem("GuideSystem")          ◁── Creates the actor system that will contain the actors

  val guideProps: Props = Props[Guidebook]          ◁── Props define a recipe for creating instances of the Guidebook actor.

  val guidebook: ActorRef =
➡ system.actorOf(guideProps, "guidebook")          ◁── Creates an actor based on the Props, returning a reference to the actor

  val tourProps: Props =
➡ Props(classOf[TouristActor], guidebook)          ◁── The Props for a Tourist include a reference to the Guidebook actor.

  val tourist: ActorRef = system.actorOf(tourProps)

  tourist ! messages.Start(Locale.getISOCountries)          ◁── Sends an initial message to the tourist actor
}
```

There's nothing special about the driver. Because it extends the `App` trait, it automatically has a `Main` function, like any other Scala or Java application.

2.3.2 *Running the driver*

The output of the build is a Java Archive (JAR) file. You could use sbt to generate the build and then use the `java` command to launch it, but during development, it's easier to let sbt take care of that job too. Use

```
sbt run
```

to build and launch the application. As with nearly any framework, building the application the first time may take a while, because the dependencies need to be downloaded. The sbt tool uses Apache Ivy (http://ant.apache.org/ivy) for dependency management, and Ivy caches the dependencies locally.

Here's the part you've been waiting for: if you built everything successfully, you should see the `Guidebook` printing a message for every inquiry it receives, and the `Tourist` printing concise travel guidance for every country. Congratulations! You've started your first actor system. A more sophisticated application would send another message to tell the actors to shut themselves down gracefully. For now, press Ctrl-C to stop the actor system.

2.4   *Distributing the actors over multiple systems*

Actors are lightweight objects. At about 300 bytes, the memory overhead required per actor is a small fraction of the stack space consumed by a single thread. It's possible to hold a lot of actors in a single Java virtual machine (JVM). At some point, a single JVM still isn't enough. The actors have to scale across multiple machines.

You've already put into practice the most important concepts that make distributed actors possible. Actors refer to one another only via actor references. The `Tourist` actor refers to the `Guidebook` by using an `ActorRef` supplied to the constructor, and the `Guidebook` actor refers to the `Tourist` only through the sender `ActorRef`. An `ActorRef` may refer to a local actor or to a remote actor, so both actors are already capable of working with distributed actor systems. Whether the references are to local or remote actors makes no difference to the code.

The first step you took toward making the messages work across multiple machines was making them immutable. It wouldn't be possible to change the content of a message after it's been sent from one machine to another. The remaining step toward making the messages fully self-contained is making them serializable, so that they can be transmitted and reconstructed by the actor system that receives the message. Once again, Scala case classes come to the rescue. As long as the properties within the case class can be serialized, the whole class can be serialized, too.

Finally, the system needs some way to resolve references to actors in remote actor systems. You learn how in the following sections.

2.4.1 *Distributing to two JVMs*

When the example moves from one to two JVMs, the actors and messages remain the same. What changes? The new version is shown in figure 2.6. The primary difference

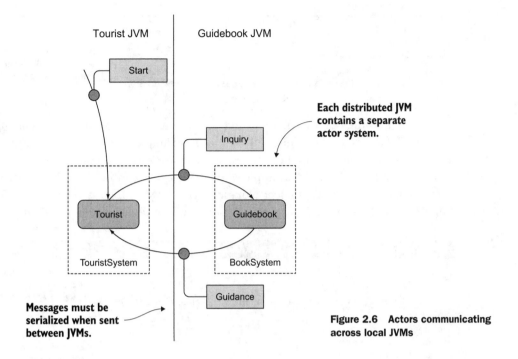

Figure 2.6   Actors communicating across local JVMs

between figure 2.6 and the example shown in figure 2.5 is that figure 2.6 shows two actor systems. Each JVM needs its own actor system to manage its own actors.

If you cloned the original example from the Git repository, you can use the source in the chapter2_002_two_jvm directory.

2.4.2   Configuring for remote actors

As you might expect, distributing actors requires a little more setup than when everything is in one JVM. The process requires configuring an additional Akka library called `akka-remote`. The affected files are

- *build.sbt*—Adds the dependency on `akka-remote`
- *application.conf*—Provides some configuration information for remote actors

The change from the previous build.sbt example is nothing more than the inclusion of the additional library, as shown in the following listing.

Listing 2.7   build.sbt for remote actors

```
name := "Guidebook"

version := "1.0"

scalaVersion := "2.12.3"

val akkaVersion = "2.5.4"
```

```
resolvers += "Lightbend Repository" at "http://repo.typesafe.com/typesafe/
    releases/"

libraryDependencies ++= Seq(
  "com.typesafe.akka" %% "akka-actor" % akkaVersion,
  "com.typesafe.akka" %% "akka-remote" % akkaVersion
)
```

> **Adds dependency on remote actors. The Akka version numbers should match.**

The configuration file shown in listing 2.8 is read automatically by Akka during startup. The tourist and guidebook JVMs in this example can use the same configuration file. More complex applications would require separate configuration files for each JVM, but the example is simple enough that one can be shared. The syntax is Human-Optimized Config Object Notation (HOCON), which is a JavaScript Object Notation (JSON) superset designed to be more convenient for humans to edit.

Listing 2.8   application.conf for remote actors

```
akka {
  actor {
    provider = "akka.remote.RemoteActorRefProvider"
  }
  remote {
    enabled-transports = ["akka.remote.netty.tcp"]
    netty.tcp {
      hostname = "127.0.0.1"
      port = ${?PORT}
    }
  }
}
```

> **Replaces the default LocalActorRefProvider with the RemoteActorRefProvider**

> **Enables remote communication by using the Transmission Control Protocol (TCP). Check the Akka documentation for other choices, such as Secure Sockets Layer (SSL) encryption.**

> **The remote actors in the example will run on your local machine.**

> **Obtains a port number from the PORT environment variable. If none is specified, the number defaults to 0, and Akka chooses a port automatically.**

2.4.3   Setting up the drivers

Now that the configuration steps are complete, the next step is adding a program to act as a driver for the Guidebook actor system.

THE GUIDEBOOK DRIVER

The driver for the Guidebook actor system is a reduced version of the original driver for the entire system. Other than removing the Tourist actor, the only change is to provide unique names for the actor system and for the Guidebook actor. The names make it easier for the Tourist actor to obtain an ActorRef to the Guidebook. The complete code is shown in the following listing.

Listing 2.9   Driver for the Guidebook JVM

```
import akka.actor.{ActorRef, ActorSystem, Props}

object GuidebookMain extends App {
  val system: ActorSystem = ActorSystem("BookSystem")
```

> **Names the actor *system* uniquely**

```
    val guideProps: Props =Props[Guidebook]
    val guidebook: ActorRef =
➡ system.actorOf(guideProps, "guidebook")
}
```

◁——┐ **Produces an ActorRef the same as in the single JVM example**

◁——┘ **Names the *actor* uniquely**

Now that the Guidebook driver is complete, you can move on to the Tourist driver.

THE TOURIST DRIVER

The constructor for the Tourist actor requires a reference to the Guidebook actor. In the original example, this task was easy because the reference was returned when the Guidebook actor was defined. Now that the Guidebook actor is in a remote JVM, this technique won't work. To obtain a reference to the remote Guidebook actor, the driver

1 Obtains a URL-like path to the remote actor
2 Creates an ActorSelection from the path
3 Resolves the selection into an ActorRef

Resolving the selection causes the local actor system to attempt to talk to the remote actor and verify its existence. Because this process takes time, resolving the actor selection into a reference requires a timeout value and returns a Future[ActorRef]. You don't need to worry about the details of how a future works. For now, it's sufficient to understand that if the path resolves successfully, the resulting ActorRef is used as it was in the single JVM example. The complete driver is shown in listing 2.10.

> **NOTE** The scala.concurrent.Future[T] used here isn't the same as a java.util.concurrent.Future<T>. It's closer to—though not the same as—the java.util.concurrent.CompletableFuture<T> in Java 8.

Listing 2.10 Driver for the Tourist JVM

```
import java.util.Locale


import akka.actor.{ActorRef, ActorSystem, Props}
import akka.util.Timeout
import tourist.TouristActor


import scala.concurrent.ExecutionContext.Implicits.global
import scala.concurrent.duration.SECONDS
import scala.util.{Failure, Success}


object TouristMain extends App {
  val system: ActorSystem = ActorSystem("TouristSystem")


  val path =
    "akka.tcp://BookSystem@127.0.0.1:2553/user/guidebook"
```

◁——┘ **Names the actor *system* uniquely**

◁——┘ **Specifes the remote URL path for the Guidebook actor**

```
    implicit val timeout: Timeout = Timeout(5, SECONDS)    ◁─┐  Waits up to 5 seconds for
                                                              │  the Guidebook to respond

system.actorSelection(path).resolveOne().onComplete {  ◁─┐  Converts the path
  case Success(guidebook) =>                              │  to an ActorSelection
                                                          │  and resolves it

    val tourProps: Props =
    ➡ Props(classOf[TouristActor], guidebook)
    val tourist: ActorRef = system.actorOf(tourProps)

    tourist ! messages.Start(Locale.getISOCountries)


  case Failure(e) => println(e)                     ◁──┐
  }
}
```

Annotations:
- **If the Guidebook is resolved successfully, continue as in the single JVM example.**
- **If the Guidebook fails to resolve, fail with an error.**

At this point, you have configuration and drivers to run the original `Tourist` and `Guidebook` actors in separate actor systems on separate JVMs. Notice that the messages and actors are unchanged from the original example, which isn't uncommon. Actors are designed to be distributable by default.

Now it's time to try the distributed actors.

2.4.4   *Running the distributed actors*

To run two JVMs, you need two command prompts. Start by opening a terminal session as you did for the single-actor system in section 2.3. This time, the `sbt` command line has to specify which `Main` class to use, because you have two. Recall that the application.conf file in listing 2.8 specifies that the listener port should be read from the `PORT` environment variable, so you have to specify the port as well.

Because the `Guidebook` waits forever for actors to contact it, but the `Tourist` waits for only a few seconds to find a `Guidebook`, the `Guidebook` is started first. The command line

The double quotes around the –D parameter are necessary in Windows but optional on other platforms.

```
sbt "-Dakka.remote.netty.tcp.port=2553" "runMain GuidebookMain"     ◁──┐
```

should result in several messages to the console, ending with a log entry that tells you that the book system is now listening on port 2553.

Next open a second terminal window. The command line to run the tourist is almost the same:

```
sbt "runMain TouristMain"
```

The differences are the port number and the choice of `Main` class to run.

If everything has gone as expected, the `Tourist` should print the same `Guidebook` information as in the original example. Congratulations! You've created a distributed actor system.

As an exercise, try opening a third terminal and running another `Tourist` on a different port number. The code works because the `Guidebook` always responds to the *sender* of a message; it doesn't care whether one `Tourist` is sending a message or a thousand `Tourists` are sending messages. If you have thousands of `Tourists`, however, you may want to have more than one `Guidebook` actor too. In the next section, you learn how.

2.5 Scaling with multiple actors

Shortly after Akka 2.0 was released in 2012, a benchmark (http://letitcrash.com/post/20397701710/50-million-messages-per-second-on-a-single) demonstrated sending 50 million messages per second on a single machine—far more than a single `Guidebook` actor would be able to handle. Recall that the actor system guarantees that no more than one thread has access to the actor at a time. Eventually, there'd be too many incoming messages for a single actor, and it would be necessary to have multiple `Guidebook` actors to service all the requests.

Actor systems make adding multiple actors easy. An actor-based system handles scaling to multiple actors uniformly, whether the actors are local or remote. The additional `Guidebook` actors may run in the same JVM or in separate JVMs. In the rest of this chapter, you learn to put additional instances of the same actor in the same JVM; then you learn to scale horizontally to another JVM, which is a taste of things to come. Chapter 4 revisits these concepts in greater depth.

Before extending the actor system, take a look at how traditional systems that don't use actors approach the same problem.

2.5.1 Traditional alternatives

In a traditional system, scaling is handled quite differently, depending on the decision to put additional instances in the same JVM or to deploy them remotely. If the instances are in the same JVM, a system that doesn't use actors might instead use an explicit thread pool to balance requests, as shown in figure 2.7.

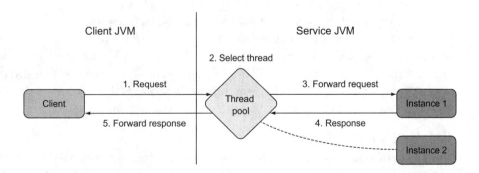

Figure 2.7   A thread pool can be used to manage access to multiple instances of a service.

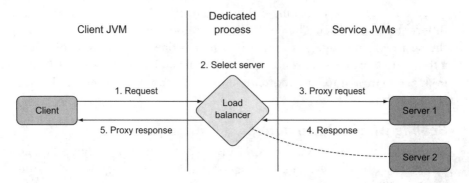

Figure 2.8   A traditional load balancer introduces a separate process between the client and server.

If the instances are in separate JVMs, the system could use a dedicated load balancer that sits between the client and service, as shown in figure 2.8. In most cases, the communication through the load balancer uses HTTP as the protocol.

Many excellent load-balancer implementations are available. HAProxy (www .haproxy.org) is a dedicated software solution, and NGINX (www.nginx.com) may be configured as a reverse proxy. Some companies even produce hardware solutions, such as the BIG-IP Local Traffic Manager from F5 Networks, Inc. Those solutions are outside the scope of this book, however, because they're not necessary. Instead, load balancing is handled by the actor system.

2.5.2   Routing as an actor function

In an actor-based system, the load balancer can be treated as an actor specialized for routing messages. The client treats the `ActorRef` to the router no differently than it treats a reference to the service itself. You've already seen that local and remote actors are treated uniformly, which continues to hold true here. The client doesn't need to concern itself with whether the router is local or remote. That decision can be made as part of system configuration, independent of how the client or service is coded.

Returning to the guidebook example, the `Tourist` actor sends an inquiry message to the router, the router selects a `Guidebook` actor, and the `Guidebook` sends the guidance directly back to the `Tourist`, all as shown in figure 2.9.

Recall from section 2.1 that the `Guidebook` actor sends its response back to the sender of a message. You may wonder how that process works when the message comes from the router rather than the original client. The answer is that the router doesn't pass a reference to itself as the sender. It forwards the *original* sender, so the routed message appears to have come directly from the client.

2.6   Creating a pool of actors

A single actor, such as the guidebook example, handles only one request at a time, which greatly simplifies coding, because the actor doesn't have to worry about synchronization. It also means that the `Guidebook` can become a bottleneck, because there's

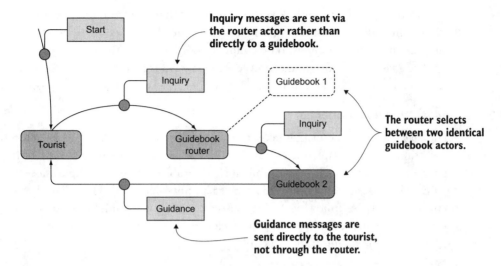

Inquiry messages are sent via the router actor rather than directly to a guidebook.

The router selects between two identical guidebook actors.

Guidance messages are sent directly to the tourist, not through the router.

Figure 2.9 Sending messages from the `Tourist` to the `Guidebook` through a router that performs load balancing

only one `Guidebook` and every request has to wait for it to become available. The simplest way to scale is to add a pool of `Guidebook` actors within the single-actor system and create a router to balance the inquiries. Figure 2.10 shows this approach.

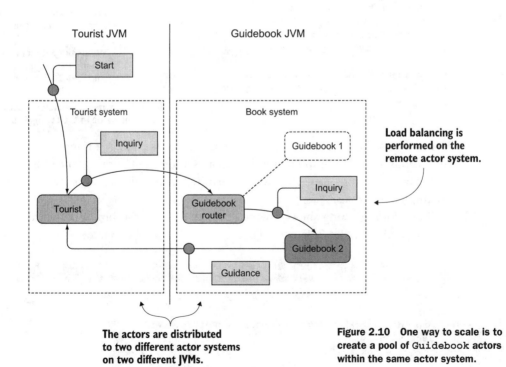

Load balancing is performed on the remote actor system.

The actors are distributed to two different actor systems on two different JVMs.

Figure 2.10 One way to scale is to create a pool of `Guidebook` actors within the same actor system.

The Tourist and Guidebook actors remain unchanged from the previous examples. In fact, the entire tourist system remains the same. As you see in the next section, only the guidebook system needs to be changed to incorporate the change.

If you cloned the original example from the Git repository, you can use the source in the chapter2_003_pool directory, which uses two JVMs and an actor pool.

2.6.1   Adding the pool router

The *pool router* is an actor that takes the place of the original Guidebook actor. As with any other actor, you need a Props for the router actor. It's possible to configure an actor pool entirely within code, but it's preferable to use a configuration file. Akka routing includes a convenient FromConfig utility that tells Akka to configure a pool. The driver in the following listing passes the original guidebook Props to From-Config so that Akka knows how to create new pool members, and everything else comes from the configuration file.

> **Listing 2.11   Driver for the guidebook JVM with a pool of guidebooks**

```
import akka.actor.{ActorRef, ActorSystem, Props}
import akka.routing.FromConfig                        ◁──── Imports library to read
                                                             the pool configuration
object GuidebookMain extends App {                           from application.conf
  val system: ActorSystem = ActorSystem("BookSystem")

  val guideProps: Props = Props[Guidebook]           ◁──── Props for the Guidebook
                                                           actor are unchanged.
  val routerProps: Props =
  ➥ FromConfig.props(guideProps)                     ◁──── Wraps the pool configuration
                                                           around the original Props for
  val guidebook: ActorRef =                                the Guidebook actor
  ➥ system.actorOf(routerProps, "guidebook")   ◁───
}
                                              The name of the actor must match
                                              the name in the configuration file.
```

Akka includes several built-in pool routers. One of the most commonly used is the round-robin pool. This implementation creates a set number of instances of the actor and forwards requests to each actor in turn. Chapter 4 describes some of the other pool implementations.

The following listing shows how to configure a round-robin pool containing five instances of the Guidebook actor. These instances are called *routees*.

> **Listing 2.12   application.conf with a pool of Guidebook actors**

```
akka {
  actor {
    provider = "akka.remote.RemoteActorRefProvider"
    deployment {                                      Configures a pool for
      /guidebook {                           ◁──────  the Guidebook actor
```

```
        router = round-robin-pool
        nr-of-instances = 5
      }
    }
  }
  remote {
    enabled-transports = ["akka.remote.netty.tcp"]
    netty.tcp {
      hostname = "127.0.0.1"
      port = ${?PORT}
    }
  }
}
```

> **Uses the built-in round-robin pool implementation with five instances in the pool**

As you can see, Akka makes it easy to create many actors in a pool. You create a pool actor, give it the `Props` needed to create new pool entries, and configure the pool as needed through the configuration file.

2.6.2 *Running the pooled actor system*

Running the pool of actors is easy, too. The process is the same as running the two-actor system example shown previously in this section. As before, the command line

```
sbt "-Dakka.remote.netty.tcp.port=2553" "runMain GuidebookMain"
```

starts the guidebook system, and the command line

```
sbt "runMain TouristMain"
```

starts the tourist system, which is unchanged. The output on the tourist console should be the same as before. The difference is on the guidebook console. Before the pool was added, each inquiry resulted in the `Guidebook` actor's printing a line such as

```
Actor guidebook responding to inquiry about AD
```

Now that the actor named `Guidebook` is a router actor, each instance of the `Guidebook` actor in the pool is assigned a different, random name. The inquiries now result in each `Guidebook` actor's printing a line such as

```
Actor $a responding to inquiry about AD
```

Because five actors are configured, the console output should show five different names for the actor, such as $a, $b, $c, $d, and $e.

> **NOTE** The round-robin pool is one of several pool implementations included with Akka. You can try some of the other types by changing the configuration file. Other choices to try include random-pool, balancing-pool, smallest-mail-box-pool, scatter-gather-pool, and tail-chopping-pool.

In this section, you scaled an actor system by replacing a single actor with a router with a pool of identical actors. In the next section, you apply the same concepts to distribute messages across multiple-actor systems on multiple JVMs.

2.7   *Scaling with multiple-actor systems*

The router actor is responsible for keeping track of the routees that handle the messages that it receives. The pool routers in the preceding section handled this task by creating and managing the routees themselves. An alternative approach is to provide a group of actors to the router but manage them separately. This approach is similar to how a traditional load balancer works. The difference is that a traditional load balancer uses a dedicated process to manage the group membership and perform the routing, whereas in the actor-based system, the routing may be performed by a router actor within the client, as shown in figure 2.11.

The two approaches aren't mutually exclusive. It's reasonable to have a router on the client select a remote actor system to service the request and then have another tier of routing in the service actor system select a specific actor instance from a pool. The response message still flows from the service actor directly to the original client actor.

If you cloned the original example from the Git repository, you can use the source in the chapter2_004_group directory, which keeps the pool router on the guidebook systems and adds a group router to the tourist system.

2.7.1   *Adding the group router*

The driver for the `Tourist` actor system is simpler with a group than in the initial system with a single remote actor. In the original example (listing 2.10), the driver

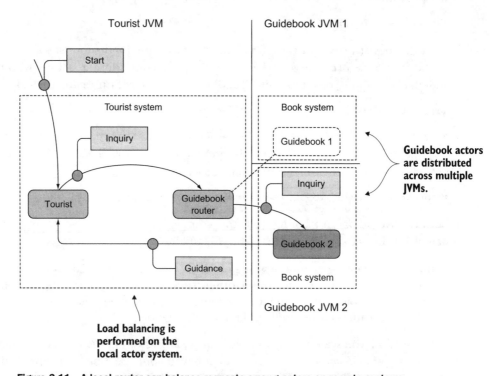

Figure 2.11   A local router can balance requests among actors on remote systems.

resolved the remote actor path by using a `Future[ActorRef]`, and the system waited for confirmation that the remote actor system had been verified before creating the `Tourist` actor. With a group router, all that work is handled by the group router, as shown in the following listing.

Listing 2.13 Driver for the `Tourist` JVM with a group of `Guidebook` systems

```
import java.util.Locale

import akka.actor.{ActorRef, ActorSystem, Props}
import akka.routing.FromConfig

import Tourist.Start

object TouristMain extends App {
  val system: ActorSystem = ActorSystem("TouristSystem")

  val guidebook: ActorRef =
    system.actorOf(FromConfig.props(), "balancer")

  val tourProps: Props =
    Props(classOf[Tourist], guidebook)

  val tourist: ActorRef = system.actorOf(tourProps)

  tourist ! Start(Locale.getISOCountries)
}
```

Imports library to read the pool configuration from application.conf

Uses a different name to distinguish this router from the router pool used by the Guidebook driver

The remaining steps are the same as the single JVM driver shown in listing 2.6.

Configuration of the router group is handled by the configuration file.

The group configuration for the balancer uses the round-robin-*group* rather than the round-robin-*pool*, as shown in the following listing. Group routers expect the routees to be provided, and they're provided via `routees.paths`. Some of the other group implementations are described in Chapter 4.

Listing 2.14 application.conf with a group of guidebook systems

```
akka {
  actor {
    provider = "akka.remote.RemoteActorRefProvider"
    deployment {
      /guidebook {
        router = round-robin-pool
        nr-of-instances = 5
      }
      /balancer {
        router = round-robin-group
        routees.paths = [
          "akka.tcp://BookSystem@127.0.0.1:2553/user/guidebook",
          "akka.tcp://BookSystem@127.0.0.1:2554/user/guidebook",
          "akka.tcp://BookSystem@127.0.0.1:2555/user/guidebook"]
      }
    }
  }
```

Leave alone the pool for the guidebook actor. It will continue to be used by the guidebook.

Creates a round-robin group router named balancer with three group members

```
    }
    remote {
      enabled-transports = ["akka.remote.netty.tcp"]
      netty.tcp {
        hostname = "127.0.0.1"
        port = ${?PORT}
      }
    }
}
```

The rest of the configuration file remains the same.

2.7.2   *Running the multiple actor systems*

The configuration in the preceding section instructed the balancer to look for three guidebooks by contacting the `BookSystem` actor systems listening on ports 2553, 2554, and 2555. Open three terminal windows, and start those three systems by using the following commands:

```
sbt "-Dakka.remote.netty.tcp.port=2553" "runMain GuidebookMain"    Run each of these
sbt "-Dakka.remote.netty.tcp.port=2554" "runMain GuidebookMain"    commands in a
sbt "-Dakka.remote.netty.tcp.port=2555" "runMain GuidebookMain"    separate terminal.
```

Next run the tourist system on a fourth terminal:

```
sbt "runMain TouristMain"
```

You should see the usual guidance on the tourist console.

Now switch to each of the terminal windows running the `guidebook` instances. You should see that all three of them have responded to some messages, and you should be able to verify that each received requests for different countries.

The pools within each of these actor systems are still in place, too, so the distributed actor system you're running now includes 16 actors: 1 `Tourist` actor plus 3 `Guidebook` systems that each have a pool of 5 `Guidebook` actors. That's quite a bit for such a small amount of code.

2.8   *Applying reactive principles*

The same `Tourist` and `Guidebook` actors remained unchanged throughout this chapter. At this point, both of the driver programs take their configuration from application.conf rather than having anything hardcoded. The complete system requires surprisingly little code. The two actors and their drivers are less than 100 lines of Scala, yet this system exhibits reactive attributes.

The four attributes that lay the foundation for reactive applications were introduced through the Reactive Manifesto in chapter 1. Reactive applications are message-driven, elastic, resilient, and responsive.

The examples in this chapter are *message-driven*. Everything occurs in response to the same three immutable messages. All communication among actors is accomplished asynchronously, and there's never a direct function call from one actor to another. Only the actor system calls the actor to pass it a message. The message passing exhibits location transparency. The sender doesn't concern itself with whether the recipient of a message is local or remote.

Location transparency also allows routers to be injected into the message flow, which helps achieve another reactive attribute. The application is *elastic*, too, capable of applying more resources by expanding a pool of local actors and capable of expanding remotely by adding remote actors.

In other words, you now have an elastic, message-driven system that you can scale horizontally without writing any new code, which is quite an accomplishment. Feel free to experiment with the configuration.

If you experiment, you'll find that that the system has some attributes of resilience and responsiveness, but it could be better. Chapters 3 and 4 show you the additional pieces needed to create a fully reactive application. You'll learn more about the design of Akka and how the components work together to deliver the underpinnings of the system you created in this chapter.

Summary

- Actors have a *receive* function that accepts a message and doesn't have a return value.
- Actors are called by the actor *system*, not directly by other actors. The actor system guarantees that there's never more than one thread at a time calling an actor's `receive` function, which simplifies the `receive` function because it doesn't have to be thread-safe.
- Actors are distributable by default. The same actors and the same messages were used throughout this chapter. Only the drivers and configuration changed as the example evolved from a pair of actors exchanging messages within a single JVM all the way to 16 actors distributed across 3 JVMs.
- Immutable messages flow among actors. Immutable messages are thread-safe and safe to copy, which is necessary when a message is serialized and sent to another actor system. Scala case classes offer a safe, easy way to define immutable messages.
- Senders address messages by using an `ActorRef`, which is obtained from the actor system. An `ActorRef` may refer to a local or a remote actor.
- Actor systems can be scaled via a router to balance requests among multiple actors. A router may be configured as a pool that creates and manages the actor instances for you. A group router requires the actors to be created and managed separately.

Understanding Akka 3

This chapter covers

- The actor model
- The actor system
- Akka as concurrent and asynchronous
- Share nothing, nonblocking design
- Akka supervision and Routers

Now that you have a good understanding of what a reactive application is and why you need it, it's time to pick a toolkit for building such systems. Before you do, quickly review the traits of a reactive system to make sure that the tools you pick are up to the job.

The Reactive Manifesto (chapter 1) lays out four key traits that identify a reactive system:

- *Responsive*—The system responds in a timely manner if at all possible. Responsiveness is the cornerstone of usability and utility; more than that, it means that problems may be detected quickly and dealt with effectively.

- *Resilient*—The system stays responsive in the face of failure. Resiliency doesn't apply only to highly available, mission-critical systems; any system that isn't resilient will be unresponsive after a failure.
- *Elastic*—The system stays responsive under varying workloads. Reactive systems can respond to changes in load by increasing or decreasing the allocation of resources.
- *Message-driven*—The system is based on asynchronous communication, where the design of sender and recipient are not affected by the means of message propagation. As a result, you can design your system in isolation without worrying about the how of transmission. Message-driven communication leads to loosely coupled design that provides the context for responsiveness, resiliency, and elasticity.

In taking a close look at these four traits, notice an interesting distinction about one of them: message-driven. The first three traits—responsive, resilient, and elastic—are about how a reactive system behaves, whereas the message-driven trait operates in a supportive role, allowing the first three traits to do their jobs. You can think of this trait in terms of implementation: you implement an asynchronous, message-driven architecture to promote responsive, resilient, and elastic behavior. Therefore, one of the key capabilities of any toolkit you choose should be support for asynchronous message passing.

Although other toolkits support message passing, the one we chose for this book is Akka.[1] The basis for this decision was the distributed nature of Akka, as well as our experience with it in production. Although we dig into Akka and its many features in this chapter, the chapter isn't intended to be exhaustive. We use analogy, explanation, and some code examples to show the reactive nature of Akka. The foundation in Akka we give you here sets you up to understand all the Akka we use later in the book. Later in the book, you learn clustering and sharding, CQRS, Event Sourcing, microservice-based design, distributed testing, and other technologies to round out your reactive learning.

> **TIP** If you've read anything about Akka, the term *hAkking* is probably familiar to you. If not, you can most likely guess what it means. *hAkking* is an affectionate quip for coding or hacking in Akka, coined in 2009.

The next section describes Akka and shows how it qualifies as a reactive toolkit.

3.1 *What is Akka?*

Akka is the brainchild of Jonas Bonér, chief technology officer and co-founder of Typesafe. Being an experienced enterprise Java architect and competent with distributed application technologies such as CORBA, EJB, and RPC (heavyweight protocols

---

[1] Programming with actors (http://en.wikipedia.org/wiki/Actor_model).

with concrete local and remote interfaces), Bonér grew frustrated with older technologies' limitations on scalability and resilience, along with its synchronous nature. He began to realize that these technologies, as well as the standards and abstraction techniques used to approach distributed computing on the JVM, weren't going to work as the level of distribution increased.

Not one to give up, he began looking outside the Java enterprise space for answers, and he came upon Erlang and Erlang Open Telecom Platform (OTP)-style supervisors. Erlang is a programming language used in telecommunications, banking, and other industries to build scalable, soft (a systemic approach for tackling real-world problematic situations), real-time systems that are meant to have high availability. It supports the traits of the Reactive Manifesto through the Erlang OTP libraries. OTP is designed to be middleware that provides the tools necessary for development. Bonér realized that the approach used by Erlang for failure management and distribution of critical infrastructure services such as telecommunications could be applied to mainstream enterprises as well. From the Akka perspective, OTP is best known for its actor implementation with supervision trees that provide the semantics for self-healing that make both Erlang and Akka resilient.

One component of Erlang in particular captured Bonér's attention: the actor model, a mathematical model of concurrent computation in which decisions are made locally within an actor and then transmitted as a lightweight message. From the actor model, he realized that it was possible to build loosely coupled systems with "let-it-crash" semantics that embrace failure and allow deterministic reasoning in a multi-threaded environment.[2] For him, this was a light-bulb moment, and after several months of hAkking, he released the first version of Akka (v0.5) on June 12, 2009.[3]

As a testament to the enduring design of Akka, the following snippet from the v0.5 README.md still holds true today:

The Akka kernel implements a unique hybrid of

- The Actor model (Actors and Active Objects).
- Asynchronous, non-blocking, highly concurrent components.
- Supervision with "let-it-crash" semantics. Components are loosely coupled and restarted upon failure.

What is a kernel?

A *kernel* in computer science is the central part of the operating system that manages tasks of the computer and hardware, and is the most fundamental part of the system. Kernels come in two forms:

- *Microkernel*—Contains only core functionality
- *Monolithic kernel*—Contains core functionality and many drivers

---

[2] Akka 5 Year Anniversary - htttp://goo.gl/WXRYxI
[3] Akka v0.5 - https://github.com/akka/akka/releases/tag/v0.5

Monolithic kernels are useful primarily for the core of an operating system, such as Linux, and extensible through a set of drivers. Microkernels, on the other hand, focus on specific problems, such as controlling memory or CPU cycles in the case of an operating system. The term *microkernel* often applies to more than one OS, as is the case with Akka. In Akka, the microkernel is a bundling mechanism that allows you to deploy and run your application without the need for an application server or launch script.

3.2 Akka today

In today's world, the demand for distributed systems has exploded. As customer expectations such as immediate response, no failure, and access anywhere increase, companies have come to realize that distributed computing is the only viable solution. In turn, the requirements placed on distributed technologies have become more rigorous. Application clustering, distributed persistence, distributed caching, and Big Data management are fast becoming expected members of any competent toolkit.

The core Akka library akka-actor provides all the semantics for the message passing, serialization, dispatch, and routing. To satisfy these increasing requirements, toolkits such as Akka must continually react by enhancing existing tools and adding new ones. Over the past couple of years, the Akka team has added some of the highest-quality distributed tools available to the toolkit. The following subsections give you a high-level overview of several of those tools, many of which we discuss in detail throughout the book.

3.2.1 Becoming responsive

Reactive applications are message-driven and use different design patterns from traditional synchronous approaches. The first set of tools contains the building blocks of reactive applications.

FUTURES

Reactive applications have seamless integration with Futures (data structures used to retrieve the result of some concurrent operations). As a result, you can synchronously reason about asynchronous computations and safely modify shared state.

ROUTERS AND DISPATCHERS

The Routers and Dispatchers implementation in Akka provides a powerful mechanism for parallel programming.

AKKA STREAMS

Akka Streams is a recent addition to the Akka toolkit. Its goal is to govern the exchange of stream data across asynchronous boundaries by managing backpressure. This technology is so profound that many other tools in Akka—such as Akka persistence, Spray.io (now Akka HTTP), and products such as the Play framework—will be updated to take advantage of Akka Streams.

AKKA HTTP

Akka HTTP is based on the Spray.io library and provides an HTTP request/response model that incorporates streamed data on demand. Relying on Akka Streams under the covers, backpressure is implicitly managed, bringing significant enhancements in responsiveness to the HTTP paradigm.

3.2.2 *Retaining data reliably*

In the actor model, actors manage state. If an actor fails, it no longer has whatever it was holding. Akka addresses this data reliability with both in-memory and on-disk replication.

AKKA DATA REPLICATION

Akka Data Replication is Akka's answer to conflict-free replicated data types (CRDTs). CRDTs allow for replicated in-memory data storage that's eventually consistent and has low latency and full availability. You can think of CRDTs as being a distributed cache.

AKKA PERSISTENCE

Persistent state management is a staple in most applications. Akka persistence provides not only this management, but also automatic recovery when a system restarts due to failure or migration. In addition, Akka persistence provides the foundation for building CQRS- and Event Sourced-based systems.

3.2.3 *Increasing resiliency and elasticity*

Akka adopts a distributed-by-default mentality through a unified programming model with referential or location transparency. Local and remote scenarios use the same API and are distinguished by configuration, providing a more succinct way to code message-driven applications. The remoting capabilities provide the basis for advanced clustering and persistence features that allow Akka systems to withstand failure and scale as needed.

AKKA CLUSTER

Akka Cluster, a loosely coupled group of systems that present themselves as a single system, provides a resilient, decentralized, peer-to-peer-based cluster membership service with no single point of failure or single point of bottleneck. Akka Cluster works by using gossip protocols and an automatic failure detector.

CLUSTER AWARE ROUTERS

Akka's Cluster Aware Routers take Akka Routers to the next level by automatically rebalancing load whenever a new member joins the cluster.

CLUSTER SINGLETON

Sometimes, you need exactly one instance of a process running in a cluster, such as a single point of entry to an external system. Akka provides the Cluster Singleton for such use cases.

CLUSTER SHARDING

Cluster Sharding allows you to interact with actors that are distributed across several nodes in a cluster by a logical identifier. This access by logical identifier is important when your actors in aggregate consume more resources than can fit on one machine. A system may have sufficient memory for only a fraction of the actors, for example. Sharding allows the actors to be distributed across many nodes without your having to embed additional logic in the clients to find the correct node for each actor.

3.2.4 Supporting Big Data with Spark

Spark is a library that turns data operations on their head by moving the computation to the data rather than having the computation read the data, and for that reason, it's performant for data-intensive operations and transformations. Big Data management is quickly becoming one of the most important requirements placed on distributed systems. Fortunately, there are technologies such as Spark (a Big Data streaming compute engine), a Scala application that leverages Akka. Although it's not officially part of the Akka toolkit, Spark feels right at home in any reactive environment, due to its Akka foundation.

Today, Akka is defined as a toolkit and runtime for building highly concurrent, distributed, resilient, message-driven applications on the JVM. In the following section, we look at the philosophy behind this definition and establish some terminology that helps you tie Akka's features to the reactive paradigm as you move through the chapter.

3.3 Akka terminology

Now that you've been introduced to Akka's origins and seen some of its advanced features, you're ready to dig into the methods employed to make Akka reactive. In this section, we define some important terms.

> **Where did Akka get its name?**
>
> Akka (the Swedified form of Ahkka from the Sámi language) is a massif (a compact group of mountains, distinct from other groups) in the northern part of Sweden. It contains 10 glaciers and 12 peaks, with Stortoppen being the highest.
>
> Akka is also the name of a goddess in Swedish mythology who stands for all the beauty and good in the world. The mountain can be seen as the symbol of this goddess.

3.3.1 Concurrency and parallelism

Concurrency and parallelism are sometimes confused as meaning the same thing, but although the terms are related, they have some differences. Figure 3.1 shows how a single toll booth becomes a blocker and slows the entire line of traffic. Adding a second toll booth removes the block and allows much greater traffic flow.

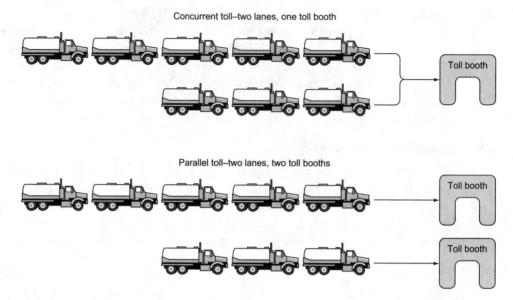

Concurrent toll–two lanes, one toll booth

Parallel toll–two lanes, two toll booths

Figure 3.1   Concurrency and parallelism compared

- *Concurrency* improves throughput by allowing two or more tasks to make progress in a nondetermined fashion, which may or may not run simultaneously. As a result, concurrent programming focuses on the complexity that arises from that nondeterministic control flow, as we discussed in chapter 1 in the section on tightly coupled middleware.
- *Parallelism*, on the other hand, occurs when execution of the tasks happens simultaneously. Parallel programming focuses on improving throughput by making flow control deterministic.

Concurrency and parallelism are key to reactive systems, as they promote responsiveness, support elasticity, and are part of the Akka DNA. On the flip side, they introduce nondeterminism and isolated processing, which require management in the aggregate, meaning that you have no guarantees of where and when a process will occur. As you work through the book, we show you how Akka leverages these constructs, as well as the best way to implement and manage them through the application you'll build.

3.3.2   *Asynchronous and synchronous*

Concurrency and parallelism are about how to process throughput; asynchronous and synchronous are about how to access that throughput. A method is said to be *synchronous* if the caller of that method must wait for a return or failure condition. The opposite is true of asynchronous. An *asynchronous* method doesn't require its caller to wait.

If the caller wants a response, a form of signal completion is required, such as a callback, future, or message passing. Figure 3.2 shows some common forms of signal completion for asynchronous methods.

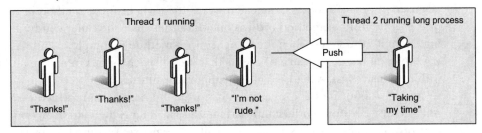

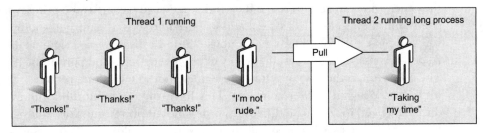

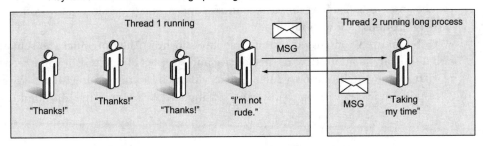

Figure 3.2 Different forms of signal completion

Blocking occurs when the sender wants to wait for the result of an asynchronous call by wrapping it in a blocking construct. This block stops all processing of not only the sender, but also the entire thread, which most likely has other processes running. As you might expect, blocking isn't a good idea, as it can have nontrivial performance implications and is a major roadblock (no pun intended) to elasticity. You simply can't go anywhere (scale up or out) if something is blocking your way. Blocking in this context should be avoided unless necessary and is frowned upon in a message-passing toolkit such as Akka.

Registered callbacks are constructs whereby the caller gives the asynchronous method with the means to signal completion. As a result, the caller doesn't have to wait for completion and may continue processing. When the asynchronous method is complete, it uses the callback to push the signal to the caller. Akka uses callbacks with its futures construct.

A *future* is a data structure that's used to capture the result of a concurrent operation and provide a callback for its access. In asynchronous methods, the future is usually used in one of two ways: the caller wraps the asynchronous method in the future, or the asynchronous method returns one. In either case, the caller continues processing and pulls the signal when the asynchronous method is complete. Futures are great ways to compose a sequence of events that aren't synchronous in nature and to help with responsiveness. Akka has built-in support for futures.

We talk about message passing in detail in the next section, which discusses the Akka actors. For now, understand that message passing is the core of any actor system and provides actor-based semantics to call an asynchronous method by sending the owner of that method a message. The means of that transmission are transparent to the caller, which in actor terms is the sender. Message passing is the primary means of communication in an Akka system and will become second nature to you by the time you complete this chapter. Asynchronous method calls provide a significant boost to responsiveness, and, as a result, are key to reactive systems and part of the Akka core. The caller (or, in the case of actors, the sender) doesn't wait for a response; therefore, it's free to deal with other concerns. This form of communication, however, introduces the need to reconcile the results independent of transmission. You've seen that blocking against asynchronous calls (one way to reconcile) is a major no-go, as it hobbles responsiveness and kills elasticity. The good news is that you've also seen that other methods (such as callbacks, futures, and message passing) allow you to manage asynchronous calls without impedance.

So far, we've discussed terminology around how Akka provides the semantics for building applications that are responsive and support elasticity. But you may not know what we meant by support for elasticity. Elasticity is the notion that a system stays responsive under varying loads by increasing and decreasing the allocated resources.

In other words, the responsiveness of the system is proportional to the system's ability to give and take resources. This allocation can occur locally, in the case of vertical scaling, or horizontally, in the case of distribution.

As a result of this definition, you can surmise that the two concepts are related in a reactive system. In addition to being related, they have a common enemy that, if it isn't managed properly, may significantly impede their capabilities. In the following section, we explore this common enemy—contention—and show you how to deal with it.

3.3.3 *Contention*

Contention (or, in computer science terms, *resource contention*) is a conflict that arises over access to shared resources such as random access memory, cache memory, and disk access. You briefly saw contention in figure 3.1 earlier in this chapter, in which two lines of cars attempt to share a toll booth. Contention at this level is primarily the responsibility of the underlying operating system; therefore, you usually don't have to deal with it. Contention, however, arises at another level that you must concern yourself with: the application level. At the application level, contention almost always results from mismanagement of shared state across multiple threads. This condition results in what you know as

- Deadlock
- Livelock
- Starvation
- Race condition

A *deadlock* is a situation in which several participants are frozen, waiting for one another to reach a specific state. All participants stop progress, and the entire subsystem stalls.

A *livelock*, like a deadlock, is a scenario in which all participants make no progress. The primary difference is that instead of being frozen, participants in a livelock situation continually change their state to allow other participants to proceed.

Starvation, on the other hand, is different, but in the aggregate has the same effect. Starvation is a scenario in which some participants are always given priority over others, preventing the others from making progress.

Race conditions are particularly nasty because they give the illusion of progress. A race condition occurs when multiple participants have access to unguarded shared mutable state, and the mutation of that state is assumed to be deterministic. This situation results in interleaved changes that may not be in the correct order, corrupting the state, which can lead to unexpected results. The illusion is that although progress is being made, it's most likely to be erroneous and no good in the end.

Figure 3.3 is a good illustration of the types of contention scenarios.

Deadlock scenario: both participants waiting on the other to change state

Livelock scenario: both participants change state for each other

Starvation scenario: priority given to some participants but not others

Race condition: mutation of ordered shared state has unexpected results

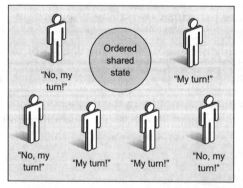

Figure 3.3   Different types of contention

As you can see, contention is a problem to avoid as much as possible. It has significant consequences for responsiveness and in turn constrains the capability to be elastic. How do you get around this problem? Surely, you need concurrent processing, and you need to manage state that in some sense is shared. We're talking about reactive systems that embrace distribution, aren't we? We are, and the answer is to share nothing.

3.3.4 Share nothing

Almost every application written requires some form of state, and that state more often than not needs access by multiple participants. The canonical example is a concurrent counter that tracks the number of visits to a given resource and updates correctly without blocking, so it stays responsive. In a language like Java, you could use a construct such as `AtomicInteger` to solve this problem. `AtomicInteger` provides a safe way to mutate the counter's value in a concurrent environment. The implication is that all mutations occur atomically. In other words, while mutations occur, no interference from the outside occurs. What happens when you have a more complex state model, such as an employee? An employee state model may contain multiple variables (first-Name, lastName, address, and so on), as well as support for different states (active, inactive, and so on). All these variables and state transitions need access by multiple participants. Unfortunately, Java has no `AtomicEmployee` in Java. What do you do?

One approach is to descend into the world of concurrent programming through synchronization and locking constructs. Although this approach is quite common for dealing with state models in a concurrent environment, it's tedious and notoriously difficult to debug, and it can cause contention. The challenges and details of this approach are more than we can cover in this book, but many resources are available if you're interested.

Another approach to managing state, and the one we will stress throughout the book, is to share nothing. Sharing nothing may sound a little extreme at first, but it's not what you may think. When we say *share nothing*, we're talking about three concepts:

1. Isolation by single source of truth
2. Encapsulation of mutation
3. Immutable state transference

In the following sections, we explain what we mean by these terms.

ISOLATION BY SINGLE SOURCE OF TRUTH

Isolation by single source of truth is a design pattern in which a state model is isolated within a single authority and that authority is solely responsible for all mutations, including creation. This pattern guarantees that there's always only one record of truth and minimizes contention through encapsulation.

ENCAPSULATION BY DEFINITION

Encapsulation by definition means restricting access to a state model by anyone other than the authority. How, then, do participants use the state model? The answer is defensive copy.

Defensive copy is the notion that any time the authority receives a request, it first makes an immutable copy of its state model. In the case of mutation, this copying involves creating a new instance by applying the mutation through constructor semantics that replace the original. (We talk about constructor semantics later in the chapter.) The authority also ensures that all mutations process in sequential order by reconciling or discarding ones that didn't process due to asynchronicity. In the case of a nonmutating request, such as a get, the authority essentially does the same, but doesn't need to replace the original, due to the lack of mutation. Defensive copy allows access to state in a safe fashion, and through immutable transference guarantees that outsiders can't fiddle with state.

IMMUTABLE STATE OF TRANSFERENCE

Immutability transference is the only safe way to share state. If a state structure is immutable, it's impossible for anyone to alter it, and you're free to share without worrying about contention. In message passing, immutability is how you guarantee that the message you send is the same message that your recipient receives. By making the message immutable, you ensure its accuracy and eliminate the possibility of contention.

The share-nothing approach may seem to be cumbersome, especially when considered in light of CRUD semantics that historically rely on object relational mappings (ORMs). That being said, we show you an alternative in chapter 5: Event Sourcing. We believe that Event Sourcing is not only a great fit for reactive environments, but also a superior way to reason about state and the management thereof.

You've seen that with Akka concurrency, parallelism, and asynchronous messages, you have the foundation for building responsive applications that support elasticity. You've also seen that you must manage these concepts to avoid contention by adopting a share-nothing mentality. So far, you've made a good start on establishing your toolkit's credentials with regard to reactive behavior. We have a lot more to cover, especially with regard to distribution, which we discuss in chapter 5. In this next section, we take a look at the core of Akka: actors.

3.4 *The actor model*

Actors aren't new, having been around in various forms since the 1970s. In fact, Scala included an earlier, more primitive version of actors before Akka fully matured and became a replacement for them. *Actors* are small capsules of programming logic that contain behavior and state, and communicate via message passing. In Akka, actors are built on top of two primary concepts: the actor model and the actor system.

According to its inventors, the *actor model* is a mathematical theory of computation that treats actors as the universal primitives of concurrent digital computation, inspired by the theory of general relativity and quantum mechanics.[4] We know that this definition may be a little scary, but it's not too complicated, at least at the application level.

---

[4] Carl Hewitt, Peter Bishop, Richard Steiger (IJCAI, 1973), "A Universal Modular ACTOR Formalism for Artificial Intelligence."

The primary purpose of an actor is to provide two concepts:

- A safe, efficient way to reason about computations in a concurrent environment
- A common way to communicate in a local, parallel, and distributed environment

To better understand how Akka actors support these concepts, look at the main components of an actor:

- State
- Actor reference
- Asynchronous message passing
- Mailbox
- Behavior and the `receive` loop
- Supervision

3.4.1 State

The first thing to look at is the state model, because we've discussed the challenges behind its management in a concurrent environment. Actors provide the semantics to encapsulate state in such a way that the actor becomes the single source of truth for its state model based on the share-nothing mentality.

Akka isolates each actor on a lightweight thread that protects it from the rest of the system. The actors themselves (housed inside a lightweight thread) run on a real set of threads; a single thread may house many actors, with subsequent invocations for a given actor occurring on a different thread.

Under the covers, Akka manages all the complexities of these concurrent interactions, removing the need for you to use synchronization and locking semantics for concurrency. As a result, you have a safe, efficient way to reason about computation in a concurrent environment.

3.4.2 Actor reference

In the original Scala actor implementation, actors were instantiated directly with concrete reference. This concrete reference required a different implementation and API for local and remote actors, and in the end, it became unwieldy. Akka chose another approach to designate instances of actors, known as `ActorRef`. When you use `ActorRef`, you don't need different implementations, which results in a single API for both local and remote.

`ActorRef` is an immutable handle to an actor that's serializable and may be local or on a remote system. Functionally, an `ActorRef` operates as a kind of proxy mechanism for the actor it represents. This proxy behavior is important in the context of remoting, as the `ActorRef` can be serialized and sent across the wire on behalf of its actor. For the remote actor acquiring the `ActorRef`, the location of the real actor (the one that the `ActorRef` represents) is transparent. This feature of Akka is called *location transparency*. Suffice it to say that location transparency is key to resilience and elasticity.

3.4.3   *Asynchronous message passing*

One of the four traits of the Reactive Manifesto is that reactive architectures should be message-driven, which is how actors communicate. Using asynchronous message-passing semantics, actors interact by sending messages to one another's `ActorRefs`. This design allows for loosely coupled systems that support elastic scaling (out or up). Akka actors support two operators, or, in the case of Java, two methods for sending messages:

- `!` (Scala) or `tell` (Java) is used to asynchronously send a message. This is often called fire-and-forget.
- `?` (Scala) or `ask` (Java) is used to asynchronously send a message and expect a reply in the form of a `Future`.

Behind Akka's message-passing semantics are two rules: *at-most-once* delivery and *message ordering per sender-receiver pair*. We explain the first rule here and the second rule in the next section.

To explain *at-most-once delivery*, we need to do so in the context of delivery mechanism categories, of which there are three:

- *At-most-once* delivery means that each message handled arrives at the recipient zero or one times. The implication is that during transit, the message may get lost.
- *At-least-once* delivery means that for each message handled, multiple send attempts may occur until delivery is successful. The implication is that the recipient may receive duplicate messages.
- *Exactly-once* delivery means that for each message handled, the recipient receives only one copy. The implication is that the message won't be lost or duplicated.

You may be asking, "Why at-most-once? I want a guarantee." Akka does support *at-least-once* delivery through its persistence library. To address the question, we start by explaining the costs of these methods in table 3.1.

Table 3.1   Message-delivery methods

Costs	Delivery method
- Least expensive - Performs best - Lowest implementation overhead - Doesn't require state management, due to fire-and-forget semantics	at-most-once
- More expensive - Performance varies based on recipient's acknowledgement - Medium implementation overhead - Requires sender state management for message reconciliation - Requires recipient to acknowledge for sender reconciliation	at-least-once
- Most expensive - Worst performance - Highest level of implementation overhead	exactly-once

Table 3.1 Message-delivery methods *(continued)*

Costs	Delivery method
▪ Requires sender state management for message reconciliation ▪ Requires recipient to acknowledge for sender reconciliation ▪ Requires recipient state management for message reconciliation	exactly-once

In a distributed environment, you want to minimize overhead as much as possible to stay responsive. One of the most costly forms of overhead is the management of communication state that the last two delivery mechanisms require. The topic of guaranteed message delivery is complex and beyond the scope of this book, but if you're interested, read a great post on InfoQ titled Nobody Needs Reliable Messaging.[5] The Akka documentation also has a great section titled Message Delivery Reliability.[6]

3.4.4 *The mailbox*

Actors communicate by passing messages back and forth, much as people do with email or letters sent via the postal system. In both cases, you need a way to receive messages, and like people, actors use a mailbox. Each actor has one mailbox that enqueues all messages in the order received. This order of reception has an interesting implication in a concurrent environment that may not be apparent. For a given sender, the recipient always receives the messages sent in the proper order—the *message order per sender-receiver pair* we mentioned earlier.

The same isn't true of messages sent in aggregate. If a single recipient receives messages from multiple senders, due to the randomness of threading, the messages in aggregate may be interleaved. Figure 3.4 should clarify.

Guaranteed order of messages

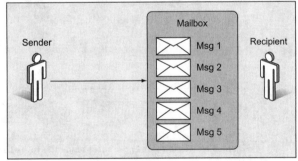

Guaranteed order of messages with interleaving

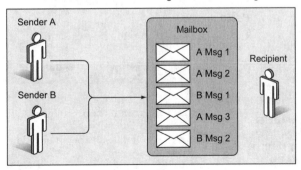

Figure 3.4 Guaranteed order of messages

---

[5] http://www.infoq.com/articles/no-reliable-messaging
[6] http://doc.akka.io/docs/akka/current/general/message-delivery-reliability.html

Don't be confused by this figure. The recipient always receives messages in order from a given sender. When multiple senders are involved, as the figure shows, interleaving can occur.

3.4.5   *Behavior and the receive loop*

Akka also provides the semantics for actor behavior. Each time an actor receives a message, it's processed against its behavior in a method known as the `receive` loop.

We explore the `receive` loop in code by giving you a brief introduction to behavior management with actors, modeling a `Greetings` actor that supports two types of messages (`Hello` and `Goodbye`) in Java and Scala, as shown in figure 3.5.

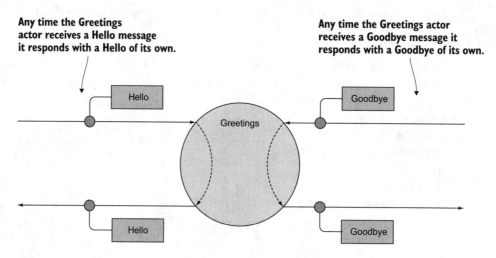

Figure 3.5   The `Greetings` actor responds to `Hello` and `Goodbye`.

HELLO IN JAVA

Listing 3.1 shows the `Hello` message.

Listing 3.1   `ImmutableHello` message in Java

```java
public final class ImmutableHello {
  private final String name;

  public ImmutableHello(String name) {
    this.name = name;
  }

  public String getName() {
    return name;
  }
}
```

Class variables are final, making them immutable.

The class is marked final, so it can't be extended.

Prefix the class with Immutable. This convention isn't required but is good practice.

Class constructor that requires a variable

Getters only

The following list walks you through the details of the Java version:

1 The first thing you notice is that the class is marked `final` so that no one extends it and potentially violates your immutability requirement.

2 Next the class is prefixed with `Immutable`. The prefix is a convention that has no effect on the class other than to make it easily identifiable as a class that shouldn't be altered.

3 Next all class variables are made `final`. In Java, the keyword `final` ensures that when a variable is set, it can't change for the life of the variable.

4 Next is a constructor that requires all class variables to enforce its creation as intended. Also, it's the only way to set the value of variables marked final.

5 Finally, you have a getter without a setter. This use is convention. A setter would be of no value, as you can't set variables marked `final`.

There's another way to model a Java class to enforce immutability, but some people regard it with disdain, as it doesn't follow accepted practices for Java class design.

The primary differences with the alternative are the lack of getters and the public variables. These differences also change how you access the classes' data. In listing 3.1, you must call a getter, whereas in listing 3.2, you use the variable directly. In the end, the effect is the same: both classes are immutable. The goodbye message `Immutable-Goodbye` is the same, the only difference being the name of the class and the constructor, so for brevity, we don't model it here.

Listing 3.2 `ImmutableHello` message in Java (alternative)

```
public final class ImmutableHello {
    public final String name;

    public ImmutableHello(String name) {
        this.name = name;
    }
}
```

Class variables are final, making them immutable.

The class is marked final, so it can't be extended.

Prefix the class with Immutable. This convention isn't required but is good practice.

Class constructor that requires a variable

HELLO IN SCALA

The following listing shows the Scala version.

Listing 3.3 `Hello` message in Scala

```
final case class Hello(name: String)
```

Class name Hello. You don't need an Immutable prefix, as Scala case classes are immutable by design.

This version is pretty different from the Java version, isn't it? If you're new to Scala, this version—a single line of code—may be surprising. But a single line of code is correct and the power of a Scala case class. A *case class* is a regular class that applies some syntactic sugar (magic) when compiled that enforces immutability. Using the example from listing 3.3, the following list walks you through the steps that the compiler applies:

1 The class becomes `final` and implements `scala.ScalaObject` and `scala.Serializable`.
2 The constructor arguments export as public final variables.
3 The compiler adds generated `toString`, `equals`, and `hashCode` methods.
4 The compiler adds an apply method that allows creation without the `new` keyword.
5 Other magic applied here isn't important for this discussion.

If you're interested in seeing what a compiled Scala case class looks like under the covers, the JVM provides a nice utility called `javap`. Simply run `javap <the name of your case class.scala>`, and output will print to the console. Again, for brevity, we don't model the `Goodbye` case class.

In the next section, you look at `GreetingsActor`, modeled first in Java and then in Scala.

GREETINGSACTOR IN JAVA

The following listing sets up `GreetingsActor` in Java.

Listing 3.4 `GreetingActor` with simple `receive` loop in Java

```
import akka.actor.AbstractActor;              Actors are implemented in Java
import akka.event.Logging;                    by extending AbstractActor.
import akka.event.LoggingAdapter;             Logging is implemented with
                                              Logging and LoggingAdapter.

public class Greeting extends AbstractActor { ??
    LoggingAdapter log = Logging.getLogger(getContext().system(), this); #?

    @Override                                 Actors also require the Receive
    public Receive createReceive {            method, which uses receiveBuilder.
      return receiveBuilder()
        .match(ImmutableHello.class, ih -> {          getSender gets a reference to the
          log.info("Received hello: {}", ih);          actor that sent the message.
          ImmutableHello ih2 = new ImmutableHello("Greetings Hello");
          getSender().tell(ih2, getSelf());
      })
        .match(ImmutableGoodby.class, ig -> {    tell uses "fire-and-forget" semantics
          log.info("Received goodbye: {}", ig);   to send the message asynchronously.
          ImmutableGoodbye ig2 = new ImmutableGoodbye("Greetings Goodbye");
          getSender().tell(ig2, getSelf());
      })
        .matchAny(o -> log.info("received unknown message: {}", ig))
        .build;                                       
    }
}
```

getSelf references the actor that's receiving the message.

matchAny will log unknown messages logged at info.

GREETINGSACTOR IN SCALA

The following listing shows GreetingsActor in Scala.

Listing 3.5 GreetingsActor with simple receive loop in Scala

```
import akka.actor.Actor                       ⟵   Actors are implemented in
import akka.actor.ActorLogging                     Scala by extending Actor.
                                               ⟵   Logging is implemented
class Greetings extends Actor with ActorLogging {   by mixing in the
                                                    ActorLogging trait.
  def receive = {                              ⟵   Actors also require the receive
    case msg: Hello =>                             method, which defines which
      log.info(s"Received hello: $msg")            messages the actor handles.
      sender() ! Hello("Greetings Hello")
    case msg: Goodbye =>                        ⟵  ! (the bang operator) uses fire-
      log.info(s"Received goodbye: $msg")          and-forget semantics to send
      sender() ! Goodbye("Greetings Goodbye")      the message asynchronously.
    case ukm:      _ => log.info(s"Received unknown message: $ukm")   ⟵
  }
}                                                   Scala _ (underscore notation) is used to
                                                    match and log any unknown messages.
```

sender gets a reference to the actor that sent the message.

COMPARING JAVA AND SCALA FOR THE GREETINGS ACTOR

The following list walks you through the difference between the Java and Scala versions of the Greetings actor:

1 The first difference is that Scala actors use akka.actor.Actor instead of akka.actor.AbstractActor due to the fact that it's quite difficult to implement a Scala PartialFunction in Java 7 and earlier. With the advent of Java 8, this situation will most likely change, but for now (per the Akka documentation), this is the way it's done.

2 Next, there's no need to instantiate a Logger, as it's included by mixing in the ActorLogging trait.

3 The receive semantics are different as well, again because Scala can handle PartialFunction. The receive method matches against a series of case statements, as opposed to the if statement in the Java version.

4 Finally, if you received a handled message, you respond to the sender by using the bang operator. The sender method is pretty much the same as getSender in Java. Scala also supports operator notation—thus, the ! instead of .tell. Any unhandled messages are matched with Scala underscore notation and subsequently logged.

In both of these examples, only one receive loop captures all behavior that responds to a message. Within that loop, you respond with Hello or Goodbye, depending on the message you receive. But is this behavior? At some level, you could argue that it is, but in both cases the action is the same: a response. We would argue that behavior is role-based and that the actions within a role are simply the execution of that behavior.

GREETINGSACTOR CHANGES

With this idea in mind, change the `GreetingActor`'s role from always responding, to one that is as follows:

1 The `GreetingActor` starts in a role in which it accepts only `Hello` messages.
2 When the `GreetingActor` receives a `Hello` message, it changes its role to accept only `Goodbye`.
3 When the `GreetingActor` receives a `Goodbye` message, it reverts to its initial role of accepting only `Hello`.

The internal `Hello` and `Goodbye` roles are represented by two `receive` functions, as shown in figure 3.6. The actor swaps between them by using the `become` operation. The semantics behind swapping are a little complicated, but Akka uses a `Stack` to keep track of the hot-swapped code as it's pushed and popped. In this section, we show you what this looks like, first in Java (listing 3.6) and then in Scala (listing 3.7).

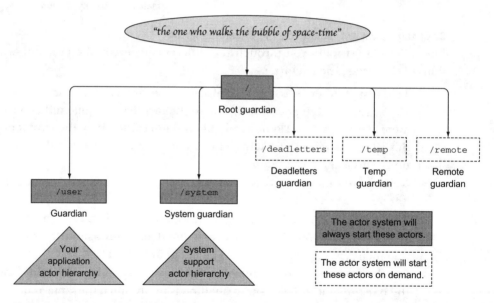

Figure 3.6   The `Greetings` actor responds to `Hello` or `Goodbye` only when it's in the corresponding state.

Listing 3.6   `GreetingsActor` with `become` operation in Java

```
import akka.actor.AbstractActor;
import akka.event.Logging;
import akka.event.LoggingAdapter;
import akka.japi.Procedure;
```

Procedure trait; similar to a function but doesn't have a value

```java
public class Greeting extends AbstractActor {
  LoggingAdapter log = Logging.getLogger(getContext().system(), this);
  private AbstractActor.Receive hello;
  private AbstractActor.Receive goodbye;

  public Greeting() {

    hello = receiveBuilder()
      .match(ImmutableHello.class, ih -> {
        log.info("Received hello: {}", ih);
        ImmutableHello ih2 = new ImmutableHello("Greetings Hello");
        getSender().tell(ih2, getSelf());
        getContext().become(goodbye);
      })
      .matchAny(o -> log.info("received uknown message: {}", ih))
      .build();

    goodbye = receiveBuilder()
      .match(ImmutableGoodbye.class, ig -> {
        log.info("Received goodbye: {}", ig);
        ImmutableGoodbye ig2 = new ImmutableHello("Greetings Goodbye");
        getSender().tell(ig2, getSelf());
        getContext().become(hello);
      })
      .matchAny(o -> log.info("received uknown message: {}", ig))
      .build();

  };

  public Receive createReceive() {
    return hello;
  }
}
```

- The hello procedure for the receive loop
- **context.become(goodbye)** replaces the top of the stack, hello, with goodbye.
- the goodbye procedure for the receive loop
- **context.become(hello)** replaces the new top of the stack, goodbye, with hello.
- Sets the default behavior for createReceive() to hello

Listing 3.7 `GreetingsActor` with `become` operation in Scala

```scala
import akka.actor.Actor
import akka.actor.Props
import akka.event.Logging

class GrettingsActor extends Actor {
  val log = Logging(context.system, this)

  override def receive = hello

  def hello = {
    case msg: Hello =>
      log.info(s"Received hello: $msg")
      sender() ! Hello("Greetings Hello")
      context.become(goodbye)
    case _       => log.info("received unknown message")
  }

  def goodbye = {
```

- Overrides the default receive loop provided by the Actor trait with the hello
- The hello receive loop
- **context.become(goodbye)** replaces the top of the stack, hello, with goodbye.
- The goodbye receive loop

```
    case msg: Goodbye =>
      log.info(s"Received goodbye: $msg")
      sender() ! Hello("Greetings Goodbye")
      context.become(hello)
    case _      => log.info("received unknown message")
  }
}
```

**context.become(hello)
replaces the new top of the
stack, goodbye, with hello.**

`GreetingsActor` is a brief introduction to behavior management with actors. As you work through the book, we show you more examples of how you can use this powerful feature of Akka.

3.4.6 *Supervision*

One of the most powerful features that Akka provides for actors is supervision. We dig into this feature in detail in the next section, as it's better understood in the context of the actor system, but we mention the basics here.

Akka allows any actor to create child actors for the purpose of delegating subtasks. In this context, the spawning actor becomes known as a supervisor and has authority over the children. Supervision is a powerful metaphor that provides the mechanics taking Akka beyond fault tolerance to resilience.

> **Resilience versus fault tolerance**
>
> Of the four traits in the Reactive Manifesto, resilience is the most often misunderstood, usually being defined as fault tolerance. Although resilience and fault tolerance have a lot in common, they're not the same.
>
> In computer science, fault tolerance is defined as an aspect of the system that allows continued operation in the event of failure of some of its components. So far, so good. Resilience covers this too, but now for the distinction.
>
> Fault tolerance contains an implied caveat: in a fault tolerant system, the degradation of quality is proportional to the severity of the failure. The larger the failure is, the worse the system behaves. In the dreaded cascading failure scenario, one server fails, and the load balancer shifts traffic to another. Now the new server is handling not only its original load, but the new load as well, and eventually, the entire server bank craters.
>
> Resilience, on the other hand, means reacting to failure by springing back into shape. Rather than pass the buck to the next guy in line, a resilient system self-heals. Self-healing is achieved by repairing the failed component or spinning up a new one as a replacement.

Akka actors bring many features to the table in support of the reactive paradigm. In the next section, we look at how Akka manages all these features through the actor system.

3.5 *The actor system*

In Akka, the actor system is the setting in which actors exist. It's a heavyweight construct that manages concurrency, actor lifecycles, and execution context (among other things), and it forms a boundary that's both spatial and temporal. To give you an overview of how an actor system works, in this section we review four key concepts:

- Hierarchical structure that contains the bubble walker and top-level actors
- Supervision
- Actor paths
- The actor lifecycle

3.5.1 *Hierarchical structure*

The structure of an actor system is hierarchical in nature, much like that of a modern corporation. A corporation usually has a single person at the top: the chief executive officer (CEO), who is responsible for the success or failure of the company. To manage this responsibility, the CEO devises an overall strategy that covers both scenarios.

Below the CEO is a group of executive officers who are tasked with implementing the strategy in their areas of responsibility, and on down the chain responsibility goes. This entire hierarchical structure in a corporation or actor system has one underlying means of carrying out the strategy: splitting up and delegating tasks as small chunks.

Figure 3.7 illustrates the executive team of an actor system.

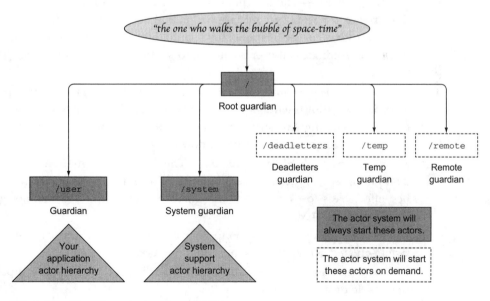

Figure 3.7 The Akka actor system hierarchy

BUBBLE WALKER

At the highest level of the hierarchy resides a unique object called a *bubble walker* (affectionate shorthand for "the one who walks the bubble of space-time"). This term may sound a little crazy, but it makes a lot of sense. Every real actor within the actor system has to have a supervisor. We talk about supervision later, but for now, follow along. The supervisor is responsible for managing exceptions thrown by the actors that it supervises.

ROOT GUARDIAN

At the top of the actor stack is the root guardian, which must have a supervisor as well. The problem is that the root guardian is at the top. What is its supervisor? That role is played by the bubble walker, which is a synthetic `ActorRef` that monitors and stops the root guardian at the first sign of trouble. As soon as the root guardian is terminated, the bubble walker sets the system's `isTerminated` status to `true`, and the actor system officially shuts down.

TOP-LEVEL ACTORS

In addition to the bubble walker, Akka provides a set of top-level actors that are responsible for different areas of the system. Here's what these actors do:

- `/` (*root guardian*)—The root guardian is the CEO of the actor system, supervising all the top-level actors listed below it. Whenever one of the other top-level actors throws an Exception, the root guardian terminates it. All other throwables escalate up to the bubble walker.
- `/user` (*guardian*)—The guardian actor is the parent of all user-created actors that are created with `system.actorOf()`. When the guardian escalates a failure, the root guardian responds by terminating the guardian. As a result, the guardian terminates all user-created actors, effectively shutting down the actor system.
- `/system` (*system guardian*)—The system guardian is a special actor that provides an orderly shutdown sequence; logging remains while user-created actors terminate. The system guardian monitors the system, and, when completed with its responsibilities, initiates its own shutdown.
- `/deadletters` (*deadletters guardian*)—The deadletters guardian is a special guardian where all messages sent to stopped or non-existent actors go. It uses a best-effort basis to capture the orphaned messages, which sometimes get lost within the local JVM.
- `/temp` (*temp guardian*)—The temp guardian is a top-level actor for short-lived system-created actors, such as those that use `ask`.
- `/remote` (*remote guardian*)—The remote guardian is for actors with supervisors that reside on a remote system.

This hierarchical structure is one of the key concepts of Akka's resilience. By having a supervised structure, Akka can embrace failure by delegating the appropriate action.

Now that you have a good sense of the hierarchy of Akka's actor system, we describe supervision in the next section.

3.5.2 Supervision

You probably have a good idea from the hierarchy discussion of what supervision is in terms of Akka. All real actors must have a supervisor. This supervisory relationship establishes a dependency among actors, as follows:

- The supervisor delegates tasks to its subordinates and responds to their failures.
- Whenever a subordinate detects a failure, it suspends itself and all its subordinates, and reports back to its supervisor.
- The supervisor receives the failure, and, based on the default or overridden strategy, applies a directive.

Following are the strategies available to a supervisor:

- `OneForOneStrategy` (default)—This strategy operates as its name implies. The supervisor executes one of four directives (listed later in this section) against the subordinate and all of the subordinate's children in turn.
- `AllForOneStrategy`—Under this strategy, the supervisor executes one of the four directives against the subordinate that failed and also against all subordinates that the supervisor manages—hence, the name `AllForOneStrategy`.

The default strategy for all supervisors it `OneForOneStrategy`. You can create your own supervisor strategy by extending the `akka.actor.SupervisorStrategy` class. We show you how strategies are implemented a little later in the chapter. For now, look at the directives that the supervisor can take:

1 `Resume` the subordinate, keeping its accumulated internal state.
2 `Restart` the subordinate, clearing its accumulated internal state.
3 `Stop` the subordinate permanently.
4 `Escalate` the failure, thereby failing itself.

The supervision strategy and directives semantics provide a powerful mechanism for the transparent handling of faults, which enables the self-healing of resilience. We should note that communication between supervisors and their subordinates comes in the form of special messages managed in mailboxes separate from the actors. The implication is that the ordering of supervision-related messages isn't relative to normal ones.

3.5.3 Actor paths

So far, you've seen what actors are, the hierarchical system in which actors exist, and how to manage actors through supervision. In this section, we show you how to access actors within the hierarchy.

In any good hierarchy, you find a trail of names that you can follow recursively. From the root guardian down through the hierarchy, you can reach any actor in the system by following the actor path. The *actor path* consists of a root that is the actor system, followed by a concatenated sequence of elements delineated with a forward slash. You can liken an actor path to a URL, as shown in figure 3.8.

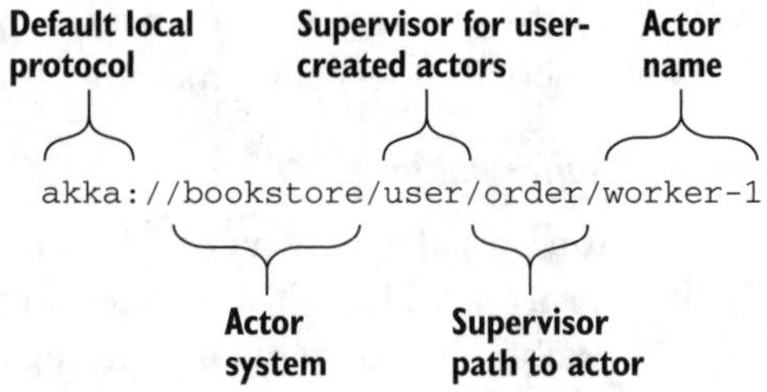

Default local protocol   Supervisor for user-created actors   Actor name

akka://bookstore/user/order/worker-1

Actor system   Supervisor path to actor

Figure 3.8   Local actor paths follow hierarchical syntax.

- The first part of the path establishes the protocol as akka, which refers to a local actor system. In chapter 6, you learn how to specify remote protocols by using TCP or UDP.
- The next part establishes the actor system name, because there may be more than one locally.
- All user-created actors fall under the user supervisor, which is created automatically by Akka. The order actor is one that you'd add to supervise the worker actors: worker-1, worker-2, and so on.

The result of accessing an actor by its path is an ActorRef, which you can obtain in two ways: looking them up or creating them. To look up an actor, Akka supports relative and absolute paths through ActorSystem.actorSelection and Actor-Context.actorSelection. In addition to obtaining an ActorRef, you can use actorSelection to send a message to an actor directly.

The following listing shows an example of using actorSelection to send an actor a message by using relative and absolute paths.

Listing 3.8   Using actorSelection with relative and absolute paths

```
context.actorSelection("../worker-1") ! msg          // relative
context.actorSelection("/user/order/worker-1") ! msg   // absolute
```

To create an actor, you use ActorSystem.actorOf or ActorContext.actorOf. ActorSystem.actorOf is generally used to start the system, whereas the latter is used from within existing actors. Unlike actorSelection, actorOf requires Props, which is an immutable class that specifies options for the creation of an actor.

The following listing shows an example of using ActorContex.actorOf with Props for creation.

Listing 3.9   Using actorOf with Props to create an actor

```
class Manager extends Actor {
  context.actorOf(Props[Worker], "worker-1")
  // other code …
}
```

Listing 3.9 sets the type of `Props` to be the actor class—in this case, `Worker`. In the `actorOf` method, you first pass in the `Props` object, followed by the name of the actor (`"worker-1"`).

Although this approach is certainly acceptable, best practice is to establish a factory to generate the `Props` values from your actor's companion object, as shown in the following listing.

Listing 3.10 Using `actorOf` with actor `Props` factory

```
object Worker {
  def props = Props[Worker]
}

class Worker extends Actor {
  def receive = {
    case order:Order => // do something ...
    // other code …
  }
}

class Manager extends Actor {
  context.actorOf(Worker.props, "worker-1")
  // other code …
}
```

3.5.4 Actor lifecycle

An actor runs through three phases: starting, restarting, and stopping. These phases tie back to the supervisor directives discussed earlier in this chapter. We discuss the phases in the following sections.

STARTING

When the actor system starts an actor with `actorOf`, the following sequence of events occurs:

1 `actorOf` is called.
2 The actor path is reserved.
3 A random UID is assigned for the actor instance.
4 The actor instance is created.
5 The `preStart()` method is called on the actor instance.
6 The actor instance is started.

This sequence of events can occur under two conditions: when an actor is started or when an actor is restarted by the supervisor. Before we talk about restarting, we talk about stopping, which is included in restarting.

STOPPING

When an actor is stopped, the following sequence of events occurs:

1 The actor instance is asked to stop with `Stop`, `context.stop()`, or `Poison-Pill`.

2 The postStop() method is called on the actor instance.

3 The actor instance is terminated.

4 The actor path is usable again.

RESTARTING

Restarting is an interesting combination. When a supervisor restarts an actor, the following sequence of events occurs:

1 The postRestart() method is called on the old actor instance.

2 The old actor instance is asked to stop with Stop.

3 The postStop() method is called on the old actor instance.

4 The actor path of the old instance is reserved for the new instance.

5 The UID of the old instance is reserved for the new instance.

6 The old actor instance is terminated.

7 The new instance is created.

8 The preStart() method is called on the new instance.

9 The new actor instance is started.

When the actor system executes the restart directive, it replaces the faulty actor with a new one. This replacement may sound a little odd, but that's the design. The important thing to note is during restart, the postRestart() method is called on the old instance rather than the new.

3.5.5　*Microkernel container*

Software as a tool probably should hold the title of "most used and versatile invention ever created." Tens of millions of software applications are running today, solving a wide range of problems, from the mundane to the complex.

Software in many ways can be likened to the human body. The human body is an incredible machine that can be trained to do just about anything, but it must have one thing to operate: an oxygenated environment. In software lingo, we call this requirement the *runtime*. Every application ever written requires a runtime, and without one, the application is nothing more than a bunch of bits. Fortunately, Akka includes a runtime. The runtime in Akka—the microkernel—is designed and optimized to offer a bundling mechanism that allows single payload distribution atop the JVM without the need for an application container or startup script.

We've spent a good deal of time in this chapter establishing the rationale behind using Akka as a reactive toolkit. Now it's time to put the toolkit to use and have some coding fun. Starting in chapter 5, we establish an analogy to help you reason through the process of building a reactive application. We start small and expand the analogy throughout the book while applying techniques in code.

Summary

- Akka's design concepts originate with Erlang and the OTP. Akka evolved to keep pace with the growing demands of computing.

- Asynchronous communication is managed through blocking, callbacks, futures, and message passing.
- Akka embraces a share-nothing approach through isolation and immutability. This approach produces systems that are less prone to errors and that are easier to understand and reason about than traditional approaches based on explicit synchronization and locking.
- The actor model encapsulates system state within supervised actors, which are referenced indirectly and communicate asynchronously via messages to an actor's mailbox.
- The actor system imposes a hierarchical path structure on the actors it contains. The actor system manages individual actors throughout their lifecycle by using predefined supervision strategies and directives. The top-level actors are built into Akka and managed by a microkernel that's part of Akka.

Part 2

Building a reactive application

This rest of the book shows you what we believe are the most important things to know about writing reactive applications.

Domain-driven design is particularly useful for reactive applications. Chapter 4 illustrates this design by mapping a domain onto an actor model, including translating some features onto behavior of the toolkit rather than things you have to write yourself. Chapter 5 solidifies your understanding by formalizing key concepts and useful patterns. In chapter 6, we turn to a more concrete programming example, using remote actors to demonstrate how working with asynchronous peers is different from traditional service call-and-response. In chapter 7, you learn about streams and the role of backpressure, and examine the Reactive Streams API for interoperability among different reactive implementations. Chapter 8 addresses the difficult topic of working with persistent data and the different roles of commands and events in your design. Chapter 9 covers alternatives for exposing your reactive services so that they can be consumed by external clients. Finally, chapter 10 puts you on the path to production readiness with brief discussions of testing patterns, application security, logging, tracing, monitoring, configuration, and packaging.

Mapping from domain to toolkit

4

This chapter covers

- Choosing reactive components to represent the domain
- Designing a message protocol
- Modeling system state
- Scaling to many actors
- Recovering from faulty actors

We believe that one of the best ways to learn is through the process of analogical reasoning—comparing the known with the unknown. An analogy is like a handle on a heavy bucket. Although you may still be able to pick up the bucket without one, your chore will be more difficult. The use of analogies in graduate school is quite common, especially in the disciplines of science and engineering. In these disciplines, an analogy is referred to as a *succedaneum,* which means *substitute.* The poet William Wordsworth captured it best:

> *Science appears as what in truth she is,*
> *Not as our glory and our absolute boast,*

But as a succedaneum, and a prop
To our infirmity.

To begin learning by succedaneum, we use a simple analogy to reason about and model an Akka-based reactive application, starting with what you've learned so far. As you work your way through the book, the complexity of the analogy increases step by step. With each increase in complexity, you learn a new reactive concept to evolve the application layer upon layer until the idea is complete. As a result of this learning style, you'll be able to craft your design in a way that translates the theory into succinct code that's easy to maintain and enjoyable to write.

4.1   Designing from a domain model

Suppose that an ambitious bookstore owner who specializes in antique books decides to start a question-and-answer service. Being an expert on antique books, the owner quickly obtains two customers who are delighted to have found a specialist, and he hires a librarian to do the legwork. To facilitate communication with his clients, the owner decides to use a whiteboard in the back room of a local coffeehouse to set a schedule. Every other day, a customer posts a question by noon, and the librarian answers it later that day. The customer who posted the question returns by 8 p.m. to retrieve the response.

Not long after starting this process, the owner encounters a problem. His regularly scheduled customer posted a question at 9 a.m. as usual. Unbeknownst to the librarian, the second customer came in at 10 a.m. and overwrote that question with her own. When the librarian came in that afternoon, not realizing what had happened, he posted his response to the second customer's question. Later that evening, the first customer returned to retrieve the librarian's answer, which was incorrect because it answered the wrong question, and the customer promptly filed a complaint.

As a developer, you recognize the problem: access to the whiteboard isn't thread-safe.

4.1.1   A better solution

The first solution that the owner considered was hiring a guard to lock the door after each customer posted a question. Locking the door would prevent another customer from getting access to the board before the first question was answered. Although this solution would work, it was dismissed quickly because it would be costly. Also, the owner realized that it would more tightly couple the business to the use of the coffeehouse's back room, which would hinder future expansion of the business.

As a developer, you recognize the solution, too: it's a lock. The lock might be implemented explicitly or by using *synchronized* access, which keeps a lock behind the scenes. Had the whiteboard been synchronized, the confused second customer would have been forced to wait until the first customer retrieved the librarian's answer. The solution would work as long as customers were willing to do nothing but wait a full day in the coffeehouse for the whiteboard to become available.

After much thought, the owner realized that he didn't need the whiteboard. A much better approach was to use the services of the post office. By relying on a written question sent through the mail, he was assured that each request would be the correct one for a given customer. Unlike a whiteboard, a letter is immutable. Furthermore, neither the owner nor his customers would be bound to the use of the coffeehouse, thereby establishing a loosely coupled relationship that would help the business grow.

Now that we've baselined the analogy, we'll break it down in reactive terms.

4.1.2 Moving from analogy to application

The first thing to do is see which parts of the analogy would suit the role of an actor. Recall from chapter 1 that actors are lightweight objects that encapsulate state and behavior, and communicate solely through asynchronous message passing. In looking at the participants, you see these candidates:

- RareBooks owner
- Librarian
- Card catalog
- Customers
- Post office

Compare each member with the features of an actor in table 4.1, and validate the assumptions. The table shows that the three fitting candidates for actor modeling are the RareBooks owner, the librarian, and the customers. All three represent distinct identity, behavior, and potential state management. The catalog doesn't send or receive messages or change state, so it isn't an actor. The post office routes messages, but doesn't meet the test because it doesn't receive or originate messages of its own.

Table 4.1 An actor needs to have behavior, state, and asynchronous messages. Check which candidates have all three features to decide which could be implemented as actors.

Has all features?	Candidate	Behavior	State	Asynchronous messaging
✓	RareBooks owner	Assigns questions for librarians to answer	Tracks which librarians are on duty and hires new librarians as needed	Asynchronous messages direct to librarian
✓	Librarians	Respond to a customer's question	Encapsulate state as the single source of truth for the answer	Respond through the post office
X	Card catalog	Source of book information for librarians to consult	Contains a card entry for each book	Doesn't send or receive messages

Table 4.1   An actor needs to have behavior, state, and asynchronous messages. Check which candidates have all three features to decide which could be implemented as actors. *(continued)*

Has all features?	Candidate	Behavior	State	Asynchronous messaging
✓	Customers	Send a question and expect an answer	Are single source of truth for their questions	Send questions and receive answers
X	Post office	Delivers the mail	Tracks which messages have been delivered to each participant	Doesn't produce messages of its own

Based on the mapping exercise, you decide to model the application as the three actors shown in figure 4.1. You also can begin to map the rest of the system to reactive constructs, as shown in table 4.2.

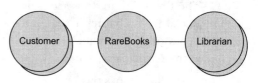

Figure 4.1   The `RareBooks` actor system

Table 4.2   When you have identified the primary actors, begin mapping other parts of the domain to roles in a reactive system.

Domain analogy	Reactive translation
RareBooks	Top-level actor representing the owner
Librarians	Actors that are supervised by RareBooks
Customers	Top-level actors representing individual customers
Card catalog	Immutable data structure
Customer question sent by mail	Immutable case class
Librarian answer sent by mail	Immutable case class
Post office	Messaging framework

4.1.3   Creating the catalog

Before modeling the actors in detail, you need to understand what they'll tell one another. In this case, the content is information related to rare books, which in library terms is known as a card catalog. A real card catalog would be implemented as a database, but for the purpose of this analogy, an in-memory representation of the card catalog as a singleton `Map` is sufficient.

The `Map` consists of a key, which is the book's International Standard Book Number (ISBN) as a `String`, and a `BookCard`, which is an immutable record of information relating to a book. As you can see in the partial listing that follows, the catalog at this stage of design consists of a few basic data structures.

Listing 4.1 The card catalog implemented as an in-memory `Map`

```
package com.rarebooks.library

import RareBooksProtocol.BookCard

object Catalog {
  val phaedrus = BookCard(
    "0872202208",
    "Plato",
    "Phaedrus",
    "Plato's enigmatic text that treats a range of
    ⇨ important ... issues.",
    "370 BC",
    Set(Greece, Philosophy),
    "Hackett Publishing Company, Inc.",
    "English",
    144)

  val theEpicOfGilgamesh = BookCard(
    "0141026286",
    "unknown",
    "The Epic of Gilgamesh",
    "A hero is created by the gods to challenge the arrogant King Gilgamesh.",
    "2700 BC",
    Set(Gilgamesh, Persia, Royalty),
    "Penguin Classics",
    "English",
    80)

  //... other BookCard instances

  val books: Map[String, BookCard] = Map(
    theEpicOfGilgamesh.isbn -> theEpicOfGilgamesh,
    phaedrus.isbn -> phaedrus,
    theHistories.isbn -> theHistories)

  //... other code used to fetch BookCard items from the map
}
```

The message protocol is shown in the next section.

The singleton Catalog

BookCard is a case class defined in the message protocol.

The state map representing the BookCards in the catalog

This code is a good start. You know what the actors will be and have a rough idea of the message that will be needed. In the next section, you'll design the message protocol in more detail.

4.2   *Becoming message-driven*

`Customers` send inquiries and receive entries from the catalog. These inquiries are modeled as immutable messages. From a programming point of view, you can think of the messages as being forms of application programming interfaces (APIs) for a given actor. For brevity's sake, we'll model two types of `Find` messages that `RareBooks` is

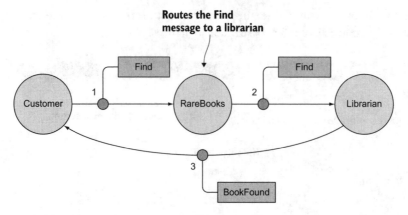

Routes the Find message to a librarian

Figure 4.2 `RareBooks` **routes book requests to a** `Librarian` **for processing, and the response flows from the** `Librarian` **directly back to the** `Customer`.

expected to answer. The flow of a `Find` message through `RareBooks` and onward to a `Librarian` is shown in figure 4.2.

It's considered to be a best practice to define the messages an actor receives either in a protocol object or in the actor's companion object. Listing 4.2 is a partial implementation of the `RareBooksProtocol` object, which is a singleton; it contains the majority of messages and abstractions that your actors will use. One of those abstractions is the trait `Msg`, which is used for matching. We explore this generalization more with the notion of commands and events in chapter 6.

> **NOTE** A *protocol object* contains the messages that are used within the actor system. In computer science, a *protocol* is defined as the rules that allow two entities to communicate with each other. These rules or standards are the syntaxes and semantics of acceptable communication. Actors can have a dependency on the protocol without having direct dependencies on one another.

Listing 4.2   Messages between `Customers` **and** `Librarians` **defined in a protocol object**

```
package com.rarebooks.library

import scala.compat.Platform          Used for time
                                      stamps

object RareBooksProtocol {            Protocol object establishing
                                      base messages for all actors

  sealed trait Topic
  case object Africa extends Topic
  case object Asia extends Topic      Enumerate the topics
  case object Gilgamesh extends Topic in the library.
  //... other topics
```

```
trait Msg {                                    All messages have
  def dateInMillis: Long                       a time stamp.
}

final case class FindBookByIsbn(               Message to request
    isbn: String,                              book by ISBN
    dateInMillis: Long = Platform.currentTime)
  extends Msg {
  require(isbn.nonEmpty, "Isbn required.")
}

final case class FindBookByTopic(              Message to
    topic: Set[Topic],                         request book
    dateInMillis: Long = Platform.currentTime) by Topic
  extends Msg {
  require(topic.nonEmpty, "Topic required.")
}

final case class BookCard(
    isbn: String,
    author: String,
    title: String,
    description: String,
    dateOfOrigin: String,                      Card for a book
    topic: Set[Topic],
    publisher: String,
    language: String,
    pages: Int)
  extends Msg

//... other message implementations
}
```

Ensure that message contains search criteria.

With this immutable message structure, you've taken a small but important step toward a reactive design. By adopting the share-nothing mentality, in the sense that messaging structures are immutable, you avoid the many pitfalls of concurrent programming.

Unlike messages, actors do have state. In the next section, you learn how to implement actor states and control the state with messages.

4.3   *Controlling actor state with messages*

So far, RareBooks has hired only two Librarians—enough to handle questions during normal business hours but not enough to stay open all the time. The model needs to include the concept that RareBooks is either open or closed. In addition, the Librarians are efficient, but researching each question does take some time. A Librarian is either ready to receive a question or busy working on a request. You can model this situation by creating two *states* for each of those actors, as shown in figure 4.3.

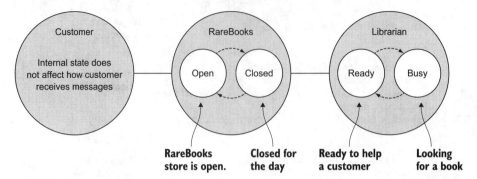

Figure 4.3 `RareBooks` and the `Librarian` change how they process messages when they change state.

4.3.1 *Sending messages to yourself*

How does `RareBooks` know when to open and when to close? `RareBooks` is an actor, and actors are message-driven, so `RareBooks` opens and closes when it receives a message telling it to open or close. The owner wants a report at the end of each day, so there's a message for that purpose too.

Because these messages are used only by the `RareBooks` actor, it makes sense to define them in the companion object rather than going to the trouble of creating a separate protocol object. The `Open`, `Close`, and `Report` messages don't have any properties, so you don't need more than one instance of each message. You can use case *objects* rather than case classes to declare them. See the following listing.

```
object RareBooks {
  case object Open
  case object Close           Messages to open, close,
  case object Report          and produce a daily report

  def props: Props = Props(new RareBooks)        Provides a properties
  // ... more definitions                        factory for actor creation
}
```

> **TIP** It's good practice to put functions that return actor `Props` in the companion object. This practice ensures that the function can't inadvertently create *closure* over the actor state, which could create difficult-to-find bugs when Akka uses it to create instances of the `Actor` type.

As shown in figure 4.4, `RareBooks` schedules the `Open` and `Close` events for itself. Akka conveniently provides a scheduler that makes the process easy. When `Rare-Books` opens, it schedules a message to tell itself when to close. When it receives the `Close` event, `RareBooks` immediately schedules the next `Open` event and sends another message to itself to run the end-of-day report.

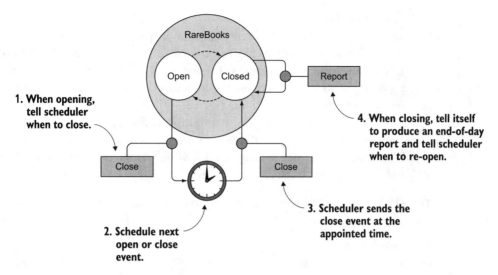

Figure 4.4 `RareBooks` **sends messages to itself for opening and closing the reference service and for running daily reports.**

It's clear from good design principles that generating the report should be separated into a separate function, but it may seem a little strange to use a separate message to trigger that report. For a simple example such as this one, a report could be generated immediately as part of handling the `Close` event. By making the event a separate message, you gain additional flexibility. Perhaps later, you'll have additional messages to invoice `Customers` or send out daily special offers. You can add multiple activities that take place concurrently at the end of the day. Or you can decide to run a report at some other time.

4.3.2 Changing behavior with state

The `RareBooks` actor needs to handle messages differently depending on whether it's open or closed. Now that you have messages that tell `RareBooks` when to open and close, the next step is defining the behaviors for the open and closed states. When `RareBooks` is open, `Librarians` are available to process requests. When `RareBooks` is closed, it sets aside new requests until the next time it's open, and while `RareBooks` is closed, it needs to run the report.

REPLACING THE RECEIVE FUNCTION

To change what an actor does when it receives a message, replace the actor's receive function. The `RareBooks` actor defines both an `open` receive function, used when `RareBooks` is open, and a `closed` receive function, used when it's closed. `Rare-Books` switches between the functions depending on the desired state. The simplest way to switch from open to closed is to invoke `ActorContext.become(closed)`. Similarly, when it's time to reopen for the day, the actor invokes `ActorContext.become(open)`.

SAVING MESSAGES FOR LATER

While `RareBooks` is closed, the receive function can't process new requests from `Customers` because no `Librarians` are available. Those requests don't have to be rejected, however; instead, they can be stashed away safely for later processing. When the state switches back to open, those requests can be unstashed, and Akka takes care of sending them to the receive function a second time.

To add stash functionality to your actor, inherit the `Stash` trait. When the actor encounters a message that it can't handle in the current state, it can call `stash()` to save it. When the actor switches state again, calling `unstashAll()` causes all the previously stashed messages to be submitted again.

> **TIP**   The `unstashAll()` function is often called immediately before a call to `become()`, and receive functions often call `stash()` from a wildcard match.

PUTTING IT TOGETHER

Now you're ready to implement the `RareBooks` actor, as shown in listing 4.4. The state transitions are the ones depictured in figure 4.4 earlier in this chapter:

- When `RareBooks` begins, it immediately creates a `Librarian`, schedules the first `Close` event, and starts receiving messages in the open state.
- While `RareBooks` remains open, it forwards protocol messages to the `Librarian`. When it receives the scheduled `Close` event, it schedules an `Open` event, becomes closed, and sends another message to itself to produce the daily report.
- While `RareBooks` is closed, it processes the daily `Report` event and waits for an `Open` event. When the `Open` event arrives, it schedules reopening, unstashes saved messages, and becomes open. Any other messages that it receives while it's closed are stashed.

Listing 4.4   The `RareBooks` actor

```
class RareBooks extends Actor with ActorLogging with Stash {

  import context.dispatcher
  import RareBooks._                          Imports message definitions from the
  import RareBooksProtocol._                  protocol object and the companion object

  private val openDuration: FiniteDuration = ...
  private val closeDuration: FiniteDuration = ...    Defines how long various
  private val findBookDuration: FiniteDuration = ... events take in the simulation

  private val librarian = createLibrarian()          One Librarian
                                                      for now

  var requestsToday: Int = 0
  var totalRequests: Int = 0      Running totals

  context.system.scheduler.scheduleOnce(
    openDuration, self, Close)    Schedules the first close event
```

```
                override def receive: Receive = open          ◁——     Begins in the
                                                                       open state
             private def open: Receive = {
               case m: Msg =>
                 requestsToday += 1              Forwards protocol
                 librarian forward m             messages to the Librarian


               case Close =>
                 context.system.scheduler.scheduleOnce(
                 ➥ closeDuration, self, Open)            On close, schedule when to reopen.


                 context.become(closed)          ◁——     Closes the shop


                 self ! Report        ◁——   RareBooks tells itself
             }                              to run the report.

         private def closed: Receive = {

             case Report =>
               totalRequests += requestsToday
               log.info(s"$requestsToday ...           Updates the running
               ➥ requests processed = $totalRequests")  totals, prints the report,
               requestsToday = 0                       and resets the daily total

             case Open =>
               context.system.scheduler.scheduleOnce(
               ➥ openDuration, self, Close)          On open, schedule when to close.

               unstashAll()             ◁——     Unstashes messages that arrived
                                                 while the shop was closed
               context.become(open)     ◁——  Opens the shop

             case _ =>
               stash()          ◁——  Stashes other messages that
           }                          arrive while the shop is closed
         protected def createLibrarian(): ActorRef = {
           context.actorOf(
           ➥ Librarian.props(findBookDuration), "librarian")   Utility to create a
         }                                                      Librarian actor
       }
```

A lot is happening in the RareBooks actor. Study it for a few moments to ensure that you understand how the pieces interact, and give yourself a pat on the back when you do. You can grab the source code from the book's website, www.manning.com/books/reactive-application-development, or http://mng.bz/71O3.

4.3.3 *Managing more complex interactions*

You may have noticed that when RareBooks is open, all the protocol messages are forwarded to the Librarian, and when it's closed, those messages are stashed for the Librarian to receive when it reopens. The Librarian has a lot of work to do.

You don't have to implement complex behavior all at once. Instead, implement simple behavior and add more as needed. For the `Librarian`, start with finding a book, as shown in the fragment of the `Librarian` actor in the following listing.

Listing 4.5   Handling a request if searches are instantaneous and never fail

```
override def receive: Receive ={
  case f: FindBookByIsbn(isbn, _) =>
    val book = Catalog.books(isbn)             Looks up by key,
    sender() ! BookFound(List(book))           using Map.apply()
  // ... handle other messages              Sends the result
}
```

This example assumes that the ISBN in the message always refers to a book in the catalog, which is easily remedied.

HANDLING ALTERNATIVES

Merely changing the call from `Map.apply(isbn)` to `Map.get(isbn)` produces an `Option[BookCard]`, which is preferable to throwing an exception, but still not satisfactory. Rather than send a `BookFound` message with an empty list, the `Librarian` should send a `BookFound` message or a `BookNotFound` message. Introduce a helper to perform the conversion. The `Either` class has a `fold` function that holds two alternatives and makes processing the results easy. See the following listing.

Listing 4.6   Using `Either` and `fold()` to process alternative results

```
def optToEither[T](v: T, f: T => Option[BookCard]):
  Either[BookNotFound, BookFound] =
  f(v) match {                                       Found returns Right.
    case b: Some[BookCard] => Right(BookFound(b.get))
    case _                 => Left(BookNotFound(s"Book(s)
      not found based on $v"))                       Failure returns Left.
  }

override def receive: Receive ={
  case f: FindBookByIsbn(isbn, _) =>
    val r = optToEither(isbn, Catalog.books.get)
                                             Folding over either is a convenient
    r fold (                                 way to process the alternatives.
      f => sender() ! f,
      s => sender() ! s                      Book not found
    )                             Book found
  // ... handle other messages
}
```

Performs the lookup

This pattern is common. A requested operation either produces a result or doesn't, and you want to send different messages in response. As `Option` has subtypes `None` and `Some`, `Either` has subtypes `Left` and `Right`. The convention is to use `Right` to represent default values and `Left` to represent failures, so `None` usually is mapped to `Left`.

TIP   Use `Either` to provide a richer, self-contained message rather than a simple failure or an empty message.

WAITING FOR A RESULT

Using an in-memory `Map` to represent the card catalog makes it possible for the `Librarian` to respond to every request immediately. In a more realistic model, performing research and preparing a result would take time. One approach would be to tell the actor thread to sleep for a while. Don't do this! See the following listing.

Listing 4.7   Blocking threads in an actor

```
override def receive: Receive ={
  case f: FindBookByIsbn(isbn, _) =>
    val book = Catalog.books(isbn)
    Thread.sleep(findBookDuration)          ◁────┐  Bad idea
    sender() ! BookFound(List(book))
  // ... handle other messages
}
```

Under the covers, Akka schedules actors to run on a thread pool that it manages internally by using a *dispatcher*. The number of threads in that pool normally is based on the number of processing cores available. It's not unusual for an actor system to have thousands of actors on a single processor, which means that each thread handles requests for many actors. Actors blocking threads can quickly cause your entire application to grind to a halt. We revisit dispatchers in section 4.4.

WARNING   Actors shouldn't block threads. A blocking operation in one actor prevents other actors from executing on that thread, which can upset the entire application, not just the blocked actor.

The concept of not blocking threads in an actor extends beyond explicitly blocking operations such as `Thread.sleep()`. Any synchronized operation or function that performs file or network I/O is blocking and should be avoided. Instead, use `Promise` and `Future` from the `scala.concurrent` package. For more information on using that package, refer to the Scala language documentation at http://docs.scala-lang.org/overviews/core/futures.html.

TIP   Logging can be a hidden source of blocking operations. Chapter 10 shows you how to use Akka's capabilities to avoid blocking log messages.

STACKING STATES

How do you enable your busy `Librarian` to spend time on research without blocking the whole system? As you might expect, the solution is to use messages and states. The `Librarian` moves to the busy state while performing research and moves back to the previous state when the research is complete. You already know how to change state by using the `become()` function. The `RareBooks` owner could assign additional tasks for the `Librarian` to perform when not busy. There could be states for adding books to the catalog, preparing invoices for Customers, or perhaps writing a monthly news-letter. After completing a research assignment, the Librarian should return to what-ever the previous state was.

Multiple previous states could exist, however. The Librarian could be working on the monthly newsletter when a new shipment of books arrives to be cataloged, and in the middle of that process, a research request from a Customer arrives. As an expe-rienced developer, you recognize that the data structure is a *stack*. Akka can manage a stack of previous states for you. By default, Akka discards the previous state, but you can change that behavior by passing discardOld=false to the become() function. When it's time to return to the previous state, use the unbecome() function to pop the previous state off the stack and return to it, as shown in figure 4.5.

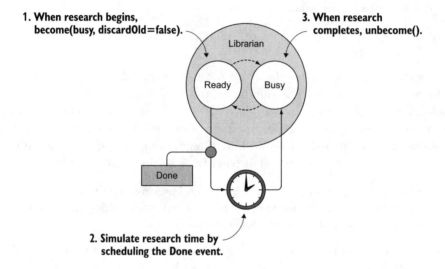

1. When research begins, become(busy, discardOld=false).

3. When research completes, unbecome().

Librarian

Ready   Busy

Done

2. Simulate research time by scheduling the Done event.

Figure 4.5   The Librarian can receive messages while busy.

A nice thing about this approach is that it's easy to extend the behavior of an actor without always having to update every receive function or manage a complex state dia-gram. Following are some guidelines that (if followed) produce stackable states:

- No state exists before the initial state, so the initial receive function should never call unbecome().
- Other receive functions should have a wildcard message handler that calls stash().
- To complete the current state, call unstashAll() followed by unbecome().
- If a message arrives that sends the actor to a higher-priority state, call become(*higherPriorityState*, discardOld=false), so that the actor returns to the current state when the higher-priority state is complete.

- To abandon the current state, call become(*newState*, discardOld=true), and when the next state completes with unbecome(), it returns to the previous state instead of the current state.

Not everything requires multiple receive functions to manage actor state. Sometimes, it's better to use one receive function and keep track of state by using variables. We explore that approach in the next section.

4.3.4 *Keeping it simple*

Like RareBooks, Customer is a top-level actor. Customers send research requests to RareBooks, and the requests are forwarded to individual Librarians. When a Librarian is unable to find a book, the Customer may complain. Then the Librarian may issue a credit to the Customer. As shown in figure 4.6, the complaint and credit interaction occurs directly between the Customer and the Librarian, not through the RareBooks actor, as in the original request.

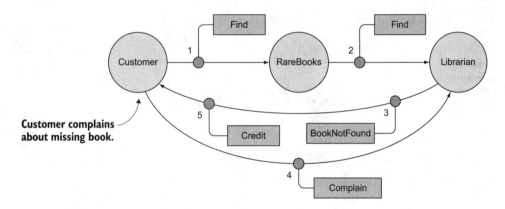

Figure 4.6 **The Customer may complain when the Librarian is unable to find a book, and the Customer receives a credit in recompense.**

For this discussion, we'll use a simplistic model of the Customer. Some Customers have more difficult research requests than others, so their odds of a successful research request are lower. In addition, some Customers are more tolerant of unsuccessful requests than others, so each Customer actor has its own tolerance property to reflect that fact. If a Customer's tolerance for unsuccessful requests is exceeded, the Customer complains and stops sending new requests. If the Customer receives a credit from the Librarian, the Customer is satisfied, and the count of unsuccessful requests is reset to zero.

Functions that model and manage the state of the Customer are defined in the companion object, as shown in the following listing. Notice that CustomerModel and State are both immutable. CustomerModel tracks the parameters that describe the

Customer.State holds the latest CustomerModel, a time stamp, and a function that produces an updated CustomerModel when a message is received.

Listing 4.8   Customer **companion object defining** Customer **state behavior**

```
object Customer {

  import RareBooksProtocol._

  def props(rareBooks: ActorRef, odds: Int, tolerance: Int): Props =
    Props(new Customer(rareBooks, odds, tolerance))

  case class CustomerModel(
    odds: Int,
    tolerance: Int,
    found: Int,
    notFound: Int)

  case class State(model: CustomerModel, timeInMillis: Long) {

    def update(m: Msg): State = m match {

      case BookFound(b, d) =>
        copy(model.copy(found = model.found + b.size), d)

      case BookNotFound(_, d) =>
        copy(model.copy(notFound = model.notFound + 1), d)

      case Credit(d) =>
        copy(model.copy(notFound = 0), d)
    }
  }
}
```

Probability that the Customer will submit a successful research request

Tolerance for unsuccessful research requests

Running count of successful research requests

Running count of unsuccessful research requests

Produces a new state based on the current state and a received message

Adds the number of books that were found

Increments the count of unsuccessful requests

Resets the count to zero

Using this state model results in a straightforward Customer actor. The important things to notice in the actor implementation shown in listing 4.9 are as follows:

- A var rather than a val is used for state.
- The Customer makes an initial call to requestBookInfo() to initiate the message flow.
- Only one receive function is needed, with no calls to become() or unbecome().
- The receive function implements the interaction shown in figure 4.6 earlier in this chapter.

Listing 4.9   Customer **actor's variable state**

```
class Customer(rareBooks: ActorRef, odds: Int, tolerance: Int)
    extends Actor with ActorLogging {

  import Customer._
  import RareBooksProtocol._
```

```
private var state =
➡ State(CustomerModel(odds, tolerance, 0, 0), -1L)        Starts in a neutral state

requestBookInfo()                        ◄──┐  Sends an initial request
                                             │  to start the message flow
override def receive: Receive = {
  case m: Msg => m match {              ◄──┐  Gate to ensure that only protocol
                                           │  messages are processed
    case f: BookFound =>
      state = state.update(f)                      Matches guard to process
      requestBookInfo()                             NotFound message when
                                                    tolerance hasn't been exceeded
    case f: BookNotFound
    ➡ if state.model.notFound < state.model.tolerance =>   ◄──
      state = state.update(f)
      requestBookInfo()
                                         Processes NotFound when
    case f: BookNotFound =>      ◄──┘    tolerance has been exceeded.
      state = state.update(f)
      sender ! Complain()        ◄──┐  Sends a complaint
                                     │  back to the Librarian
    case c: Credit =>        ◄──┐
      state = state.update(c)    │
      requestBookInfo(}          Resumes sending
  }                              research requests
}

private def requestBookInfo(): Unit =          Helper to send a research
  rareBooks ! FindBookByTopic(Set(pickTopic))   request on some topic

private def pickTopic: Topic =
  if (Random.nextInt(100) < state.model.odds)    Helper to pick a random
    viableTopics(Random.nextInt(viableTopics.size))  and possibly unknown topic
  else Unknown
}
```

> **What is a match guard?**
>
> In Scala, a *match guard* is syntactic sugar that provides more readable syntax for case statements. You can think of match guards as filters. You can place a guard on a match so that the match is made only if the pattern matches and the guard condition is true. Otherwise, matching moves on to the next case and tries again.

As mentioned at the beginning of this section, the Customer actor is similar to the Librarian, with one distinct difference: the management of local mutable state. As the analogy progresses, you add to this notion of state management by adding more properties. In chapter 6, we introduce storing state with Akka persistence.

4.3.5 *Running the application*

To run the application, use sbt as shown in chapter 2. (You can find full details and documentation on sbt at www.scala-sbt.org.) From a terminal window, change the directory to the root application reactive-application-development-scala, and start sbt. You should see the following output:

```
[info] Loading global plugins from ...
[info] Loading project definition ...
[Info] Set current project to ...
>
```

At the > prompt, type `project chapter4_001_messaging` to change the project to the one you laid out. Next, type run, and you should see the following:

```
[info] Running com.rarebooks.library.RareBooksApp
...
Enter commands [`q` = quit, `2c` = 2 customers, etc.]:
```

Enter 2c (for two customers), and the application starts passing messages among RareBooks, the Librarian, and the Customers. You haven't output yet, but the code in the online repository logs all results to rarebooks.log in the root directory. A good way to watch what's happening is to tail the log file while the app is running, like so:

```
$ tail -f rarebooks.log
```

In the log file, you should see the actor system starting up, including the creation of the RareBooks, Librarian, and Customer actors. In addition, you see a sequence of messages flowing back and forth, and the simulation of RareBooks opening and closing. One thing to note is the throughput. Depending on your machine's specifications, performance may vary, but you should see around 10 or 11 messages processed per simulated day.

Congratulations!

4.3.6   *Reviewing progress*

The next section shows you how to make an application more elastic by adding Librarian actors to the example. Then you see how to make an application more resilient by replacing a faulty Librarian actor. Before continuing, consider what you've accomplished reactively so far:

Responsive
- The participants communicate asynchronously through message passing, which removes delays due to synchronous processing.
- The immutable message structure prevents delays that otherwise could occur due to concurrency faults.

Resilient
- The share-nothing philosophy through isolation of state prevents concurrency faults that could occur due to shared mutable state.
- The immutable message structure removes the possibility of mutations in the state that's messaged, preventing potential concurrency faults.

Elastic

- The loosely coupled design through message passing supports vertical and horizontal scaling.

Message-driven

- The actor model provides the message-passing semantics for message-driven architecture.

4.4 *Increasing elasticity*

We've spent a great deal of time laying out the analogy and establishing the overall system in a reactive format. As a result, you have the groundwork to explore more complex concepts (such as elasticity) in detail. As you may recall from chapter 1, *elasticity* means that the system stays responsive under varying workloads. Reactive systems can respond to changes in load by increasing or decreasing the allocation of resources.

How do you make the application elastic? From the owner's perspective, it's obvious that `RareBooks` needs to hire more `Librarians`. In computational terms, the application needs to process requests in parallel.

4.4.1 *Akka routing*

By hiring more `Librarians`, the owner reduces overall response time for `Customer` requests by processing them simultaneously. Akka uses a *router* to achieve parallelism among multiple actors. The purpose of a router in Akka is to pass messages to a set of other actors, called *routees*.

ROUTING LOGIC

The router uses one of several routing logic strategies to manage the distribution of these messages. The router implementation in Akka provides a variety of routing logic strategies that can be applied based on an application's needs, or you can create a custom router. Table 4.3 shows the routing implementations that ship with Akka.

Table 4.3 Akka routing logic

Routing logic	Description
`RoundRobinRoutingLogic`	Processes items that are encountered (messages) sequentially, in a circular manner
`RandomRoutingLogic`	Uses a random number with a range bound by the number of routees to select the routee to employ
`SmallestMailboxRoutingLogic`	Attempts to send to the nonsuspended routee with the fewest messages in its mailbox
`BroadcastRoutingLogic`	Broadcasts the message to all routees
`ScatterGatherFirstCompleted-RoutingLogic`	Broadcasts the message to all routees and replies with the first response

Table 4.3 Akka routing logic *(continued)*

Routing logic	Description
TailChoppingRoutingLogic	Sends the message to a random picked routee and waits for a specified interval; then sends to another randomly picked routee until one cycle is complete
ConsistentHashingRoutingLogic	Uses consistent hashing to select a routee based on the message received

The routees themselves are ordinary child actors wrapped with the `ActorRefRoutee` trait, which denotes an actor as a routee. `ActorRefRoutee` also provides value members for referencing the routee (`ref`) and sending messages (`send`).

Routers come in two categories: pooled and group. We describe both types in the following sections.

POOLED ROUTERS

Pooled routers create and manage the routee actors as children and are responsible for their supervision, as shown in figure 4.7. The settings for pooled routers are based on configuration or code, with the requirement that a router be created programmatically.

Chapter 2 shows how to define settings for a pooled router by using a configuration file. Akka looks for a file called application.conf at the root of the class path. The

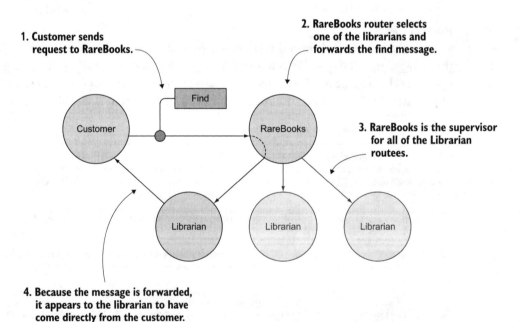

1. Customer sends request to RareBooks.

2. RareBooks router selects one of the librarians and forwards the find message.

3. RareBooks is the supervisor for all of the Librarian routees.

4. Because the message is forwarded, it appears to the librarian to have come directly from the customer.

Figure 4.7 The RareBooks actor supervises a pool of Librarians.

application tells Akka to read the properties from the configuration file by using `FromConfig`, as shown in the following listing.

Listing 4.10 Router loaded from the configuration file

```
val librarian: ActorRef =
  context.actorOf(FromConfig.props(              Loads from the
                                                 configuration file
    Librarian.props(findBookDuration), "librarian"))
                                                 Generates instances of the
                                                 Librarian itself, using props
                                                 from the companion object
```

The configuration shown in the following listing defines a round-robin pool of 10 `Librarian` actors in the `rarebooks` actor system.

Listing 4.11 Configuration for a pool router with routing logic and routee count

```
akka.actor.deployment {
  /rarebooks/librarian {              The path to
                                      the router pool
    router = round-robin-pool                        Type of router pool
    nr-of-instances = 10
  }                                   Number of routers
}                                     in the pool
```

An alternative to using a configuration file is to create the router programmatically, which requires a small change (see the following listing).

Listing 4.12 Configuring a pool router programmatically

```
val librarian: ActorRef =
  context.actorOf(RoundRobinPool(5).props(          Defines the round-robin
    Librarian.props(findBookDuration), "librarian")  pool in code
```

Whether the router is configured through a configuration file or programmatically, no changes are made in the `Librarian` actor. In both cases, that actor is defined by using `Props` generated by the `Librarian` companion object.

GROUP ROUTERS

Group routers differ from pooled routers in that they allow routees to be created externally. After the routees are created, they're associated with a router by their actor path. The router isn't the parent of the routees and isn't responsible for their supervision. As with a pooled router, a group router's settings are defined in configuration or code. The configuration for a group router is similar to the pool router that you saw previously (see the following listing).

Listing 4.13 Configuration for a group router with routing logic and routee locations

```
akka.actor.deployment {
  /rarebooks/librarian {              Uses a group rather
    router = round-robin-group        than a pool
```

```
    routees.paths = [
        "/user/rarebooks/librarian-1",
        "/user/workers/librarian-2",            The workers may have        Provides paths
        "/user/workers/librarian-3"]            different supervisors.       to the actors
    }
}
```

There's no difference between loading the pool router from a configuration file and loading the group router from a configuration file. The code is the same code presented in listing 4.12. If you want to create the group router programmatically, you need to make a few code changes, as shown in the following listing.

Listing 4.14   Configuring a group router programmatically

```
val paths = List(                                         List of paths
    "/user/rarebooks/librarian-1",                        for the actors
    "/user/workers/librarian-2",
    "/user/workers/librarian-3")          Creates a round-robin      Generates instances
val librarian: ActorRef =                 group for the actors       of the Librarian itself,
  context.actorOf(RoundRobinGroup(paths).props(                      using Props from the
    Librarian.props(findBookDuration)), "librarian")                companion object
```

Whether the router was created with a configuration or programmatically, and whether the router is a pool or a group, individual instances of the `Librarian` actor are created by using the same `Props`. The individual `Librarians` are unaffected by the routing strategy or supervision. If you stop and think about this situation for a moment, you'll find it to be surprising. By modifying your configuration file and making a slight change in the way the actor is created, you implement parallelization by using two different supervision strategies.

4.4.2   Dispatchers

Dispatchers are the heart of Akka's messaging system. *Dispatchers* coordinate communication among actors, implementing `scala.concurrent.ExecutionContext` and registering an actor's mailbox for execution. They work in concert with an *Executor*, which is essentially a grouping of threads, and provide the execution time and context in which actors operate. In doing so, they provide the foundation for parallelism via the Executor, in that they can be tuned to the underlying cores within a machine. Akka provides four types of dispatchers, as shown in table 4.4.

Table 4.4   Akka dispatchers

Name	Description	Mailbox	Sharing	Backing	Uses
Dispatcher	Default	Per actor	Any number of actors	`fork-join-executor` or `thread-pool-executor`	Bulkheading, optimized for nonblocking

Table 4.4 Akka dispatchers *(continued)*

Name	Description	Mailbox	Sharing	Backing	Uses
Pinned-Dispatcher	Dedicates a unique thread per actor	Per actor	Can't be shared	`thread-pool-executor`	Heavy I/O blocking operations
Balancing-Dispatcher	Redistributes work from busy actors to idle actors	Shared	Only actors of the same type	`fork-join-executor` or `thread-pool-executor`	Work sharing
Calling-Thread-Dispatcher	Runs on the current thread only	Per thread, on demand	Any number of actors	Calling thread	Testing

LIBRARIAN ROUTER

Now that you understand how parallelization works in Akka by way of routers, we'll address throughput. To achieve multiple `Librarians` with a router in code, you change two files: application.conf and Librarian.scala. The changes in application .conf are shown in the following listing.

Listing 4.15 application.conf specifying router configuration

```
rare-books {
  open-duration = 20 seconds
  close-duration = 5 seconds
  nbr-of-librarians = 5          ⟵──┐ Number of Librarian
  librarian {                         routees to create
    find-book-duration = 2 seconds
  }
}
```

You may be thinking, "Wait a second; I thought the router settings went under `akka.actor.deployment`." You'd be correct, but in this case, routees are created and configured programmatically. The `nbr-of-librarians` setting is a convenience for adjusting the number of routees created by the code, as shown in the updated `RareBooks` actor (in the following listing).

Listing 4.16 `RareBooks` reading router configuration from application.conf

```
import akka.actor.{ Actor, ActorLogging, Props, Stash }          ⟵──┐
import akka.routing.{ActorRefRoutee, Router, RoundRobinRoutingLogic }  │
                                                      Removes the
                                                      ActorRef import
  private val nbrOfLibrarians: Int =
  ⇒ context.system.settings.config
  ⇒ getInt "rare-books.nbr-of-librarians"    ⟵── Gets the number of
                                                 Librarian routees to create
                                                 from the configuration
```

```
var router: Router = createLibrarian()        ◁─┐ Local mutable reference is a
                                                 │ Router instead of an ActorRef.
private def open: Receive = {
  case m: Msg =>                         ┌─ Routes the message
    router.route(m, sender())      ◁─────┘  instead of forwarding

protected def createLibrarian(): Router = {    ◁─┐ Returns a Router
                                                 │ instead of an ActorRef

  var cnt: Int = 0
  val routees: Vector[ActorRefRoutee] =    ◁──┐ Vector of ActorRefRoutee
➥ Vector.fill(nbrOfLibrarians) {
➥ val r = context.actorOf(                      ┌─ Creates an
➥ Librarian.props(findBookDuration), s"librarian-$cnt") │ individual Librarian
    cnt += 1
    ActorRefRoutee(r)                   ◁─┐ Wraps the Librarian
  }                                       │ in ActorRefRoutee
  Router(RoundRobinRoutingLogic(), routees)          ◁──────┐
}                                                            │
                                    Creates a Router with RoundRobin-
                                    RoutingLogic and the list of routees
```

The owner is happy now, because `RareBooks` can satisfy many more customers in parallel. The reason we chose to programmatically configure the router is to have more control of supervision of the routees, which is coming up next.

4.4.3   *Running the application with routers*

Assuming that you're still in sbt, change the project to `chapter4_002_elasticity` and run it again. This time, enter more customers by typing 5c for five customers. Tail the log file again, and take note of the significant increase in performance. Even with more than double the number of customers, the result you get is almost five times higher performance—pretty amazing for a few lines of new code.

4.5   *Resilience*

So far, we've explored the basis of reactive programming via message-driven communication (the base) and elasticity (a pillar). Now we look at the other pillar: resilience. Before we get started, however, we need to update the example to simulate a fault in the code that reflects the real-world interactions the owner would have with his employees and customers.

Successful business owners usually put their heart and soul into their endeavors, so quality is of the utmost importance. As the company grows and additional resources come on board, however, compromises in quality sometimes occur. You can expect this result to some extent, because some new employees don't have the necessary experience, and the learning curve can be lengthy. In this section, we simulate that situation as a fault in Akka and show how you can overcome these problems through the use of supervision.

When the business owner was a sole proprietor, he prided himself in always responding to the customer. When a customer reached her tolerance for "books not found," the owner sent her a credit, which resolved the issue. He never allowed the number of complaints to stress him, because he considered complaints to be a standard part of doing business. Unfortunately, the newly hired librarians don't share this outlook. Although they're committed to doing a good job, they don't have the owner's stamina for grievances. As a result, after a certain number of complaints, the employees become frustrated. When they're frustrated, they must take a break, during which time they're unable to process requests; worse, they lose track of the current complaint, resulting in the customer never receiving a credit. This problem is a serious one. A frustrated employee will recover and start working again, but a frustrated customer may not. Because the customer never received a credit (because the worker lost track of complaints), eventually, that customer's requests will stop.

4.5.1 Faulty Librarian actor

In Akka, this situation is called a *fault*, and we model it in this section as an exception. When one of the `Librarians` exceeds its tolerance for complaints, it becomes frustrated and throws a `ComplainException`. When this exception occurs, Akka pauses the `Librarian` routee and escalates to the parent, which is `RareBooks`. Because `RareBooks` uses the default supervision strategy (which we talk about in the next section), it restarts the paused `Librarian`, effectively resetting that `Librarian`'s `complainCount` to zero. At this point, the `Customer` that complained is in a state in which it no longer requests information, as it didn't receive a credit. The `RareBooks` owner can correct that situation.

Start by adding some declarations to the companion object, as shown in the following listing.

Listing 4.17 Faulty `Librarian` parameters

```
object Librarian {
  // ...
  final case class ComplainException(
      c: Complain,                                        Immutable
      customer: ActorRef)                                 exception
      extends IllegalStateException("Too many complaints!")   descriptor
  // ...
  def props(
      findBookDuration: FiniteDuration,
      maxComplainCount: Int): Props =                     Adds maxComplain-
    Props(new Librarian(findBookDuration, maxComplainCount))   Count parameter
  // ...
}
```

Next, add the complaining misbehavior to the `Librarian`, as shown in the following listing.

Listing 4.18 Faulty `Librarian` behavior

```
class Librarian(
    findBookDuration: FiniteDuration,
```

```
        maxComplainCount: Int)                              ◄──┐  Adds maxComplainCount
        extends Actor with ActorLogging with Stash {           │  to the constructor
 //...
 private var complainCount: Int = 0              ◄──┐  Local mutable state
 //...                                              │  for number of
 private def ready: Receive = {                     │  complaints received
   case m: Msg => m match {
     case c: Complain if complainCount == maxComplainCount =>      ◄──┐  Matches
         throw ComplainException(c, sender())                         │  guard on
     case c: Complain =>                                              │  complaint
         complainCount += 1                                           │  count
         sender ! Credit()
 //...
```

Too many! points to `throw ComplainException(c, sender())`

Otherwise, process the complaint messages normally. points to `case c: Complain =>`

Finally, a small change makes the `RareBooks` actor fetch the `max-complain-count` and pass it to the `Librarian` on creation (shown in the following listing).

Listing 4.19   `RareBooks` actor changes

```
class RareBooks extends Actor with ActorLogging with Stash {
  //...
  private val maxComplainCount: Int =                  ◄──┐  Fetches the max-
    context.system.setting.config getInt                  │  complain-count from
    ➥ "rare-books.librarian.max-complain-count"           │  application.conf
  //...
  protected def createLibrarian(): Router = {
    //...                                               Passes maxComplainCount upon
    val r = context.actorOf(Librarian.props(            creation of Librarian routee
    ➥ findBookDuration, maxComplainCount), s"librarian-$cnt")   ◄──
    //...
```

Configure the simulation by making the number of tolerable complaints a property of `Librarian` in application.conf and add it to the properties factory as a parameter, as shown in the following listing.

Listing 4.20   Faulty `Librarian` actor application.conf changes

```
//...
rare-books {
  open-duration = 20 seconds
  close-duration = 5 seconds
  nbr-of-librarians = 5
  librarian {
    find-book-duration = 2 seconds
    max-complain-count = 2          ◄──┐  Maximum number of tolerable
  }                                      complaints for a given Librarian
}
```

Now that the `Librarian` simulation has a maximum tolerance for receiving complaints before giving up and failing, see how it behaves when you run it.

4.5.2 *Running the faulty application*

As before, make sure that you're at the sbt prompt and set the project to chapter4_003_faulty. Run the application with two Customers, but this time, set their tolerance for books not found to 2, as follows:

```
Enter commands [`q` = quit, `2c` = 2 customers, etc.]:
2c2
```

Tail the log file, and let the application run for a while. Notice that after one of the Librarians throws the ComplainException, the Customer that the Librarian was serving stops requesting information, and eventually, all Customers stop. The application continues running, but the number of Customer requests processed per day will be zero!

4.5.3 *Librarian supervision*

The owner implements a simple rule to overcome this small but serious issue. Whenever a Librarian becomes frustrated and needs a break, it must first inform the owner of the situation. That way, the owner can proxy for the Librarian and issue the credit on that Librarian's behalf. In Akka terms, you achieve this result by implementing the appropriate supervision process. You may recall from the discussion of Akka supervision in chapter 3 two strategies that you can use out of the box:

- *OneForOneStrategy*—This strategy (the default) operates as its name suggests. The supervisor executes one of four directives (listed in this section) against the subordinate and in turn executes all the subordinate children.
- *AllForOneStrategy*—In this strategy, the supervisor executes one of the four directives not only against the subordinate that faulted, but also against all subordinates that the supervisor manages.

These strategies have four directives:

- *Resume* the subordinate, keeping its accumulated internal state.
- *Restart* the subordinate, clearing its accumulated internal state.
- *Stop* the subordinate permanently.
- *Escalate* the failure, thereby failing itself.

In this case, the default OneForOneStrategy and the Restart directive are fine. You need to intercept the exception and extract the Customer, however, so that the owner can send a credit while the faulty Librarian is recovering. To do so, use a *decider*, which decides what to do in the case of failure.

From an Akka point of view, a decider represents a PartialFunction[Throwable, Directive] that applies at the time of failure. The Decider maps the child actor's fault to the directive that's taken. If you declare the strategy inside the supervising actor as opposed to within a companion object, its decider has access to all internal states of the actor. In addition, this is thread-safe, including obtaining a reference to the currently failed child, which is available as the sender of the failure message. You create a decider to intercept and handle the `ComplainException`, as shown in the following listing.

Listing 4.21 RareBooks supervision implementation

```
class RareBooks extends Actor with ActorLogging with Stash {
    //...
    override val supervisorStrategy: SupervisorStrategy = {      ⟵ Overrides the default
                                                                    supervision strategy
        val decider: SupervisorStrategy.Decider = {

            case Librarian.ComplainException(complain, customer) =>      ⟵ Decides what to do
                customer ! Credit()      ⟵ Sends the                       with a ComplainException
                SupervisorStrategy.Restart      Customer a
        }                                       Credit message

        OneForOneStrategy()(
            decider orElse super.supervisorStrategy.decider)      Returns the
    }                                                             OneForOneStrategy with
                                                                  the decider or applies
                                                                  the default strategy
```

Creates a Decider for the strategy → (points to `val decider: SupervisorStrategy.Decider = {`)

Invokes the Restart directive → (points to `SupervisorStrategy.Restart`)

This seemingly simple but powerful model of hierarchical supervision is the key to resilience in Akka. As mentioned in chapter 3, this style of oversight is much more than fault tolerance. Although fault-tolerant systems imply the degradation of quality proportional to the severity of the failure, such is not the case with resilience. Resilience embraces failure through expectation and in turn self-heals in the face of failure.

4.5.4 *Running the application with resilient supervision*

Now that you've fixed the faulty `Librarian` problem, run the application once more. From the sbt prompt set the project to `chapter4_004_resilience`. Run the application with two `Customers` and a low tolerance, as before:

```
Enter commands [`q` = quit, `2c` = 2 customers, etc.]:
2c2
```

Tail the log file, and let the application run for a while. You see that when one of the `Librarians` throws the `ComplainException`, `RareBooks` steps in and issues a credit to the complaining `Customer`.

Summary

- Reasoning by use of an analogy that explains how people solve a problem manually can lead to solid reactive design.
- You can extend a simple solution to accommodate progressively more detail.
- You should use protocol objects to define messages used by multiple actors. Companion objects can be used to define protocols used in limited scopes.

- Controlling actor state with `become()`, `stash()`, and `unstash()` produces simple state transitions. Using the context stack with `unbecome()` enables more-sophisticated and extensible state management.
- It's often useful for an actor to send a message to itself.
- Match guards are syntactic sugar that can simplify matching logic.
- Akka has several built-in strategies for routing messages among multiple worker actors. Pool routers are for worker actors that are also supervised by the pool owner. Group routers provide the same routing logic without requiring supervision.
- Dispatchers manage how actors are scheduled on threads by using an execution context.
- Actors can be allowed to fail. Failures are managed by a combination of supervision strategies, directives, and deciders.

Domain-driven design

5

Sometimes, humans require some distance to fully comprehend a thing. An example is an impressionist painting. When you look at one of these paintings up close, all you see are colored dots and small brushstrokes; you don't see a clear image. When you back away from the painting, it becomes clear, and you can see a child on a swing, a park, or a lake. This situation is similar with a large architecture, a reactive architecture being no exception. In this spirit, we take some steps back in this chapter to look at a reactive application from a distance, starting with the next item in the reactive toolbox, domain-driven design.

In building reactive architectures, you need not venture into unknown territory. Helpful patterns and technologies already exist that allow you to program the

116

reactive way with a lot less effort than you think—if you learn to use and embrace some well-known standard items in your toolbox. As with the construction of a house, if you know how to build a wall, a floor, and a roof, building the entire house isn't too much of a stretch. With this approach to domain modeling, you can begin building systems that adhere to the Reactive Manifesto, giving you message-driven, elastic, responsive, and resilient capabilities.

Domain-driven design is a set of domain development terms, tools, and ideas formalized by Eric Evans in the early 2000s to simplify complex domain modeling.

This chapter discusses these tools and methodologies, and describes how they work in a traditional sense and in the reactive world.

5.1 *What is domain-driven design?*

Domain-driven design (DDD) is a valuable tool for fleshing out domains and their behavior, a *domain* being a discrete area of functionality designed to solve a software problem. DDD applies to many domains and programming languages. (You see it applied to Scala and Akka in this chapter.) The phrase *domain-driven design* was first used in a book bearing the same name by Eric Evans, the father and pioneer of the domain-driven-design philosophy.

DDD helps you build reactive applications incorporating the key traits of the Reactive Manifesto:

- *Elasticity* (reacting to load)—Elasticity means an easily distributable and individually scalable domain model.
- *Message-driven*—Immutable, one-way messages reduce side effects between domains.
- *Resilient*—Failing sub-domains don't degrade the system behavior as a whole.
- *Responsive*—Well-organized and well-subdivided domains are more performant than monolithic domains.

DDD is the practice of modeling complex systems with the goal of mapping real-life domain behavior to system behavior. Many of us have been practicing these techniques without knowing that they had a name; some people might call the use of DDD good architecture. *Immutability*, which we discuss in chapter 2, describes objects that are created only once and never mutated or changed. Immutable domain design means that *domain entities* (meaningful items in a domain model) are created only once, and all attributes are set on creation, allowing easy sharing across multiple computer threads and processes. Immutable objects have fewer side effects, as there are no setters (mutator functions that update the state) on any of the attributes on the object. This fact doesn't mean that a domain entity can't be changed, but doing so is different from performing a traditional setter type update; instead of mutating the current state of the object, the object provides a copy of itself with the desired change.

DDD is a structure of practices and a set of vocabulary called the *ubiquitous language* that maps software to a real-life domain. Using DDD practices results in an evolving domain model patterned as closely as possible on the functions of the physical domain, whether that domain is a postal service or an airport (which we use as a domain example in this chapter).

DDD isn't meant for trivial architectures, but what reactive architecture is trivial? One important prerequisite of DDD is access to domain expertise. It's possible to apply the practice by becoming an expert in the domain yourself, but that process is difficult and carries some amount of risk due to substitution of actual domain expertise for a developer's best guess. In the absence of business expertise in an airport domain model, for example, an attribute belonging clearly to ground control may inadvertently be added to the tower. Each of these mismatches of the domain versus real-life counterparts obscures the design and makes the overall application of DDD less valuable. In short, do DDD, but do it right or not at all.

DDD sets up a solid foundation at the beginning of a distributed software design, because the domain is divided into more easily digestible pieces and also easily distributable pieces, helping satisfy the important elasticity aspect of going reactive.

One of the first steps in creating an accurate domain model is dividing the functions of the domain into discrete parts, known as *bounded contexts*, so that each can be understood as an independent piece, and the interactions among these pieces can be mapped into the model of the entire domain.

We look at bounded contexts in section 5.1.7, but first we look at what happens in the absence of such DDD: incorrectly planned and monolithic designs, characterized in the following section as a Big Ball of Mud.

5.1.1   The Big Ball of Mud

The absence of proper application design has been called a *Big Ball of Mud*, meaning a domain design that is "haphazardly structured, sprawling, sloppy, duct-tape and bailing wire, spaghetti code jungle" (Brian Foote and Joseph Yoder, http://www.laputan .org/mud/). This is due to the fact that monolithic domain designs seldom (if ever) work and quickly become unmanageable. These types of designs are continually in need of quick repairs and are not well thought out as part of the architecture as a whole; as these accumulate, the system starts its inevitable decline.

WHAT CREATES A BALL OF MUD?
The forces that contribute to this Ball of Mud are

- *Time*—Perceptions, real or imagined, that there isn't enough time to do the best job or that there's some mad rush to get software out to market before a given season are usually an indication of not having enough time to do the job properly.
- *Experience*—Insufficient programmer aptitude, inexperience, and lack of supervision contribute to a Ball of Mud.
- *Cost*—Cost is the perception that higher-quality software will bear too high a cost, which is interesting because most of the time, inferior software costs

substantially more than software done right in the first place. Sometimes, there isn't enough money to fund anything more than a rushed project for a startup that's concerned only about fiscal survival.

- *Visibility*—Software, especially back end software, can't be seen or touched. A messy user interface would draw criticism and immediate correction, whereas the back end can be built in the shadows, waiting to fail.
- *Complexity*—Complexity is a killer. Sometimes, software needs to be somewhat complex to solve a problem, but when the software houses multiple complexities (bad encapsulation design) or is overly complex, it becomes confusing and unmanageable. Complex code is hard to look at and discouraging to maintain.
- *Change*—Software changes; requirements change. If software is built in a tightly coupled fashion, without expectation of change, there will be mud.

WHAT DOES THE MUD BALL LOOK LIKE?

The Big Ball of Mud is characterized by the following problems:

- *Throwaway code*—This is caused by an attempt to solve the immediate problem without regard for the overall design because of the perceived simplicity of a change or to make the change as noninvasive as possible. Throwaway code is never thrown away, as time is never taken to refactor it the right way because of the same short-term thinking that caused it in the first place. This perception of investment in software is known as the *sunk-cost fallacy*—an overwhelming and irrational feeling in management that because so much money has been spent on a bad project, it's too expensive to throw away.
- *Piecemeal growth*—Piecemeal growth is growth and evolution of a thing over time. New York City is an excellent example of piecemeal growth of a city. The city started out organized and then spread inward and outward from what used to be New Amsterdam, the present-day Canal Street area, and up through Harlem. The city's streets are disorganized from Downtown to Midtown; Broadway even travels diagonally at some point. The city expanded according to need, not according to some grand plan. This same "sprawl" may occur in your codebase. Los Angeles, another example of uncontrolled urban sprawl, is pictured in figure 5.1.

  On one hand, a grand master plan may seem like it would result in a more organized city and code, but the reality is that all things change, and planning on a moving target is setting yourself

Figure 5.1   Los Angeles urban sprawl

up for failure. On the other hand, growth without planning ends up as a mess. What do you do? The solution is *atomicity* of design, which means designing closely related sections of your system compartmentalized from other parts of the system. Keep the system up-to-date by relentlessly refactoring locally.

- *Keeping the code working*—The software is important; your customers, workers, and money depend on it. Necessary improvements are desired, but they're not made for fear of breaking the system. Everyone from the top down is afraid of having the code touched or touching it himself. Often the resulting code is throwaway (discussed earlier in this list).

- *Sweeping it under the rug*—If you can't make the dirt go away, you can hide it from plain sight. Unrealistic deadlines, insufficient requirements, and the feeling that a little more hidden dirty code won't hurt anything or be noticed can cause people to keep code they shouldn't. It's usually thought that removing this type of code is cost-prohibitive, but the cost of maintaining such a codebase shouldn't be ignored.

HOW CAN YOU AVOID THE BALL OF MUD?

Following are some techniques for avoiding the Big Ball of Mud:

- *Control fragmentation with continuous integration.* When large teams work on a domain (even a team of three people may be considered large), the potential exists for fragmentation, due to the divergence of ideas within the team. Because the domain is continuously *discovered*, different developers may come up with divergent ideas. Breaking the domain down further isn't the way to solve the problem. The domain is broken down to a level that still maps to a real-life domain problem, and when attempts are made to break it down further and artificially, that domain loses cohesion.

- *Continuous integration comes to the rescue.* Developers working on any given domain should come together at least daily, merging their code and ideas—and (most importantly) keeping the ubiquitous-language document updated with their evolved ideas. When code is merged often, emerged divergence is guarded against and removed. As you can see, continuous integration allows close collaboration among the team members.

- *Avoid anemic domain models.* An *anemic domain model* is one that hasn't been thoroughly thought through in terms of DDD and is an antipattern. This type of domain model may appear at first glance to be reasonable and map somewhat to real-life objects, but when you examine it closely, you find that it has no real behavior. An example anemic domain object resembles a data structure with getters and setters rather than some entity with behavior and complex characteristics. These models don't fully benefit from object-oriented design in that the data and behavior aren't encapsulated together; they're more a half-step that match a procedural style more than object-oriented design does.

- *Design shearing layers.* You can mitigate or prevent a Ball of Mud by designing shearing layers. If you look at a building as being an analogy for software, there is an argument that there isn't anything that is a building. The building is really the combination of many components, such as the foundation, wiring, roof, rafters, and walls. These components have their own rates of change and their own life spans, which implies that software components should be grouped according to their own rates of change and life spans. These components with differing rates of change also apply to discrete areas of a domain as well as areas of abstractions, because abstractions change much more slowly than most other types of logic; therefore, they should exist and be maintained separately. A Big Ball of Mud is an attempt to build the building without regard to layering.

- *Perform reconstruction.* The only real cure for a Ball of Mud is reconstruction. If your system has declined to the point that it has become a Big Ball of Mud, it's often best to throw it all out and start over. This situation, which is always a hard pill to swallow, is created by
  - Obsolescence of tools and technology
  - Long absence of original maintainers
  - Real requirements emerging during the building of the throwaway system
  - Dramatic design change that renders the original architectural assumptions useless

ARCHITECT'S MOST USEFUL TOOLS

An architect's most useful tools are an eraser at the drafting board and a wrecking ball at the site.

Frank Lloyd Wright[1]

Now that you've seen the problem with improper domain design, you're ready to design your domains in a domain-driven way. When you do so, your domain cityscape ends up looking like the one in figure 5.2, starting with bounded context.

Figure 5.2   Utopian cityscape (Photo: Partizánske by Marián Zubák is licensed under CC BY 2.5 [https://creativecommons.org/licenses/by/2.5/deed.en])

---

[1]   http://www.laputan.org/mud/mud.html#reconstruction

5.1.2 *Bounded context*

A *bounded context* describes a discrete area of functionality or a domain within a domain. You begin modeling a domain by dividing major areas of the application into a set of bounded contexts.

An example of this approach is modeling aircraft and airports, which we'll call the Flight domain. Rather than attempt to model everything in a large, cross-contaminated mishmash, divide an application built for the flight domain into three major areas of behavior:

- Aircraft, which is concerned with flying
- Tower, which is concerned with multiple aircraft arriving, departing, and in the air
- Ground control, which concerns itself with moving multiple aircraft and vehicles around the airport

The airport is implicit in this example, as no behavior has been identified around the airport as a whole, although it may be defined in the *ubiquitous language,* a set of terms shared and understood by both the domain experts and the developers, which we'll explain in the next subsection.[2] A great many subdomains may be identified as part of an airport, but we'll keep this example simple by working with the three subdomains defined in the preceding list. A bounded context is a DDD term describing a subdomain. This example has three contexts or subdomains: the aircraft, the tower, and ground control. These subdomains have different concerns.

The aircraft subdomain is concerned only about flying, safety, weather, and the mechanics of flight. The subdomain communicates with external bounded contexts, such as a control tower, but it does so in the simplest manner necessary to carry on the business of flying. The inner workings of control are left to the control tower bounded context. If communication is required between bounded contexts, as when a control tower instructs a plane to descend 2,000 feet, in our system this would translate to the control tower context communicating some message it understands to the aircraft context.

You may be seeing the connection between the flight domain and any complex domain in the business world. You see how we've broken the complex business of flight into digestible pieces. By doing so, we naturally make the domain more distributed as well because the domain can be split into three independent pieces: aircraft, tower, and ground control. Each piece can exist at runtime on separate hardware and in different physical locations.

As we mentioned in the preceding section, the aircraft context or subdomain communicates with the other contexts (tower and ground control), and when it does, it

---

[2] To attempt to define the airport as an aggregate root, or container of domain functionality as we'll discuss very soon, would result in combining the ground control and tower contexts. This is undesirable, as these are separate concerns, and the domain models would clash and cause confusion, such as ground control's treatment of a plane as just another vehicle, whereas the tower concerns itself with aircraft.

uses what DDD calls an anticorruption layer to translate the incoming messages. An anticorruption layer is an outer layer that sits inside a bounded context to convert and validate data going to and from other contexts and external systems. A command might be sent by an external party for a reduction of altitude by 2,000 feet; it's up to the aircraft context to determine whether this command is reasonable and won't drive the craft into the ground.

The control tower and ground control contexts contain their own complexities for controlling aircraft and vehicles in all aspects of flight as well as on the ground. To help discover and identify these domains, use a bounded-context diagram. Figure 5.3 illustrates the use of a bounded-context diagram for flight.

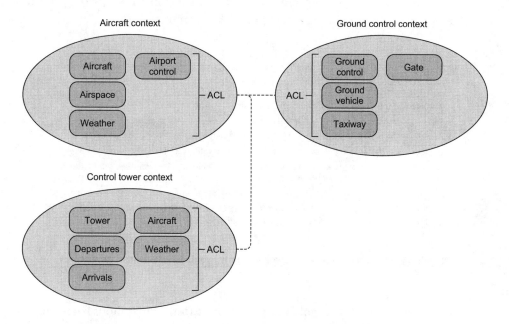

Figure 5.3   Flight domain contexts show the entire system from a bird's-eye view.

You can see in figure 5.3 that each context can be thought out and developed in isolation from the other contexts, and eventually hooked to them through their anticorruption layers (ACL). Developing such subdomains is much simpler to tackle than the entire thing at once.

You get a glimpse of how DDD makes a large application more distribution-friendly: the overall domain is decoupled into various bounded contexts, which can operate independently and in different application spaces, communicating only through messages with the outside world.

Next, we look in greater detail at the ubiquitous language, which is a glossary of domain terminology that serves as a reference for the bounded contexts.

5.1.3   Ubiquitous language

The use of the terms *aircraft, vehicle, ground control, departures*, and so on represents the use of *ubiquitous language*, which is the software terminology matching the real-life domain, and shared by the development team and the domain experts. Figure 5.3 in the preceding section illustrates this design.

The ubiquitous language is a set of terms describing all aspects of the domain that are understood by both domain experts and developers. This language is expressed in a living document that should be created as early as possible and continuously referred to by functional and technical teams. The ubiquitous language facilitates discussions with the domain experts and defines key domain concepts used in the domain model. Figure 5.4 illustrates a partial document describing the ubiquitous language of the overall flight domain in the example.

- Aircraft – Usually an airplane, but not necessarily so. Aircraft fly to and from destinations and must deal with external control within airspace and airports, but must also be concerned with weather and the operation and health of the aircraft and those aboard.
- Airspace – A geographical area in which an aircraft is under control of a tower.
- Arrivals – The area of the tower primarily concerned with aircraft arriving into the airport.
- Departures – The area of the tower primarily concerned with aircraft taking off from the airport.
- Ground Control – This operation controls and moves aircraft and other vehicles around the tarmac as well as to and from gates.
- Tower – The control tower controls aircraft during departure, arrival, and within its airspace.
- Weather – Weather is a concern everywhere, from the aircraft in the air as well as all vehicles on the ground, including plows and snow melting equipment.

Figure 5.4   Ubiquitous language document clearly defining flight domain terminology

With the terminology firmly in hand, thanks to the ubiquitous-language document, you can design your domain entities: the building blocks of the domain that map to the preceding document as well as real life. These building blocks are

- *entities*, which have identity and are persistent objects, and which
- can take the form of *aggregates* to encapsulate other entities
- and use *value objects*

We explain these building blocks in the following sections.

5.1.4   Entities, aggregates, and value objects

Entities in DDD are any objects that represent a meaningful area of the domain and that (most importantly) have identity. Each entity's identity is unique among all other entities in the domain. This uniqueness is established by the attributes of the entities, which can never be duplicated. An example of such an entity is a person. A person can have the same first and last names as another person but can never have the same Social Security number.

Sometimes, a unique ID is fabricated, such as an ID generated at the time an entity is created, but often, some meaningful attribute is naturally unique, such as a customer ID or serial number. In the flight domain example, the *id* attribute uniquely identifies aircraft. The attribute would never be reused for another aircraft, and it allows the reuse of the call sign for other flights. In practice, we always use a generated ID for all domain entities for consistency's sake, as well as ease of use within a framework. Somewhere in your framework, you handle some common functionality for creating new entities and want to guard against duplicates. When all entities consistently use the id attribute, this process becomes simple—but doesn't prevent duplicate business keys. In an employee domain, for example, each employee has a unique generated ID, but employees also have a Social Security number that must be unique. This uniqueness must be maintained somewhere in the framework, such as in a service layer. See the services section, 5.1.5.

Entities are named in some meaningful way and map directly to the ubiquitous language; they're not defined by their attributes and have real-life meaning in and of themselves. You don't need to understand the inner behavior of an aircraft to know what an aircraft is, for example. In figure 5.5, only the aircraft and passengers are entities.

In the figure, you see that `Ack`, `Meal`, and `Weather` are value objects, and as such, they have no identity, as we explain in the following sections. The aircraft, passengers, and seats are all entities and have unique identity as well as persistent state. Because

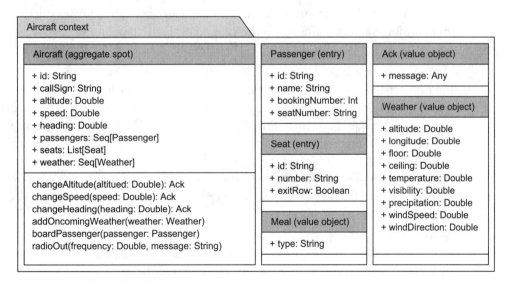

Figure 5.5   Example aggregate with value objects

the aircraft encapsulates the other entities and value objects, it's considered to be an aggregate root.

Aggregate roots, also known as *aggregates*, are domain entities that represent the top of a hierarchy of two or more entities. We highly recommend that you identify your aggregated roots as single entities and don't try to immediately identify an entity hierarchy within. This practice falls into the category of premature optimization, which is usually considered to be a bad design choice. Hierarchies naturally present themselves in due course as your design evolves.

Assume that when you designed the aircraft, you did so knowing that you'd need some domain object to model the aircraft behavior in the sky and on the ground, and you later determined that the passengers affect that behavior due to the overall weight of the aircraft and other factors. You identify the passenger entity and determine it to be part of the aircraft aggregate. Aggregate roots map directly to the ubiquitous language, such as the term *aircraft*. Aggregates are entities first, and as such, they have unique identities. Access to any encapsulated entities, such as passengers, occurs only through the aggregate.

An example of an aggregate root is a car. The car is made up of many entities—engine, electrical system, chassis, interior, and so on—but none of those entities exists in any capacity outside the car, although the entities might be modeled differently in other domains. An assembly-line domain, for example, could also have the notion of an engine, but with different meaning and behavior.

In the example bounded-context diagram in the figure above, the aircraft is the only aggregate root, encapsulating domain behavior. The aircraft aggregate has various states and many complex capabilities. In fact, an aggregate root can be considered to be a bounded context in itself. The aircraft aggregate encapsulates the many areas of behavior that it contains and is the root access to all that it holds.

STRONG CONSISTENCY WITHIN AGGREGATES

Aggregates are always strongly consistent with regard to their encapsulated data, in that any change in the aggregate is guaranteed to reflect the latest state of all data within. The addition of a passenger to the plane, for example, would result in a new version of the aggregate, including the latest speed and heading of the aircraft.

Eventually, interactions among aggregates are always consistent. An aircraft eventually receives a radio message from a tower, for example, but the state of the tower may change before the aircraft has a chance to respond. This situation in no way hampers the plane from making its maneuver, and eventually the aircraft gets more instructions.

VALUE OBJECTS

In the flight domain, `Ack`, `Meal`, and `Weather` are considered to be value objects. A *value object* represents a meaningful construct within the domain and also maps to the ubiquitous language, but it doesn't have the concept of identity and therefore isn't unique. The aircraft might have a collection of duplicate meals, and one of those meals might be considered to be equivalent to another meal without breaking DDD rules for value objects. These value objects would never exist in and of themselves—only in the context of the encapsulating aircraft.

As we mention earlier in the chapter, the meals on the aircraft are value objects. Each meal has no identity or behavior in its own right. Meals are always immutable, in that they're created once and never updated. One meal is distinguishable from another only in comparison by its type (such as chicken versus beef), because it has no identity. In short, you don't care much about one meal versus another except for the capability to delivery chicken meals to passengers wanting chicken and beef to the others. Classification doesn't equal identity!

An aggregate, its entities, and its value objects all have consistent state and are stored as a single persistent unit. In figure 5.5, you see the aircraft aggregate modeled with some basic characteristics, including the collections of the passenger and seat entities, as well as meal and weather value objects.

The following value objects are explained:

- Ack (*acknowledge)* is a value object at its most simple. It's a data structure designed to carry a radio message from the aircraft to the tower and has no behavior or identity, but it maps to the ubiquitous language and therefore is a value object, even though it isn't contained within the airplane as any attribute or collection.
- A *passenger* never exists outside this aircraft (in the model). Passengers may be added to an aircraft, but only by going through the aircraft aggregate; the passengers are never accessed directly.

In the next section, we look at services, repositories, and factories, which are best described as the rest of the application's DDD functionality that isn't contained within aggregates.

5.1.5 Services, repositories, and factories

Services are best described as processes that don't belong to any domain entity but may operate on those entities. A service operates on one or many aggregates at the same time from the outside to achieve some goal. You may have noticed that the example flight domain doesn't employ services. In our experience, you usually find that all domain logic correctly lives inside domain aggregates, which is a common object-oriented encapsulation technique. We're not saying that services are wrong; they're valuable when necessary. But we recommend using them sparingly as a rule. The reason is that over time, developers have made services the go-to area for functionality, but they should have placed that functionality within aggregates. Services are often used for functionality when developers are unfamiliar with aggregates and DDD. A helpful rule of thumb: if it's a behavior of a thing, include it in an aggregate; if not, use a service.

We once needed to use a service in an energy-optimization application. We had to reach out to various buildings and temperature zones to pull real-time temperature

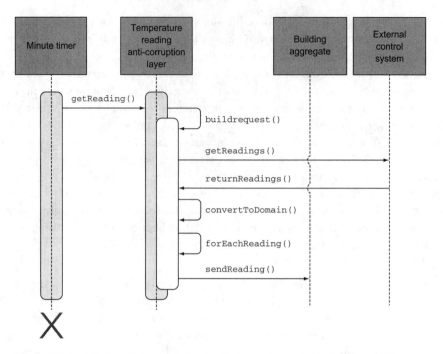

Figure 5.6   Building-reading domain service that operates on many building entities at the same time

readings and associate those readings with buildings, which we modeled as aggregates. Figure 5.6 shows how a building-reading service might retrieve all building readings each minute and then send them to each building aggregate.

As the figure shows, the design dictated making a request to the outside building control service each minute for all readings across all buildings. This functionality couldn't be within any given building; therefore, it had to be in a service. As it happened, this service was also an anticorruption layer, which (as we explained earlier) is a protective and communicative layer between the domain and the outside world. We used an anticorruption layer because the services needed to call out to an external building control system for data and that data needing validation and transformation before being allowed to enter the domain.

Repositories are similar to services because they're also outside the domain, but they're used to retrieve and instantiate domain objects from the data store.

You use repositories to get at your domain aggregates. Aggregates are persistent, and DDD applications are long-lived, which means that the systems will start and stop many times; the data drives the system and gives it ongoing life.

Suppose that Flight 300 has been created in the system and is in the air, and the system is shut down. When the system restarts, some facility must instantiate domain aggregates from the database to start working with them again, which is exactly what a repository does.

Typical repository behavior includes

- A get of a single domain aggregate by ID
- Retrieval of all aggregates
- Some sort of find operation

In the Scala programming language, putting aside the concept of actors for now, it's best and most expressive to implement repositories as companion objects. The following list explains repositories and companion objects:

- A *companion object* is a singleton with the same name as an implementation class and with special access to private functionality in that class. It's commonly used as a factory.
- A *factory* is a way of creating objects that's close in behavior to the repository pattern, but whereas the repository returns aggregates that exist in some persisted state, the factory is used only for initial creation.

The very idea of Flight 300 is conceived by using the create-factory function in the Aircraft companion object. Listing 5.1 collapses the behaviors of repository and factory in the Aircraft companion object, rather than creating a separate object such as AircraftRepository, though doing it that way would be OK. For convenience, the listing puts everything in a single object.

In the following listing, create is the factory function, and all others are repository functions. The Aircraft needs a minimum amount of data to be created: the unique id and the callsign. The listing shows how the repository/factory would normally be modeled in many languages; it uses plain Scala.

Listing 5.1   Aircraft repository and factory companion object

```scala
object Aircraft {

  def create(id: String, callsign: String): Aircraft = ...        ← The create
                                                                      factory function

  def get(id: String): Aircraft = ...                             ←

  def getAll(): List[Aircraft] = ...                              ←

  def findByCallsign(callsign: String): Aircraft = ...            ←
}

case class Aircraft (
  id: String,
  callsign: String,
  altitude: Double,
  speed: Double,
  heading: Double,
  passengers: List[Passenger],
  weather: List[Weather]
)
```

The get repository function issues a database operation to retrieve a single aircraft.

The getAll repository function issues a database operation to retrieve all aircraft.

The findByCallsign repository function issues a database operation to find an aircraft by call sign.

Now we'll look at an alternative, message-driven way to do the same things, building on what you learned in chapter 2 about Akka actors.

At various points in time, Flight 300 must communicate with the outside world; the flight needs to know about incoming weather and traffic control on the ground and in the air. To enable this communication, use an anticorruption layer, which we briefly covered earlier when describing the aircraft's communication with tower and ground control, and which we explain in more detail in the following section.

5.1.6 *Anticorruption layers*

Anticorruption layers sit atop a bounded context and convert communications and representational data to and from outside systems. This allows a level of purity within the main part of the bounded context that knows nothing about the outside system's requirements or its inner workings. In turn, the outside system has no knowledge of the inner workings of the bounded context. Maintaining purity is important because garbage going into the domain results in garbage coming out—in short, corruption.

The anticorruption layer, shown in figure 5.7, translates inbound external logic to constructs that the inner domain understands. In this case, external weather data is validated and converted to the domain representation of weather.

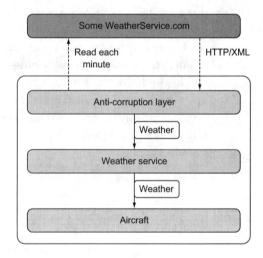

Figure 5.7   Weather anticorruption translating incoming XML to domain Weather

Conversely, the anticorruption layer translates domain logic for the outbound flows to the external constructs when sending data to external contexts or parties. The weather is requested each minute by the weather service within the domain and arrives over HTTP in an XML format known and dictated by the external weather provider, SomeWeatherService.com. The anticorruption layer knows about both the format of the XML coming in and the Weather domain value object within. This layer won't allow bad or invalid data to enter the domain.

A use case relating to figure 5.7 is the receipt of new weather data by the aircraft for airspace it's about to fly through. As the figure shows, the weather comes into the aircraft's anticorruption layer in some format, such as XML. The anticorruption layer takes this XML format and transforms it into the aircraft's idea of weather, which is the Weather value object contained in the aircraft context. As you see in figure 5.7, the aircraft context uses an anticorruption layer to communicate with an external weather service. The anticorruption layer accepts incoming weather in the XML format of the weather-service provider and translates the Weather value objects.

Next, we wrap up DDD by looking at state transitioning and layered architectures. We finish the chapter by discussing the valuable Saga Pattern for modeling long-lived domain transactions.

In addition to a typical anticorruption layer, anticorruption can be augmented by domain state transitioning. An aircraft on the ground has different behaviors from an aircraft in the air. Requesting an aircraft on the taxiway to bank left is nonsensical; therefore, having a function in place to take that command is nonsensical. To express this situation, support the aircraft in two flavors:

- `Aircraft`
- `GroundedAircraft`

Each command issued to a grounded aircraft results in an updated instance of the aircraft in ground mode. Only after a successful takeoff command does that grounded aircraft morph into an aircraft in the air; and at that point, all the commands that have to do with flying are supported.

You have various ways to achieve this in terms of implementation, and we won't list them here. But pay special attention to the `become/unbecome` discussion in chapter 4, because that is a very handy way to model this. With an actor domain implementation, the actor representing the aircraft becomes a handler of a different set of messages for each state it handles—an elegant solution.

5.1.7   *Layered architecture*

It's common in muddy designs to mix UI, database, and other nondomain logic with the domain itself. Applications should be built in layers, separating the concerns as much as possible. It should be easy to look at a domain object and quickly understand the behavior of that object. As other code is mixed in, it becomes hard to separate the wheat from the chaff, making maintenance of the code difficult and putting in place unnecessary barriers that make it hard for new staff and domain experts to understand the code.

To use the UI as an example, changes would cause possible changes and corruption in domain logic, because the UI person may not have understand the domain well enough and could break the domain rather than fulfill the UI-change requirement.

Be sure to isolate domain logic from all application underpinnings so that the domain model is as expressive and apparent as possible.

5.1.8   *Sagas*

A *saga* is a long-running business process, but don't be fooled by the word *long-running*, as a saga may complete its job in an instant. Sagas aren't strictly considered to be part of DDD, but you'll likely find them necessary in your reactive applications.

Sagas aren't domain entities but may operate on them, and they have no sort of domain identity, but may carry a transaction ID while they do their jobs.

A good example of a business saga is a bank transfer. A bank transfer can't take place solely within a single bank account, and you wouldn't want to tie up a bank-domain entity to wait for funds and acknowledgments for a single customer's transfer.

For this situation, create a saga to model the bank-transfer process from start to finish. The saga has the following steps or (more accurately) states:

1 Withdraw from the *from* account, and await the acknowledgment.
2 Deposit to the destination account, and await the acknowledgment.
3 Notify the customer of the completed transfer.
4 Kill itself.

There are as many ways to model sagas as there are computing languages, and in section 5.2.3, you see how to model sagas the Akka way.

5.1.9   *Shared kernel*

A *shared kernel* is a context shared among domain teams that contains shared code to be DRY (don't repeat yourself) and should be handled with care. This kernel should be kept as small as possible, not allowed to bloat with premature optimizations. Teams should add code to this context only in close collaboration, because breakage would have a ripple effect.

Shared kernels typically take the form of libraries named `core` or `common` and may easily lead to code smell, so tread carefully.

You have a good grasp of DDD and how helpful it is in designing reactive-friendly software, which is the simplest type to reason about and distribute. In the next section, we show you new ways (compared to a traditional Java or Scala class with getters and setters) of implementing the flight domain to make it more reactive-friendly, applying what you learned about Akka in chapters 2 and 3.

We stop short of implementing any sort or storage mechanism to persist the domain to a database, leaving that topic implied for now. We dive deep into that subject in chapter 8.

5.2   *An actor-based domain*

In this section, you design a rudimentary Akka actor-based domain model. This model, coupled with Akka clustering and persistence as described in later chapters, allows unbounded elasticity, as well as resilience, responsiveness, and the state of being message-driven.

5.2.1   *A simple Akka aircraft domain*

In listing 5.2, you lay the groundwork for a Scala case class like the ones you applied in chapter 3 (listing 3.3), representing an aircraft state for the flight domain. This case class is a construct that you'll use strictly for message passing. The aircraft protocol includes all the messages that are handled by an aircraft actor, which we model a bit later.

The following is the example code for the aircraft attributes and protocol.

Listing 5.2 The `Aircraft` case class and protocol

```
final case class Aircraft (                          ◄──┐   The Aircraft class has no behavior
  id: String,                                             now; it reflects current state.
  callsign: String,
  altitude: Double,
  speed: Double,
  heading: Double,
  passengers: List[Passenger],
  weather: List[Weather]                The messaging
)                                       protocol for       It's best practice to seal the
                                        an Aircraft        messages, which results in
object AircraftProtocol {     ◄──────┘                    Scala match errors when a
  sealed trait AircraftProtocolMessage      ◄─────────── message isn't implemented.
  final case class ChangeAltitude(altitude: Double) extends
    AircraftProtocolMessage                                        ◄──────────┐
  final case class ChangeSpeed(speed: Double) extends AircraftProtocolMessage │
  final case class ChangeHeading(heading: Double) extends
    AircraftProtocolMessage
  final case class BoardPassenger(passenger: Passenger) extends
    AircraftProtocolMessage
  final case class AddWeather(weather: Weather) extends          These messages are
    AircraftProtocolMessage                                      immutable and won't
  final case object Ok                                           result in the direct
}                                                                return of any data.
```

The code in listing 5.2 lays the groundwork for interaction with an aircraft. But where is the behavior? The behavior is all encapsulated within an actor, as we'll show you by wrapping the aircraft domain functionality within an actor. Earlier, we talked about layered architectures, which dictate that domain logic should stand out as much as possible. Some camps desire a full domain object with functions and attributes.

For this example, you do the same thing, but with a slight paradigm shift:

- Instead of functions named `changeAltitude()` or `changeSpeed()`, you use message handlers within the actor.
- We contend that modeling the domain independent of actors and then wrapping that domain within the actor is a waste of time, because we consider actors to be an extension of Scala or Java, so we assume that this architecture will have no other implementation of `Aircraft`. Follow your own heart, however, and do what feels right in your own designs.

The next section shows an `Aircraft` actor that communicates by using the `Aircraft` protocol for messaging. Because `Aircraft` is an actor, each message is a one-way communication, and each message is handled in the order received. The actor stores current state in memory, and each message received results in a modified replacement of that state.

5.2.2   *The actor*

The Akka actor encapsulates all behavior of the aircraft and does so with messaging rather than traditional function calls:

- Each processing of a message results in the new state of the aircraft within the actor.
- The sender is sent an OK reply upon processing of the message.
- That reply may be expanded upon to return the OK or a list of validation errors (or something similar).

The aircraft aggregate is modeled as an Akka actor in the following listing.

Listing 5.3   The `Aircraft` actor

```
import akka.Actor

class AircraftActor(              ◁────┐  The actor constructor arguments
  id: String,                           initialize the current state and may be
  callsign: String,                     used in creation or read from a database.
  altitude: Double,
  speed: Double,
  heading: Double,
  passengers: List[Passenger],
  weather: List[Weather]
) extends Actor (
                                         ┐ The protocol is
  import AircraftProtocol._     ◁────────┘ brought into scope.

  var currentState: Aircraft = Aircraft(id, callsign, altitude, speed,
    heading, passengers, weather)              ◁──────┐ A var is OK here and can be
                                                        accessed only by the actor
  override def receive = {                              itself when instantiated.
    case ChangeAltitude(altitude)      =>
      currentState = currentState.copy(altitude = altitude)    ◁────┐
      sender() ! OK                           ◁────────────┐         │
                                                            │   The current state is
    case ChangeSpeed(speed)            =>                   │   updated to contain
      currentState.copy(speed = speed)                      │   the new value.
      sender() ! OK                                         │
                                               The reply is OK, so the
    case ChangeHeading(heading)        =>      sender of the message
      currentState = currentState.copy(heading = heading)  knows that the message
      sender() ! OK                            was processed.

    case BoardPassenger(passenger)     =>
      currentState = currentState.copy(passengers = passenger :: passengers)
      sender() ! OK

    case AddWeather(incomingWeather) =>
      currentState = currentState.copy(weather = incomingWeather :: weather)
      sender() ! OK
  }
```

This example is thread-safe but not free of side effects. The problem is even though one atomic update of the aircraft can occur at any time, an updater may be making that update based on a stale state. To guard against this situation, use *versioning*, a method of ensuring domain consistency, as we show you in the next section.

5.2.3 *The process manager*

We talked about the Saga Pattern earlier in this chapter in a functional way. In this section, we look at an implementation that uses an actor approach: the bank-transfer example (refer to section 5.1.8). We won't go as far as modeling the accounts. Assume that each bank account is represented by an actor that accepts messages by using an account protocol. We take the liberty of simply calling the actor the `BankTransfer-Process` and drop the word *manager* for brevity.

The following listing shows the account and Process Manager protocols and companion objects.

Listing 5.4   Process Manager and account protocols and companion objects

```
import akka.actor.{ReceiveTimeout, Actor, ActorRef}
import scala.concurrent.duration._
                                               The bank-transfer
object BankTransferProcessProtocol {           Process Manager protocol
  sealed trait BankTransferProcessMessage

  final case class TransferFunds(
    transactionId: String,
    fromAccount: ActorRef,
    toAccount: ActorRef,
    amount: Double) extends BankTransferProcessMessage
}                                              The companion object, with
                                               positive and negative
object BankTransferProcess {                   acknowledgment messages
  final case class FundsTransfered(transactionId: String)
  final case class TransferFailed(transactionId: String)
  final case object Acknowledgment
}                                              The account
                                               protocol
object AccountProtocol {
  sealed trait AccountProtocolMessage
  final case class Withdraw(amount: Double) extends AccountProtocolMessage
  final case class Deposit(amount: Double) extends AccountProtocolMessage
}
```

In the following listing, you use the objects that you created in the account-transfer Process Manager actor.

Listing 5.5   The `Process Manager` actor

```
class BankTransferProcess extends Actor {

  import BankTransferProcess._
  import BankTransferProcessProtocol._
  import AccountProtocol._
```

The receive timeout allows 30 minutes for any step in the process.

The initial request to transfer funds includes all information necessary to do the job, including the sender actor reference, which is copied here to the client to enable the reply to the initial requester of the transfer across receive boundaries.

```scala
        context.setReceiveTimeout(30.minutes)

        override def receive = {
          case TransferFunds(transactionId, fromAccount, toAccount, amount) =>
            fromAccount ! Withdraw(amount)
            val client = sender()
            context become(
              awaitWithdrawal(transactionId, amount, toAccount, client
              )
        }

        def awaitWithdrawal(transactionId: String, amount: Double, toAccount:
          ActorRef, client: ActorRef): Receive = {
          case Acknowledgment =>
            toAccount ! Deposit(amount)
            context become awaitDeposit(transactionId, client)

          case ReceiveTimeout =>
            client ! TransferFailed(transactionId)
            context.stop(self)
        }

        def awaitDeposit(transactionId: String, client: ActorRef): Receive = {
          case Acknowledgment =>
            client ! FundsTransferred(transactionId)
            context.stop(self)

          case ReceiveTimeout =>
            client ! TransferFailed(transactionId)
            context.stop(self)
        }

      }
```

Await the withdrawal or fail the transfer on a receive timeout message (included in Akka framework).

Await the deposit or fail the transfer on a receive timeout.

The process self-destructs.

The process shown in listing 5.5 babysits the entire transfer from start to finish over a limited amount of time. At any point, failure is a possibility, due to inability to access an account, insufficient balance, and so on. When failure happens, the client is sent the `TransferFailed` message to perform some compensating action or retry the transfer.

When DDD is used in combination with Akka and Command Query Responsibility Segregation and Event Sourcing (CQRS-ES), a set of concepts that dictates the separation of read and write application concerns and the persistence of events rather than state (see chapter 8), you have all the tools necessary to build successful reactive applications.

Summary

- We showed how to divide and conquer a domain by using DDD.
- You learned to define an evolving ubiquitous language to describe a domain.

- We introduced the concepts of entities, aggregate roots, and value objects, which form the building blocks of your domain.
- We discussed when and how to use services, repositories, and factories to work with your domain entities.
- We showed how you might model aspects of an airport/flight domain.
- You learned to use anticorruption layers to communicate with other domains and the outside world.
- You learned the Saga Pattern for long-running transactions.
- We explored how you might design an aircraft aggregate as an Akka actor.
- We showed how you'd implement a saga by using the Process Manager pattern.

Using remote actors

6

This chapter covers

- Structuring reactive applications with sbt
- Configuring Akka with application.conf
- Remoting with Akka
- Obtaining reliability guarantees in distributed systems

Historically, a *distributed system* is defined as a software system in which components that reside on networked computers work together on a common goal. This definition, albeit somewhat generalized, captures the gist, but it has led to some unfortunate side effects, such as the belief that the programming model used for a remote object can be generalized to match that of a local one. In a distributed system, remote objects require different latency metrics, memory access models, concurrency constructs, and failure handling. The local model can't be generalized into a distributed model.

TIP For more on this subject, see the classic paper "A Note on Distributed Computing" (Sun Microsystems, 1994) at http://dl.acm.org/citation.cfm ?id=974938, which explains why the generalization approach is bound to fail.

Akka takes the opposite approach, modeling objects as though they're all distributed by default. Through Akka's toolkit and runtime design, all functionality is equally available on a single Java virtual machine (JVM) or a cluster of machines. The application programming interface (API) for elasticity and scalability, whether horizontal or vertical, is one and the same, providing the semantics for distributed interaction translated into a common API. The hard problems of optimization are managed under the covers, leaving you to focus on your application. The result is that the system can run in a local or distributed environment with almost no change in the code.

In this chapter, you convert a completely local application to a distributed, reactive application. You've already built the local version of the application: RareBooks. You refactor the project into two JVMs and learn how to configure them to communicate remotely. Finally, you look at some of the issues that arise in a distributed environment.

6.1 Refactoring to a distributed system

The RareBooks example that you developed in chapters 3 and 4 contains a single actor system. The most important aspect of distributing RareBooks is refactoring it into two actor systems. Each actor system runs in a separate JVM with its own `main()` function. To make the code for the two actor systems easier to manage, the application is also split into two sbt projects. The first step is designing the distributed actor systems.

6.1.1 Splitting into multiple actor systems

The original actor system has a simple supervision hierarchy, as shown in figure 6.1. In that hierarchy, both the `customer` and the `rare-books` actors are supervised by the `user` actor, which is supplied automatically by Akka. The two actors represent separate ideas that each contain state and identity. Each actor could run isolated and independent of the other, providing elasticity and scalability.

To transform the original actor system into a distributed system that runs in multiple JVMs, a few changes are necessary, as shown in figure 6.2. The reference from the `customer` actor to the `rare-books` actor is a remote reference rather than a local reference. Akka uses a common API and is distributed by default, so the remote reference has the same type as the local reference: an `ActorRef`. Instead of requiring code changes, distributed actors require configuration changes. (You learn more about remote references in section 6.3.)

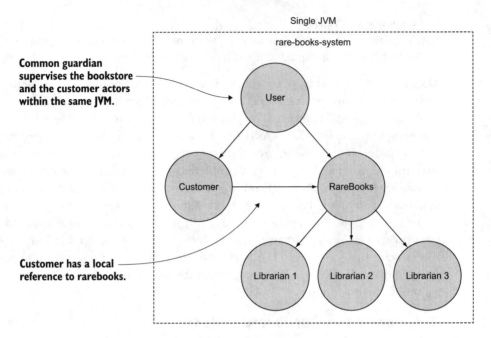

Common guardian supervises the bookstore and the customer actors within the same JVM.

Customer has a local reference to rarebooks.

Figure 6.1   Initial state of the RareBooks application

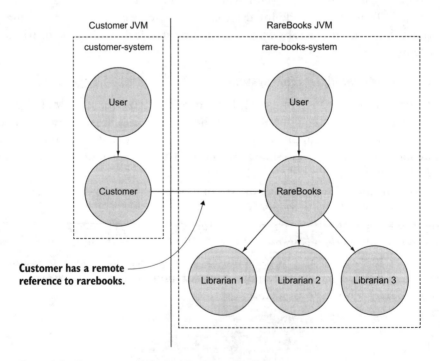

Customer has a remote reference to rarebooks.

Figure 6.2   Target state of the RareBooks application

The example system needs a bit of refactoring before it's ready for remoting. Each actor system runs in a separate JVM, and each JVM in turn requires its own application containing a `main()` driver.

6.1.2 Structuring with sbt

The first time you split a single actor system in two (in chapter 2), the actor systems were left together in a single project, which had two `main()` drivers. That arrangement becomes unmanageable in real-world projects. Before making additional code changes, refactor the project to match the domain, as shown in figure 6.3.

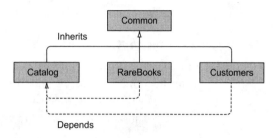

Figure 6.3   Refactoring the RareBooks application into a parent sbt project and three subprojects

sbt makes it easy to define the dependencies. Start by defining the common parent project that declares the three subprojects. A simplified version follows; the complete version is available at http://mng.bz/71O3. See the following listing.

Listing 6.1   Root build.sbt with subprojects

> **Declares the common parent used by all the examples in this book, which contains the Akka dependencies and other build parameters**

```
lazy val common = project
```
◁

```
lazy val chapter6_001_catalog = project.dependsOn(
    common % "test->test;compile->compile")
```
Declares that the catalog is a project that depends on the common parent

```
lazy val chapter6_001_customer = project.dependsOn(
    common % "test->test;compile->compile",
    chapter6_001_catalog % "compile->compile")
```
Declares that customer is a project that depends on the common parent and on the catalog

```
lazy val chapter6_001_rarebooks = project.dependsOn(
    common % "test->test;compile->compile",
    chapter6_001_catalog % "compile->compile")
```
Declares that rarebooks is a project that depends on the common parent and on the catalog

The catalog subproject is a static, compile-time dependency referenced by both the Customers and RareBooks subprojects. The actors in the Customers subproject need a reference to the RareBooks actor. You could have handled this situation with another static dependency, but it's best not to compile the location of an actor into the code. Instead, use runtime configuration to provide the reference.

6.2   Configuring the applications

If you've been around the JVM for a while, the notion of configuration isn't new to you. Many frameworks (such as Spring and Hibernate) use configuration to ease the assembly of framework objects and services in a loosely coupled fashion.

Akka configuration uses Lightbend Config Library, which is a robust general library for managing configuration on the JVM that can be used for Akka or any JVM-based application. Through this configuration library, Akka provides the means to establish logging, enable remoting, define routing, tune dispatching, and do other things, all with little or no code.

Now all you need is an application to configure.

6.2.1 *Creating the first driver application*

The next step of your remoting exercise is implementing RareBooks as an independent application. RareBooks must be able to bootstrap independently so that it can stand on its own, without the customer actors.

Figure 6.4 shows the stand-alone version of RareBooks.

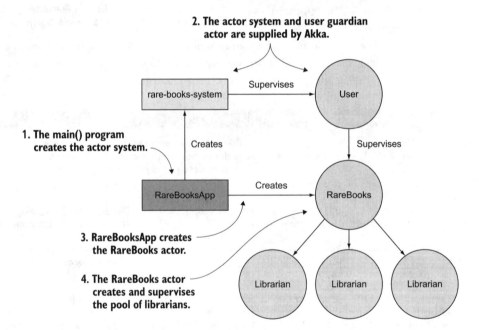

Figure 6.4   The RareBooksApp driver and RareBooks and Librarian actors

The RareBooks `main()` method is defined in the companion object and is responsible for creating the actor system, as follows.

Listing 6.2   Companion object for RareBooksApp.scala

```
package com.rarebooks.library                   Imports
                                                 removed
. . .

object RareBooksApp {
```

```
def main(args: Array[String]): Unit = {
    val system: ActorSystem = ActorSystem("rare-books-system")
    val rareBooksApp: RareBooksApp = new RareBooksApp(system)
    rareBooksApp.run()
  }
}
```

Creates the actor system → (points to `val system: ActorSystem = ActorSystem("rare-books-system")`)

Instantiates and runs the application (points to `val rareBooksApp: RareBooksApp = new RareBooksApp(system)`)

The `RareBooksApp` class is a command-line application that creates the `RareBooks` actor, as follows.

Listing 6.3 RareBooksApp.scala class

```
class RareBooksApp(system: ActorSystem) extends Console {

  private val log = Logging(system, getClass.getName)
  createRareBooks()

  protected def createRareBooks(): ActorRef = {
    system.actorOf(RareBooks.props, "rare-books")
  }

  def run(): Unit = {
    commandLoop()
    Await.ready(system.whenTerminated, Duration.Inf)
  }

  @tailrec
  private def commandLoop(): Unit =
    Command(StdIn.readLine()) match {
      case Command.Customer(count, odds, tolerance) =>
        commandLoop()
      case Command.Quit =>
        system.terminate()
      case Command.Unknown(command) =>
        log.warning(s"Unknown command $command")
        commandLoop()
    }
}
```

Console is a common superclass used by drivers in this book. (points to `extends Console {`)

Creates the RareBooks actor, which takes care of creating the librarians (points to `createRareBooks()` method)

Starts the command loop (points to `commandLoop()`)

Wait while the application runs, so it doesn't exit immediately. (points to `Await.ready(system.whenTerminated, Duration.Inf)`)

Accept simple commands from the terminal. (points to `private def commandLoop(): Unit =`)

Next you might expect to make code changes in the `RareBooks` actor. There are none! Instead, use the actor you created in chapter 4 (in listings 4.3, 4.4, and 4.5), which is the same.

6.2.2 Introducing application.conf

On startup, Akka looks for a file called application.conf. The following listing is a starting point for a custom application.conf file for an Akka application. You should find it easy to understand the syntax, although some of the parameters will be new to you.

Listing 6.4 Sample application.conf for an Akka application

```
akka {

  loggers = ["akka.event.slf4j.Slf4jLogger"]
```

Loggers to register at boot time (points to `loggers = ["akka.event.slf4j.Slf4jLogger"]`)

Logs level used by the configured loggers as soon as they've started (with options OFF, ERROR, WARNING, INFO, and DEBUG)

Logs level for the basic logger activated during ActorSystem startup before the configured loggers have been initialized; sends log messages to stdout

```
loglevel = "ERROR"
stdout-loglevel = "ERROR"

logging-filter = "akka.event.slf4j.Slf4jLoggingFilter"

actor {
  provider = remote

  default-dispatcher {
    throughput = 10
  }
}
remote {
  log-remote-lifecycle-events = off
  netty.tcp.port = 4711
  }
}
```

Filter of log events used by the LoggingAdapter before publishing log events to the eventStream

Configures Akka for remote references (with options local, remote, and cluster)

Throughput for default Dispatcher; set to 1 to tell the Dispatcher to be as fair as possible

The port clients should connect to (default is 2552)

The format for application.conf should look familiar. If you're thinking JSON, you're close; it's HOCON (Human-Optimized Config Object Notation).

6.2.3   *Using HOCON*

The primary goal of HOCON is to stay close to JSON format while providing convenient, human-readable configuration notation. To be both machine-readable and human-readable, the format should be

- *A JSON superset*—All JSON should be valid and should result in the same in-memory data that a JSON parser would have produced.
- *Deterministic*—The format is flexible but not heuristic. It should be clear what's invalid, and invalid files should generate errors.
- *Parsed with minimal look-ahead*—The file can be tokenized by looking at only the next three characters. Right now, the only reason to look at three characters is to find comments that start with //. Otherwise, parsing would require only two characters.

Paraphrased from the HOCON documentation, the following features are also desirable, to support human use:

- Less noisy/less pedantic syntax
- Ability to refer to another part of the configuration so you can set a value to another value
- Import/include another configuration file in the current file
- Map to a flat properties list such as Java's system properties
- Get values from environment variables
- Ability to write comments

Independent configuration is a powerful notion and part of what allows Akka to be distributed by design.

6.2.4 Configuring the driver application

You have one final step to complete remote setup for RareBooks configuration. Rare-Books must be configured to accept messages from other actor systems. In addition, some of the hard-coded parameters move from the domain model to the configuration file, where they're easier to manage. Following are the changes required for the application.conf file.

Listing 6.5   RareBooks application.conf

```
akka {
  loggers  = [akka.event.slf4j.Slf4jLogger]
  loglevel = DEBUG

  actor {
    debug {
      lifecycle = on
      unhandled = on
    }

    provider = remote        ⟵——  Enables remote
  }                                 providers

  remote {                                            Remote transport
    enabled-transports = ["akka.remote.netty.tcp"] ⟵—— added.
    log-remote-lifecycle-events = off

    netty.tcp {
      hostname = localhost      Specifies the listener
      port = 2551               hostname and port number
    }
  }
}

rare-books {
  open-duration = 20 seconds
  close-duration = 5 seconds
  nbr-of-librarians = 5
                                  Uses HOCON to specify
  librarian {                     parameters for
    find-book-duration = 2 seconds   the domain model
    max-complain-count = 2
  }
}
```

Consider what you've accomplished. You started with an actor that was embedded in a self-contained simulation. Now RareBooks is a stand-alone application that's prepared to accept messages from other systems. Now that the store is in business, you can give it some customers.

As with any store in the real world, it's important for customers to be able to find the store. From the perspective of the customer, RareBooks is a remote actor.

6.3   Remoting with Akka

If you've worked with HTTP, you're familiar with sending a request message to a URL and expecting a response message. A reactive system has a few differences. You already know that local and remote references to actors share the type `ActorRef`. In this section, you see that remote actor references are created with syntax similar to that of a URL. Another difference is that messages in reactive systems are one-way, which means that they are not specialized into distinct request and response message types. We cover the effect on the client design in this section.

6.3.1   Constructing remote references

In chapter 3, you learned that an actor system is hierarchical, with a unique trail of actor names that can be navigated recursively. You also saw how to construct a Uniform Resource Identifier (URI) to reference an actor in the local actor system. Figure 6.5 shows how to extend that URI to a remote actor, with these differences:

- The protocol changes from `akka` to `akka.tcp`. Akka supports both TCP and UDP for remote transports.
- The hostname or IP address is included after the actor system name.
- The listener port is included after the hostname or IP address. The default is 2552, but including it explicitly is best.

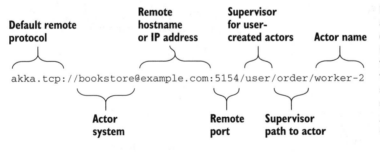

Figure 6.5   Remote actor references use a different protocol from local references, adding the hostname and port to locate the actor system. The path of supervisors leading from /user to the named actor remains the same.

Notice that the protocol for remoting is *not* HTTP.

6.3.2   Resolving the references

When you have a URI, the next step is to convert it to an `ActorRef`. The steps are often combined into a single expression, but we go through the steps individually in this section. The first step, shown in the following listing, is getting the physical base address of the remote system.

Listing 6.6   Configurable hostname and port

```
import akka.actor.Address

private val hostname: String =
⮕  system.settings.config.getString("rare-books.hostname")

private val port: Int =
⮕  system.settings.config.getInt("rare-books.port")

val rareBooksAddress: Address =
⮕ Address("akka.tcp", "rare-books-system", hostname, port)
```

Gets the hostname for the rare-books remote actor system

Gets the port number for the rare-books remote actor system

Creates the base address

The values of `hostname` and `port` are configurable and reside in the Customer's application.conf, which we review in the next section.

The next step is creating an `ActorSelection` that identifies the complete path to the remote actor. The path begins with the root, which comes from the base address that you constructed. The root is followed by `"user"`, which is the built-in guardian actor, and then by `"rare-books"`, which is the name of the actor being selected, as follows.

Listing 6.7   Selecting the path for the remote actor

```
import akka.actor.{ActorSelection, RootActorPath}

val selection: ActorSelection  =
⮕ system.actorSelection(
⮕ RootActorPath(rareBooksAddress) /
⮕ "user" / "rare-books")
```

Uses the actor system to perform the selection

Generates a root path by using the previously created rareBooksAddress

Extends the selection path through the guardian to the rare-books actor. RootActorPath conveniently declares the / operator to make paths easier to build and read.

The final step is resolving the actor selection into an `ActorRef`. As part of resolving the selection, Akka exchanges messages with the remote actor system to verify that the reference is valid. Because messages are asynchronous, the resolution takes some time. Therefore, the result of the resolution is a `Future[ActorRef]` rather than an `ActorRef`, and a timeout is specified. When the `Future` completes, the `ActorRef` is used to construct a `Customer` actor in the local system, as follows.

Listing 6.8   Resolving the actor selection

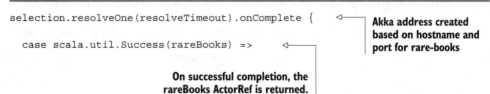

```
selection.resolveOne(resolveTimeout).onComplete {

  case scala.util.Success(rareBooks) =>
```

Akka address created based on hostname and port for rare-books

On successful completion, the rareBooks ActorRef is returned.

```
      system.actorOf(Customer.props(rareBooks, odds, tolerance))

  case scala.util.Failure(ex) =>
    log.error(ex, ex.getMessage)
}
```

When the actor resolution completes, use it to create a customer.

No changes to the customer actor are needed. You've created a new application that can be invoked remotely without changing the core domain. This notion is one of the key aspects of the Akka toolkit.

Creating actors remotely

Actor selection finds remote actors that already exist. You can also create new actors on remote systems. You could use this capability, for example, to increase the number of librarians available to the RareBooks store in the example application. To create actors remotely with Akka, add the remote actor's path to the *deployment* section of application.conf:

```
akka {
  actor {
    deployment {
      /worker-2 {
        remote = "akka.tcp://remoteWorkerSystem@127.0.0.1:2556"
      }
    }
  }
}
```

Alternatively, you can set up the deployment with code rather than configuration. The documentation for `akka.actor.Props.withDeploy()` is a good starting point.

When the deployment configuration is in place, use `ActorSystem.actorOf` or `ActorContext.actorOf` as usual to create actors remotely, like this:

```
context.actorOf(Props[Worker], "worker-2")
```

`ActorSystem.actorOf` is used for starting the system, and `ActorContext.actorOf` is used within actors that are already created. Unlike `actorSelection`, `actorOf` requires `Props`, which is an immutable class for specifying options for the creation of an actor, and the class needs to be available on the class path of the remote actor system.

6.3.3 *Replacing clients with peers*

If you're used to working with HTTP, you're familiar with the idea of having a request and a response. In reactive systems, messages are one-way. A response is nothing more than another one-way message back to the sender, as shown in this simple `Echo` actor.

Listing 6.9   Echoing the original message back to the sender

```
import akka.actor.Actor

class Echo extends Actor {
  def receive = {
```

```
    case msg =>
        sender() ! msg
    }
}
```
◁─── **Akka makes the sender available as an ActorRef through Actor.sender().**

This arrangement works because a reference to the sender is included in every message, and Akka makes it available to the receive method.

Actors are equal peers. When a response is returned, it's another one-way message from one actor to another—in this case, from the current actor to the sender. An actor may be a client for one interaction and a service to another, and it can play any other role as needed by the domain model. One consequence is that an actor sending a message doesn't necessarily expect a single message in response. Whatever responses are produced may come from the same actor or from a different actor. There could be one message, multiple messages, or perhaps none!

> **WARNING** Calls to the sender() function are valid only within the scope of the receive method. Be careful not to make the function accessible to other threads. This error happens most often when the sender is used in a Future. If you need to pass the sender, call sender() to resolve it to a value first. Akka guarantees that an actor processes only one message at a time. This restriction is essential, because if the receive method had two simultaneous callers, it would have no way to decide which ActorRef to return.

Another consequence is that like all actors, an actor in the role of a client needs to run within an actor system. In the RareBooks example, separating customer into another JVM requires creating another actor system for it, as shown in figure 6.6.

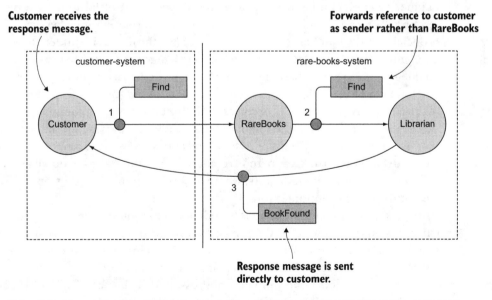

Figure 6.6 Every actor lives inside an actor system. When an actor sends a message, responses may come from the same actor, a different actor, or not at all.

In this example, a `customer` actor creates a remote reference to `rare-books` and sends a `Find` message. The RareBooks actor then *forwards* the `Find` message to the `librarian` using a router. Because the message was forwarded, the sender isn't changed, so it appears to the `librarian` that the sender was the `customer` actor. Then the `librarian` sends a new `BookFound` message directly to the `customer`.

The `librarian` in the example doesn't respond to requests instantaneously. Finding a book takes some time, and the example simulates that effect by waiting a little while before responding. In a distributed system, you can't rely on the configuration to remain static over time. Actors may fail and restart; pools of actors may grow or shrink in response to load. Some operations take a long time, perhaps long enough that the original requestor (the `customer` actor) is replaced. In a synchronous system, a client failure can be very messy. Should the server keep going or terminate the request? What if failure isn't detected until processing is complete? Where should the response be sent? The underlying problem is that requests and responses are fundamentally different, and each response message is tied inextricably to the request message.

In a reactive system, both the request message and the response message are first-class messages between peers. Request-response is a common pattern. Sending the request from `customer` to `rare-books` and then sending the response directly from `librarian` to `customer` is a variation on the pattern. Making the requester and responder peers leads to a powerful concept: the `customer` actor may have failed and restarted while the `librarian` was processing the request, but the response message still can be sent back to the newly recovered `customer`. The key is location transparency.

Location transparency is a fundamental concept in computer science, wherein a unique logical identifier is used to represent the physical location of a distributed resource. You can liken location transparency to Internal Revenue Service's (IRS) use of Social Security numbers (SSN), where the SSN is the logical identifier and your name is the physical address. Regardless of what you change your name to (assuming that you do it legally), you always have the same SSN that the IRS uses for tax purposes.

Don't confuse location transparency with *transparent remoting*—a pattern wherein a remote proxy is created that conforms to the interface of a remote object. Instead of executing the methods of the remote object locally, the parameters are serialized and sent over the network. Then the remote object deserializes the parameters, executes, and marshals a return. Transparent remoting is an attempt to generalize the model for both local and remote objects, whereas location transparency is optimization for local and remote communication.

In Akka, transparent remoting is foundational to remoting and significant for resilience. It's quite common for the physical locations of resources to change over time due to fault conditions. When a node crashes in a clustered environment, for example, the coordinator may spin up a replacement on a different machine. The result is a change in the new node's physical address, and if that physical address is in the code, the application is broken.

URI vs. URL

URI stands for *Uniform Resource Identifier*, and *URL* stands for *Uniform Resource Locator*. A URI tells you the resource that's being identified, and a URL tells you where to find it. Based on those definitions, URIs have location transparency, but URLs don't. In practice, especially with HTTP, URIs and URLs are often used interchangeably. The distinction is blurred by the presence of Domain Name System (DNS) entries and load balancers that allow one URL to reach any of multiple instances of a service.

Now that you know how to create a remote reference from a Customer to the Rare-Books actor, and you know why the Customer actors have their own actor system, all you need is a driver application for those Customer actors.

6.3.4 Creating another driver

As shown in figure 6.7, the customer driver follows the same pattern as the RareBooks driver you created in section 6.2. A CustomerApp class with a corresponding companion object contains the main() function. When CustomerApp creates the actor system, Akka automatically creates the guardian user actor.

The difference between the CustomerApp and the RareBooksApp you created in section 6.2 is that the CustomerApp resolves an ActorRef to RareBooks and creates multiple customer actors instead of the single rare-books actor. That step is shown

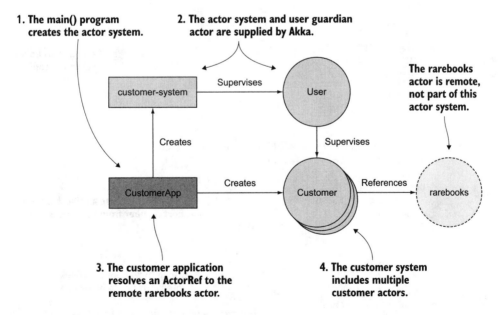

Figure 6.7 The CustomerApp driver and Customer actor

in the following listing, which combines the resolution steps and creates *count* customers. You can download the complete source from http://mng.bz/71O3.

Listing 6.10   Resolving the RareBooks actor and creating multiple Customer actors

```
protected def createCustomer
  (count: Int, odds: Int, tolerance: Int): Unit = {          Called by the command loop

  system.actorSelection(RootActorPath(
    rareBooksAddress) / "user" /"rare-books").           Combine the steps to
    resolveOne(resolveTimeout).onComplete {              resolve the ActorRef.

    case scala.util.Success(rareBooks) =>

      for ( _ <- 1 to count)
        system.actorOf(Customer.props(rareBooks, odds, tolerance))

    case scala.util.Failure(ex) =>                     Creates count customer actors
      log.error(ex, ex.getMessage)                     by using the resolved ActorRef
  }
}
```

Most of the configuration is the same, too, as shown in the following listing.

Listing 6.11   Customer application.conf

```
akka {
  loggers  = [akka.event.slf4j.Slf4jLogger]
  loglevel = DEBUG

  actor {
    debug {
      lifecycle = on
      unhandled = on                              Same as RareBooks
    }                                             application.conf

    provider = remote
  }

  remote {
    enabled-transports = ["akka.remote.netty.tcp"]
    log-remote-lifecycle-events = off

    netty.tcp {
      hostname = localhost          Both JVMs in the example use localhost, so choose
      port = 2552                   a different port number from RareBooks.
    }
  }
}

rare-books {                        How long to wait for RareBooks
  resolve-timeout = 5 seconds       remote reference to be resolved
  hostname = localhost
  port = 2551                       Hostname and port number of RareBooks
}
```

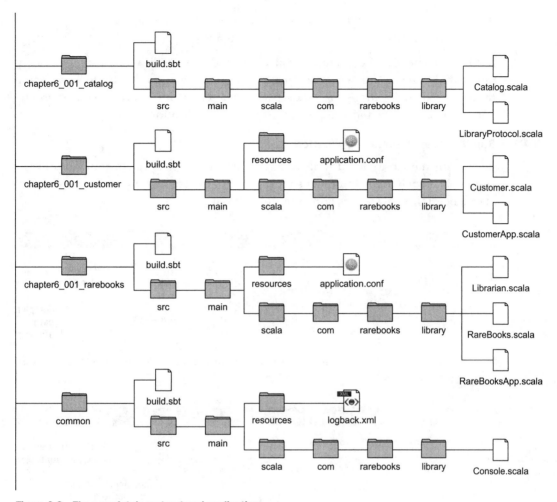

Figure 6.8   The completely restructured application

Now you have the two applications ready and configured. The result of the refactoring should contain the files shown in figure 6.8. Congratulations! The only thing left to do is try your completed example.

6.4   Running the distributed example

In chapter 4, you ran the application from a single terminal session. Because Rare-Books now supports remoting, that approach is no longer possible. You need to start separate terminal sessions for Customer and RareBooks driver applications. The sequence you use in this section is

1   Start a terminal session, and launch the Customer driver application.
2   Start a terminal session, and launch the RareBooks driver application.

3 Create some customer actors with the Customer application.

4 Start a third terminal session to review the results.

For convenience in the example, you run the driver applications from within sbt rather than directly with a Java command line so that you don't have to worry about the build target locations and class path. Chapter 10 introduces some packaging options that would be more appropriate for a real application.

6.4.1 *Starting the customer application*

Begin with the Customer driver. Because you have a root project with subprojects, launch sbt, switch to the customer subproject, and then launch the driver application. Start a new terminal session, and enter the following.

Listing 6.12   Starting sbt

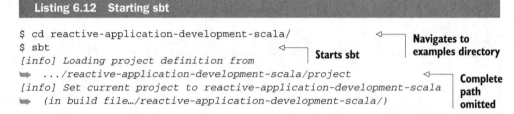

```
$ cd reactive-application-development-scala/
$ sbt
[info] Loading project definition from
➥  .../reactive-application-development-scala/project
[info] Set current project to reactive-application-development-scala
➥  (in build file…/reactive-application-development-scala/)
```

- Navigates to examples directory
- Starts sbt
- Complete path omitted

Now you're running sbt in the root of the examples project. Switch sbt to the customer subproject, as follows.

Listing 6.13   Switching to the customer subproject

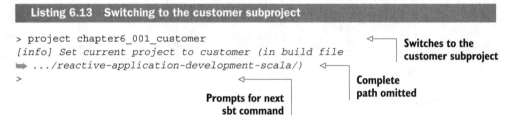

```
> project chapter6_001_customer
[info] Set current project to customer (in build file
➥  .../reactive-application-development-scala/)
>
```

- Switches to the customer subproject
- Complete path omitted
- Prompts for next sbt command

At this point, you've set the project to the customer. The next step is to start the customer application, as follows.

Listing 6.14   Starting the customer application

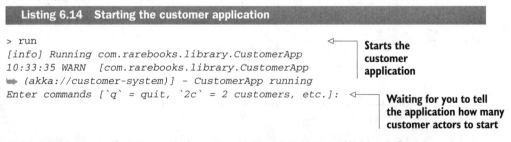

```
> run
[info] Running com.rarebooks.library.CustomerApp
10:33:35 WARN  [com.rarebooks.library.CustomerApp
➥  (akka://customer-system)] - CustomerApp running
Enter commands [`q` = quit, `2c` = 2 customers, etc.]:
```

- Starts the customer application
- Waiting for you to tell the application how many customer actors to start

If you've made it this far, pat yourself on the back. You've started the first remote application, which is ready to create some customer actors. Before you create any customers, however, you need to start RareBooks. There's no sense ordering books if the store doesn't exist!

6.4.2 Starting the RareBooks application

The steps for starting the RareBooks application are almost the same as those for starting the customer application (see the following listing).

Listing 6.15 Switching to the RareBooks project and starting the application

```
$ cd reactive-application-development-scala/
$ sbt
[info] Loading project definition from
➥ .../reactive-application-development-scala/project
[info] Set current project to reactive-application-development-scala
➥    (in build file…/reactive-application-development-scala/)
> project chapter6_001_rarebooks
[info] Set current project to rarebooks (in build file
➥ .../reactive-application-development-scala/)
> run
[info] Running com.rarebooks.library.RareBooksApp
18:04:58 WARN  [com.rarebooks.library.RareBooksApp
➥ (akka://rare-books-system)] - RareBooksApp running
Waiting for customer requests.
```

Same as starting the customer application

Switches to the rarebooks subproject

Starts the rarebooks application

Waits for the first customer

Now that you have both applications up and running, you're ready to start the ordering.

6.4.3 Creating some customers

Switch back to the terminal where you started the customer application, and enter 2c for two customers. You should see the following.

Listing 6.16 Customer output

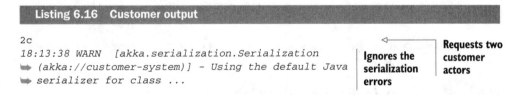

```
2c
18:13:38 WARN  [akka.serialization.Serialization
➥ (akka://customer-system)] - Using the default Java
➥ serializer for class ...
```

Ignores the serialization errors

Requests two customer actors

If you switch to the RareBooks terminal session, you see similar output.

6.4.4 Reviewing the results

Let the application run for a little while. Open a third terminal session to view the log output produced by the two applications' sending book requests and responses back and forth. The result should look something like what you see in listing 6.17. Your log output may vary from the listing depending on how long you wait before starting the actor systems and creating customers, how many customers you create, and the settings in your application.conf files. Look at both applications and the log output. Try to find examples of librarians receiving complaints, issuing credits, and even shutting themselves down and being restarted by the supervisor actor after receiving too many complaints.

Listing 6.17   Logging from the complete system

```
18:02:04 WARN   [com.rarebooks.library.CustomerApp
➥ (akka://customer-system)] - CustomerApp running
Enter commands [`q` = quit, `2c` = 2 customers, etc.]:
18:04:58 WARN   [com.rarebooks.library.RareBooksApp
➥ (akka://rare-books-system)] - RareBooksApp running
Waiting for customer requests.
18:04:58 DEBUG [akka://rare-books-system/user/
➥ rare-books/librarian-1] - started
➥ (com.rarebooks.library.Librarian@448eb83b)
...
18:04:58 DEBUG [akka://rare-books-system/user/
➥ rare-books] - now supervising Actor
➥ [akka://rare-books-system/user/rare-books/
➥ librarian-0#-2013227586]
...
18:13:38 DEBUG [akka://customer-system/user/$a] -
➥ started (com.rarebooks.library.Customer@2b07b134)
...
18:13:39 INFO  [akka.tcp://rare-books-system@
➥ localhost:2551/user/rare-books] -
➥ Closing down for the day
...
18:13:39 INFO  [akka.tcp://rare-books-system@
localhost:2551/user/rare-books] -
2 requests processed today. Total requests processed = 2
...
18:42:26 INFO  [akka.tcp://rare-books-system@
➥ localhost:2551/user/rare-books/librarian-4] -
➥  BookNotFound(Book(s) not found based on
➥ Set(Unknown),1487140944853)
```

- **Customer application startup**
- **RareBooks application startup**
- **Librarian actors starting**
- **RareBooks actor begins supervising the librarians.**
- **Customer application starts some customers.**
- **RareBooks closes for the day.**
- **RareBooks generates the daily report.**
- **A search didn't find a book.**

Pat yourself on the back a second time! You've created a reactive application that supports remoting.

6.5   *Reliability in distributed systems*

Reactive systems are message-driven, so they send a lot of messages. At the small scale of a single computer running an example application, as in the preceding section, dropped messages should be rare. Consider the ramifications of a large-scale reactive system. Reactive systems are elastic and resilient, which means that they may grow or shrink over time as actors are added and removed, and that they're expected to handle failure even while passing millions or even billions of messages. Some messages won't arrive at their intended destination the first time they're sent. You need to consider reliability as an aspect of the complete design rather than an afterthought.

6.5.1 *Reliability as a design parameter*

Ideally, every message is delivered to its intended destination immediately and exactly once. Knowing that failures do occur, you can add logic to detect failures and retransmit messages that didn't arrive on the first try. But this solution has a cost: each new piece of logic adds to system overhead, thereby decreasing total capacity and creating another component that itself can fail. In reactive systems, failure conditions are made explicit. You, as the application designer, make decisions about the message reliability that your application needs.

AT-MOST-ONCE DELIVERY

It's easy to guarantee that a message will be delivered *at most once*. If you send it only once, the message will be delivered, or it won't be delivered. Very often, the reliability of delivery is high enough and the cost of missed messages is low enough that an at-most-once guarantee is perfectly acceptable.

AT-LEAST-ONCE DELIVERY

Guaranteeing that a message will be delivered *at least once* is more difficult. You can send a message and wait for an acknowledgment that it was delivered (figure 6.9). If you don't receive an acknowledgment within some time limit, you can send the message again and again until you do receive an acknowledgment (figure 6.10).

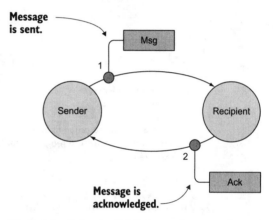

Figure 6.9   Guaranteed delivery requires some form of acknowledgment from the recipient.

That approach has a few problems, however:

- There's no guarantee of how long it will take. If the intended recipient fails or a network connection isn't repaired before your time limit expires, the message won't be delivered on time.

- The sender must keep track of all the messages it sends until it receives an acknowledgment, in case it needs to try again.

Figure 6.10   Retries can continue until an acknowledgment is received by the sender or a timeout is exceeded.

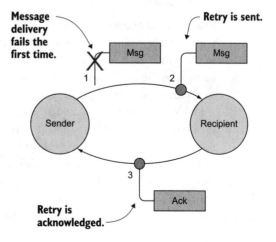

- The problem could be that the messages are being delivered but the acknowledgments aren't being returned successfully (figure 6.11). In that case, many duplicates of the same message could be delivered as the sender keeps retrying without receiving an acknowledgment.

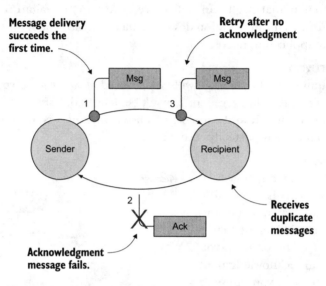

Figure 6.11   If the problem is that acknowledgments are failing to reach the sender, the recipient could receive duplicate messages.

Despite those problems, it isn't uncommon for messaging systems to provide at-least-once delivery by setting reasonable time limits and boundaries on how many unacknowledged messages the sender will retain before dropping some or refusing to accept more.

EXACTLY-ONCE DELIVERY

Guaranteeing that a message will be delivered *exactly* once adds a new difficulty. The sender may not receive all the acknowledgments in time to prevent unnecessary retries, so the *receiver* must keep track of all the messages too. The receiver needs them so it can recognize duplicates. In a busy service, that could be a lot of messages.

Worse, if you try to scale the service by adding more instances of the recipient, you face a new problem: if a message is received but the acknowledgment doesn't get back to the sender in time, the sender resends the message. The retry could be routed to a different recipient, as shown in figure 6.12. How does the second recipient know that the message is a duplicate that has already been processed by the first recipient? The second recipient needs reliable communication with the first recipient, and the coordinator becomes another source of failure.

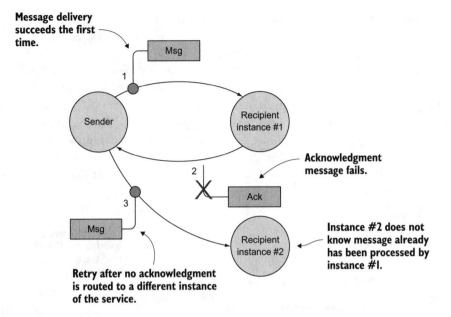

Figure 6.12   Guaranteeing that a message is received exactly once is even more difficult if multiple receivers are needed to handle the processing load.

6.5.2   Akka guarantees

It should be apparent that a complete guarantee of delivery, whether at-most-once or exactly-once, isn't possible in a real system. You don't have infinite retries available. Also, you should realize that each increment of reliability adds to system overhead, perhaps considerably. After that overhead is added, you can't recover the performance that you sacrificed. The solution in Akka is to provide the fastest option by default and layer additional reliability on top of actors as needed.

DEFAULT DELIVERY

As you learned in chapter 3, Akka messages are based on a mailbox concept. Each actor has its own mailbox that acts as a queue, and delivery to the mailbox is at-most-once. Akka adds an additional guarantee that messages delivered *directly* between two actors into the default mailbox type won't be out of order, but always added to the mailbox in the order in which they were sent.

The ordering property is useful for constructing application business logic. In the example application, at the end of each day `rare-books` receives a `Close` message to close the store, followed by a `Report` message to generate daily reports. It would be messy if the `Report` message arrived before the `Close` message. The report might not include requests that arrived after the report was generated but before the store closed for the day.

The ordering property is also useful for adding resilience features to your application. If a gap occurs in the sequence of messages, the receiver might take steps to recover. Having the original message arrive while the recipient is recovering for its absence leads to messy logic. It's much easier to reason about the recovery process knowing that the missing message will never arrive.

The ordering guarantee is valid only for direct messages from one actor to another. Inserting another actor, such as a router, between the actors can lead to unexpected results. Messages from a sender to the router remain in order, as will messages from the router to an individual recipient (routee). The catch is that messages may arrive at different routees in a different order. This situation is illustrated in figure 6.13, in which the first message may arrive at Recipient A even after the second and fourth messages are received (in that order) by Recipient B and the third message fails completely.

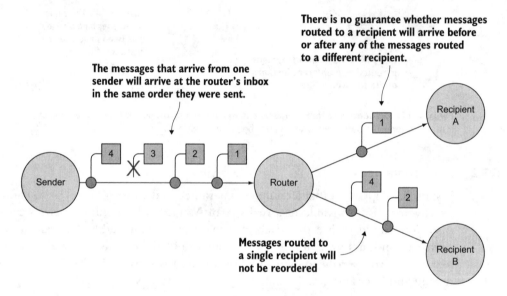

Figure 6.13   Akka defaults to at-most-once delivery with some guarantees on message ordering.

OTHER MAILBOX TYPES

The guarantee on message ordering applies to the default mailbox. Akka has more than a dozen mailbox implementations that you can choose among, and not all of them guarantee ordering in the same way. Implementations with the word *Priority* in their names reorder messages on purpose.

AT-LEAST-ONCE DELIVERY

At-least-once delivery in Akka is perhaps better described as a toolkit for building at-least-once reliability into your application rather than as a complete solution. Underlying the at-least-once delivery mechanism is Akka persistence, which is an Akka module that provides reliable state management by way of persistence across actor starts and restarts. We cover Akka persistence in more detail in chapter 8.

To implement at-least-once delivery, you create the sender as a `PersistentActor` and mix in the `AtLeastOnceDelivery` trait. `PersistentActor` extends `Actor` with persistence features, and to use it, you must include a build dependency in the Akka persistence module.

To implement at-least-once delivery, you need

- An event that can be made persistent
- A function for converting the event to a message that includes a persistence identifier
- An acknowledgment message for the receiving actor to confirm the message
- Receive functions for normal operations and for recovery

Figure 6.14 shows a successful sending cycle.

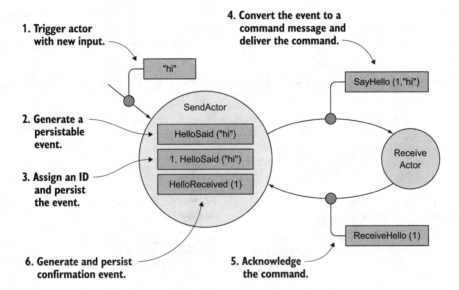

Figure 6.14   Akka at-least-once delivery uses events, which are persisted, and messages, which are delivered to other actors.

The `AtLeastOnceDelivery` trait enables resending unconfirmed messages and supports a configurable timeout. Although `AtLeastOnceDelivery` is a nice addition, it requires some work on your part. You're responsible for persisting both the message sent and the confirmation received in the case of a JVM crash, and you must provide a special receive function to assist with recovery. The receiving actor's requirement is much simpler than the sending actor's requirement. The receiving actor doesn't need the `PersistentActor` or `AtLeastOnceDelivery` traits; it only needs to confirm that it has received and processed the event. Because the guarantee is at-least-once rather than exactly-once, the recipient may receive duplicate messages. Finally, the order of messages may change. The following listing includes both the sending actor and the receiving actor.

Listing 6.18   Sample send and receive actors extending AtLeastOnceDelivery

```
import akka.actor.{ Actor, ActorSelection }
import akka.persistence.{ AtLeastOnceDelivery, PersistentActor }

sealed trait Cmd
case class SayHello(deliveryId: Long, s: String) extends Cmd
case class ReceiveHello(deliveryId: Long) extends Cmd

sealed trait Evt
case class HelloSaid(s: String) extends Evt
case class HelloReceived(deliveryId: Long) extends Evt

class SendActor(destination: ActorSelection)
    extends PersistentActor with AtLeastOnceDelivery {

  override def persistenceId: String = "persistence-id"

  override def receiveCommand: Receive = {
    case s: String =>
      persist(HelloSaid(s))(updateState)
    case ReceiveHello(deliveryId) =>
      persist(HelloReceived(deliveryId))(updateState)
  }

  override def receiveRecover: Receive = {
    case evt: Evt => updateState(evt)
  }

  def updateState(evt: Evt): Unit = evt match {
    case HelloSaid(s) =>
      deliver(destination)
      ➥ (deliveryId => SayHello(deliveryId, s))

    case HelloReceived(deliveryId) =>
      confirmDelivery(deliveryId)
  }
}

class ReceiveActor extends Actor {
  def receive = {
    case SayHello(deliveryId, s) =>
      // ... do something with s
      sender() ! ReceiveHello(deliveryId)
  }
}
```

Defines the messages that are exchanged between SendActor and ReceiveActor

Defines the objects that are persisted locally to track state

The destination actor is an ActorSelection rather than an ActorRef so that it can be persisted.

The sending actor must be a PersistentActor and extend AtLeastOnceDelivery.

Name of the unique key for entries in the persistence layer

To send a string, create the persistent event, and update the state of the actor.

To process the confirmation response, create the persistent event, and update the state of the actor.

Used to replay events when the actor is recovering from a restart

Tell the at-most-once delivery mechanism to deliver the message to the destination.

Used by the deliver function to transform the delivery ID into a message

Tell the at-most-once delivery mechanism that a confirmation message has been received.

The ReceiveActor confirms every SayHello message with a ReceiveHello message that includes the deliveryId.

Fully understanding `AtLeastOnceDelivery` requires understanding Akka persistence and Event Sourcing, which are covered in chapter 8. For now, the important thing to understand is that `AtLeastOnceDelivery` keeps track of which messages haven't been confirmed, handles resending them, and uses Akka persistence to manage storing the messages that haven't been confirmed.

Summary

- You can use sbt to define the structure of a reactive project with multiple driver applications.
- Lightbend Config Library provides a human-readable format for storing and managing runtime configuration of your applications.
- Akka uses location transparency to maintain a uniform view of actors, so an ActorRef may refer to a local or remote actor. Local and remote references share a URI syntax that doesn't use HTTP.
- Establishing a reference to a remote actor involves contacting the remote actor system to ensure that the actor exists.
- All actors are peers. If a client makes a request to an actor system and expects a reply, the client also needs to have an actor system.
- Akka provides limited delivery guarantees for messages. By default, it guarantees at-most-once delivery and guarantees that messages won't be received out of order. Akka persistence can provide at-least-once delivery, limited by timeouts and capacity.

Reactive streaming

7

This chapter covers

- Seeing the dangers of unbounded buffers
- Safeguarding your application with backpressure
- Using Akka Streams in your application
- Integrating Akka Streams with other toolkits

In chapter 6, you learned how to cross actor system boundaries and send messages to remote actors. In this chapter, you learn how to prevent an application from being overwhelmed by too many messages. The reactive approach to regulating streams of messages so that they don't become floods is called *backpressure*.

Akka applies backpressure for you through Akka Streams. On the surface, Akka Streams is similar to other libraries you may have encountered, such as the `java.util.stream` package introduced in Java 8. You can take advantage of it directly by assembling stream sources, sinks, flows, and graphs without having to worry much about what's happening below the surface, as shown in section 7.3. Alternatively, you can use toolkits that are built on top of it, such as Akka HTTP (which we cover in chapter 9).

After learning about the Akka Streams library, you take it to the next level with the Reactive Streams application programming interface (API), which provides a standard interface to asynchronous streams and, as part of the specification, requires non-blocking backpressure. Reactive Streams is supported by many toolkits, including Akka, Java 9, and .NET. You can use it to integrate with other systems and apply backpressure across the connection.

We start by examining what happens when no backpressure exists.

7.1 Buffering too many messages

If you wanted to, you could configure millions of actors distributed across thousands of servers to send messages to a single actor running on your laptop. That single actor would expect to continue receiving messages one at a time, in keeping with the single-threaded contract it has with Akka. The result would be a huge backlog of unprocessed messages. Where would those messages be?

Ideally, the backlog of messages would be safe in the actor's mailbox. The default mailbox types are unbounded, so they can grow to accommodate a considerable number of unprocessed messages. Eventually, the application will run out of available memory to hold more messages, and the server may buffer additional data in system buffers. Usually, those buffers hold a small fraction of what an actor's mailbox can hold. When those buffers overflow too, the server is forced to start rejecting incoming messages, as shown in figure 7.1.

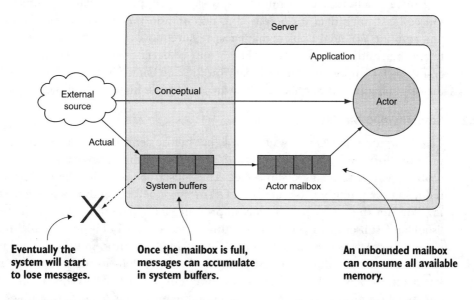

Figure 7.1   System buffers may attempt to handle messages that your application isn't ready to accept.

It may seem far-fetched to expect enough incoming data to overwhelm your system under normal load, especially if the system was designed with reactive principles and is capable of elastic growth. But consider some of the conditions that could lead to sudden increases in the numbers of messages that need to be processed:

- Your site appears in the news, and people all over the world start using it at the same time. This situation is sometimes called the "Reddit hug of death," because a link appearing on the front page of that site has been known to send surges of traffic to smaller sites that are ill-prepared to handle it.
- A system that your actor needs to complete processing is down for an extended period, so messages accumulate while recovery takes place.
- Other nodes in your application may fail or be unreachable, causing traffic to concentrate on a single node.
- Your application could be subject to a distributed denial-of-service attack. These attacks can exceed 1 terabit per second—enough to overwhelm any server they reach.

Your application may have to defend itself against unexpected increases in workload.

7.2   *Defending with backpressure*

At its root, the problem is that work is arriving faster than it's being processed. Eventually, no matter what you do, the application will be overwhelmed. The reactive solution is to slow the arrival rate of new work through backpressure.

Conceptually, the idea behind backpressure is simple. The data consumer tells the source how much data it's prepared to accept, and the source sends no more than that amount. You might object that backpressure moves the problem from one system to another, and you'd be correct. The beauty of backpressure, however, is it can keep going: each component can push back on the one before it, going all the way back to the original source if necessary, which turns out to be highly effective in real systems.

7.2.1   *Stopping and waiting*

Requiring the publisher to wait for a signal before sending each message provides a primitive form of backpressure. Figure 7.2 illustrates this approach in a publish/subscribe system with a single subscriber. The subscriber provides the backpressure by requiring the publisher to wait for an OK message before sending a message containing work for the subscriber to process, preventing a queue of messages between publisher and subscriber from accumulating. Instead, the publisher has to hold each message until it knows that the subscriber is ready to process it. Although holding each message may appear at first glance to be equivalent to the publisher's making synchronous calls to the subscriber, it is different. Publisher and subscriber are sending asynchronous messages to each other, so the message exchange is nonblocking.

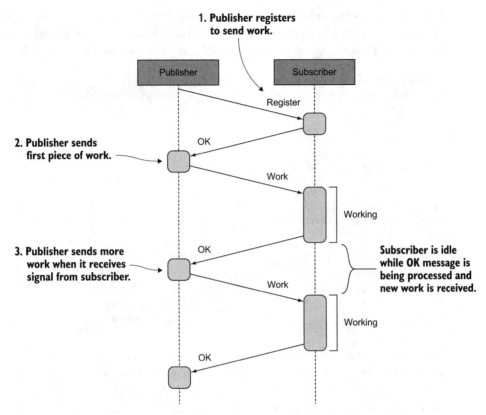

Figure 7.2 Positive acknowledgement per message idles available resources.

A minimal implementation of backpressure with positive acknowledgement could consist of a `Publisher` actor and a `Subscriber` actor. The `Publisher` waits for an OK message before sending a Work message to the `Subscriber`, as follows.

Listing 7.1 Publisher actor with OK processing

```
import akka.actor.{Actor, ActorRef}
import Subscriber.{Register, Work}

object Publisher {                      Message to tell the publisher
  case object Ok                        it's OK to send work
}

class Publisher(subscriber: ActorRef) extends Actor {
  override def preStart =               Sends an initial message
    subscriber ! Register               to start the process
  override def receive = {
    case Publisher.Ok =>                Publisher sends work when
      subscriber ! Work("Do something!")  it receives an OK message.
  }
}
```

When the subscriber completes a piece of work, it replies with an OK message signaling that it's ready to accept another, as shown in the following listing. After responding with the OK message, the subscriber waits idly for another piece of work.

Listing 7.2   Subscriber with OK response

```
import akka.actor.Actor

object Subscriber {
  case object Register
  case class Work(m: String)
}

import Subscriber.{Register, Work}
class Subscriber extends Actor {
  override def receive = {
    case Register =>
      sender() ! Publisher.Ok          <-- OK request to send
                                           initial work
    case Work(m) =>
      System.out.println(s"Working on $m")   <-- Performs the
                                                 requested work
      sender() ! Publisher.Ok    <-- Tells the publisher it's
  }                                  OK to send more work
}
```

The driver, shown in the following listing, sets up the actor system and the two actors as you'd expect: it configures the actor system, waits a few seconds for it to do some work, and shuts down. You can download the example from http://mng.bz/71O3 and run it by using the command sbt run.

Listing 7.3   Driver to start and stop the example

```
import akka.actor.{ActorRef, ActorSystem, Props}

object Main extends App {
  val system: ActorSystem = ActorSystem("StopWait")

  val subscriberProps = Props[Subscriber]
  val subscriber: ActorRef = system.actorOf(subscriberProps)

  val publisherProps =
    Props(classOf[Publisher], subscriber)    <-- The publisher gets a
  val publisher: ActorRef = system.actorOf(publisherProps)   reference to the subscriber.

  Thread.sleep(10000)          Waits a few seconds and then shuts
  system.terminate()           down the whole actor system
}
```

Congratulations—you've implemented a stream protocol with backpressure. At this stage, the example is rudimentary. You see a lot of messages scrolling when you run it, but it's quite inefficient. After completing each piece of work, the subscriber has to wait for an OK message to get back to the requestor and then wait for the message containing the next piece of work to arrive before it starts working again. Another problem evident in the driver program is that it lacks a clean shutdown, which can lead to the loss of an unfulfilled work request. You may encounter a few warnings about dead letters.

In the next two sections, we explore how to make the stream implementation slightly less rudimentary. First, we consider how to keep the subscriber busy.

7.2.2 *Signaling for more than one message*

You can reduce the subscriber's idle time by telling the publisher that it's OK to send multiple requests rather than one. The number of requests allowed can be fixed or passed as a parameter in the message. The publisher keeps a running count of the number of messages that it's allowed by the subscriber to send. The subscriber is responsible for deciding when it can allocate more messages to a publisher. In figure 7.3, each message from the subscriber back to the publisher says that it's OK to send three more work requests.

The subscriber doesn't have to wait until it receives three work requests to tell the publisher that it can send more. Requesting additional work before the subscriber fully completes processing the current requests is one way to ensure that the sub-

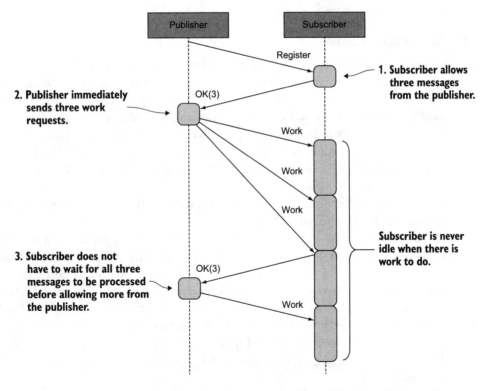

Figure 7.3   The subscriber tells the publisher how many messages it's prepared to accept.

scriber has a continuous supply of work. The additional messages sit in an inbox queue until the subscriber processes them, and the subscriber is responsible for ensuring that it doesn't request more messages than it can handle.

Similarly, when the subscriber sends a message to the publisher to inform it that three messages have been allocated for it to send, the publisher is *not* obligated to send that many messages. The number allowed is a maximum. If the publisher doesn't have that many messages left, it can end the stream.

At this point, your stream implementation can apply enough backpressure to keep the subscriber busy without being overwhelmed, but it still expects to run forever.

Signaling for multiple messages isn't microbatching

A signal that a stream is ready to receive multiple messages means that the sender is allowed to send a set number of *individual* messages. The messages are still received one at a time. This process is different from a technique called microbatching, which is commonly used to optimize big data systems. With microbatching, the system accumulates messages that are ready for processing until some limit is reached. Usually, the limit is a fixed number of messages or some maximum time between batches. When it reaches the limit, the system passes all the accumulated messages at the same time. Then the processor has to handle the microbatch as a unit, mixing infrastructure considerations with business logic.

7.2.3 *Controlling the stream*

Either the publisher or the subscriber may end the stream. Because the publisher and subscriber are asynchronous, the details of ending the stream are a little bit different, depending on which actor ends it. If the publisher is ending the stream, it has to stop sending messages. If the subscriber wants to end the stream, it sends a message back to the publisher. That message may take time to arrive and be processed by the publisher. In the meantime, messages that were sent before the cancellation was processed continue to arrive at the subscriber, as shown in figure 7.4. It's up to the subscriber to decide what to do with messages that arrive after it sent a cancellation message: ignore them or process them. The publisher has no way to know whether the messages arrived at the subscriber.

Whether the publisher or subscriber ends the stream, a completion message usually is sent at the end of the steam. This message informs the subscriber so that it can release resources and perform any final processing. The completion message may take the form of a success message (if the stream is terminating normally) or a failure message. When the completion message arrives, no further messages should follow.

When you use Akka Streams, you don't need to write code for all the intricacies of managing the request count and flow control, so we won't extend the example in this section. We return to it in section 7.4, however, when we discuss the Reactive Streams API.

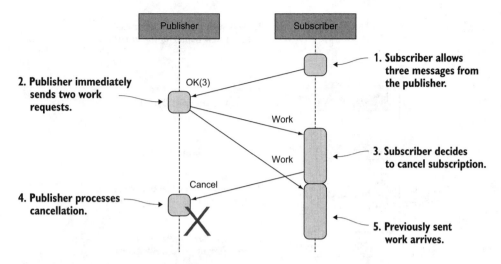

2. Publisher immediately sends two work requests.

OK(3)

1. Subscriber allows three messages from the publisher.

Work

3. Subscriber decides to cancel subscription.

Work

Cancel

4. Publisher processes cancellation.

5. Previously sent work arrives.

Publisher

Subscriber

Figure 7.4   Some messages may continue to arrive after a subscription is canceled.

7.3   *Streaming with Akka*

Akka Streams are graphs assembled from processing stages. Each stage can exert back-pressure on earlier stages. A basic stream consists of a *source* and a *sink*, which are combined to create a *flow* that you can execute. A complete stream could be as simple as

```
source.to(sink).run()
```

To see how to use Akka Streams, give the RareBooks librarians from chapter 6 a new job: loading entries to the catalog. The stream consists of a source, some intermediate flows, and a sink. The source is a stream of bytes read from a comma-separated file. Then the flows convert the stream of bytes (a continuous `ByteString`) into a stream of `BookCard` entries:

1   A *framing* flow uses the line separators that it encounters in the stream to produce a stream consisting of a separate `ByteString` for each line.
2   A *mapping* flow parses each comma-separated `ByteString` to produce a stream of arrays of `Strings`.
3   Another *mapping* flow converts each array of `Strings` to a `BookCard`, producing a stream of `BookCard` entries.

The stream of `BookCard` entries terminates with a sink. The sink sends the `BookCard` as a message to a `librarian` actor, which adds the card to the catalog. You may recall from chapter 6 that the `librarian` actor takes time to perform each task. You don't have to worry about flow control. Behind the scenes, Akka Streams applies backpressure so that `BookCard` entries don't come too fast.

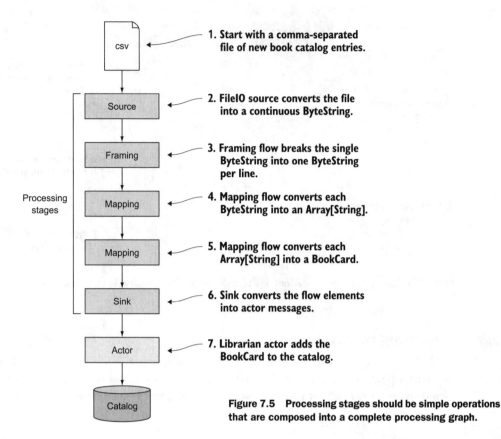

1. Start with a comma-separated file of new book catalog entries.

2. FileIO source converts the file into a continuous ByteString.

3. Framing flow breaks the single ByteString into one ByteString per line.

4. Mapping flow converts each ByteString into an Array[String].

5. Mapping flow converts each Array[String] into a BookCard.

6. Sink converts the flow elements into actor messages.

7. Librarian actor adds the BookCard to the catalog.

Figure 7.5   Processing stages should be simple operations that are composed into a complete processing graph.

Figure 7.5 shows the components you need to create. You can download the source code for this chapter from http://mng.bz/71O3.

7.3.1   *Adding streams to a project*

The catalog loader is a stand-alone application with its own `build.sbt`. Akka Streams is separate from the Akka core, so start by adding both modules as dependencies, as follows.

Listing 7.4   build.sbt for the catalog loader

```
val akkaVersion = "2.5.4"

scalaVersion := "2.12.3"

name := "catalogLoader"

libraryDependencies ++= Seq(
  "com.typesafe.akka"  %% "akka-actor"                % akkaVersion,
  "com.typesafe.akka"  %% "akka-stream"               % akkaVersion
)
```

The complete catalog loader has many moving parts, so you'll build it in phases.

TIP The Alpakka initiative (https://github.com/akka/alpakka) has connectors that handle integration with Amazon Web Services (AWS), Google Cloud, Microsoft Azure, and several queueing packages. The project also maintains a list of externally developed connectors.

7.3.2 Creating a stream source from a file

The goal of the first phase (listing 7.5) is to read a file and print the contents. The source is based on a file path, and the sink is a `println()`. Not surprisingly, running the stream requires an actor system. The actor system is no different from the actor systems for RareBooks introduced in chapter 6. The stream also requires an `Actor-Materializer`, which is new. The job of the materializer is to transform the flow into processors to be executed by actors.

Listing 7.5 Stream to read a file

```
package com.rarebooks.library

import java.nio.file.Paths

import akka.actor.ActorSystem
import akka.stream.ActorMaterializer
import akka.stream.scaladsl._

import scala.concurrent.Await
import scala.concurrent.duration.Duration

object Cataloging extends App {                    Processing
  implicit val system =                            stages execute
    ActorSystem("catalog-loader")                  in this system.
  implicit val materializer = ActorMaterializer()             Transforms the stages
                                                              into processors
  val file = Paths.get("books.csv")                    Be sure that this file is
                                                         in the current directory.
  val result = FileIO.fromPath(file)            Stream source
    .to(Sink.foreach(println(_)))               based on the file
    .run()                           Starts the stream processing

  Await.ready(result, Duration.Inf)                   Waits for the stream
  system.terminate()                                  to complete
}                          Shuts down the
                           actor system
```

Attaches the sink

Use `sbt run` to execute the stream. If everything is working, `sbt run` outputs a very long line like this:

```
ByteString(…)
```

The reason is that Akka `FileIO` produces an `akka.util.ByteString`, which is an optimized data type for working with streams of raw bytes.

7.3.3   *Transforming the stream*

The next phase of development is transforming those raw bytes into a stream of
BookCards that the librarian can add to the catalog. The transformation comprises
the three flows described in the preceding sections: converting the continuous-source
ByteString to single-line ByteStrings, parsing each line into an array of Strings,
and converting each array to a BookCard.

Decoding a continuous stream into a stream of discrete elements is called *framing*.
The Scala domain-specific language (DSL) has a function to generate a flow that
frames lines around a delimiter, which in this case is a newline. The input is a single
ByteString, and the output is a stream of individual ByteStrings.

Converting each ByteString to an array of Strings is a mapping constructed
from a couple of utility functions. Turning that mapping into a flow is easy because
Flow has a map function for that purpose. Following is the resulting application.

Listing 7.6   Transformation of a file into a stream of BookCards

```scala
// ... previous imports
//
import akka.util.ByteString          ◁——  Contains the utf8String
import LibraryProtocol.BookCard             conversion used in parsing

object Cataloging extends App {
  implicit val system =
  ⮡ ActorSystem("catalog-loader")
  implicit val materializer = ActorMaterializer()

  val file = Paths.get("books.csv")

  private val framing: Flow[ByteString, ByteString, NotUsed] =
    Framing.delimiter(ByteString("\n"),                         Declares the
      maximumFrameLength = 256,                                 framing function
      allowTruncation = true)

  private val parsing: ByteString => Array[String] =   Declares the
    _.utf8String.split(",")                            parsing function

  private val conversion: Array[String] => BookCard =
    s => BookCard(
      isbn = s(0),                                    Declares the
      author = s(1),                                  conversion
      // ... remaining fields                         function
    )

  val result = FileIO.fromPath(file)       Frames the
    .via(framing)              ◁——         ByteString by line
    .map(parsing)              ◁——  Parses each line
    .map(conversion)                into an Array[String]
    .to(Sink.foreach(println(_)))
    .run()
  Await.ready(result, Duration.Inf)
  system.terminate()
}
```

Converts to
BookCard ▷

Use sbt run to execute the stream. This time, you see individual BookCards.

Now take a step back to look at what you've accomplished. You've created five processing stages: a source, three flows, and a sink. Together, they read a file and transform it into a stream of BookCard entries for the RareBooks catalog.

> **TIP** It's worth spending some time to examining the scaladoc for Flow. It has a rich set of functions similar to those in the Scala collections library, including basics such as filter, map, fold, and reduce.

7.3.4 Converting the stream to actor messages

The next phase is replacing the sink that generates println() messages with one that sends messages to the librarian actor. The application has a reference to the actor system, so one approach is to use tell, as in the following.

Listing 7.7 Sink sending messages directly to an actor

```
// ...
val librarian: ActorRef
// ...
val result = FileIO.fromPath(file)
  .via(framing)
  .map(parsing)
  .map(conversion)                              Use tell to send the card
  .to(Sink.foreach(card => librarian ! card))  ◁──┘ directly to the Librarian actor.
  .run()
```

For a somewhat richer interface, you can use Sink.actorRef to send the messages automatically. That function adds a final message that's sent to the actor when the stream is complete. Whether you choose tell or Sink.actorRef, each message to the actor behaves in the usual way. That is, each message is nonblocking, asynchronous, and one-way, which in this case presents a problem: no backpressure!

To apply backpressure from the actor to the stream, you need to use the more complex Sink.actorRefWithAck function. This function takes several parameters:

- *ref*—A reference to the actor.
- *onInitMessage*—A message sent before any elements from the stream.
- *ackMessage*—A message returned from the actor to acknowledge each request. The sink must receive this message after it sends onInitMessage and before it sends any stream elements, and the sink also must receive this message after each stream element.
- *onCompleteMessage*—A message sent to the actor when the stream completes successfully.
- *onFailureMessage*—A message sent to the actor if the stream completes with failure.

As you can see, the `Librarian` actor has to handle a few new messages. First, add those messages to the `LibraryProtocol`, as follows.

Listing 7.8 The `LibraryProtocol` extended to interact with the stream

```
case object LibInit
case object LibAck
case object LibComplete
case class LibError (t: Throwable)
```

To make the extended protocol work, you first need to make a few changes in the Librarian's receive function so that it's prepared to accept the new BookCards and respond as follows.

Listing 7.9 `Librarian` actor extended to add catalog entries

```
// ... start with the familiar Librarian you used in chapters 3, 4, and 6
  private def ready: Receive = {
    // ... preexisting match cases elided
    case LibInit =>
      log.info("Starting load")            ⟵  Allows the stream to start
      sender() ! LibAck                        sending new books
    case b: BookCard =>
      log.info(s"Received card $b")          ⟵  Adds the new book
      Catalog.books = Catalog.books + ((b.isbn, b))    to the catalog
      sender() ! LibAck                    ⟵  Allows the stream
    case LibError(e) =>                         to send another book
      log.error("Load error", e)       No special processing
    case LibComplete =>                  is needed for
      log.info("Complete load")         completion or error.
```

Now you've done all the preparatory work to complete the final phase of the example by adding `actorRefWithAck` to the processing stream.

7.3.5 *Putting it together*

Following is the complete processing stream.

Listing 7.10 `Sink.actorRefWithAck` to exert backpressure from the actor

```
// ...
val librarian: ActorRef
import LibraryProtocol._          ⟵  Imports the messages to
// ...                                interact with the librarian
val result = FileIO.fromPath(file)
  .via(framing)
  .map(parsing)
  .map(conversion)
  .to(Sink.actorRefWithAck(                Sink with the backpressure
    librarian, LibInit, LibAck, LibComplete, LibError)   messages defined
  .run()
```

When you run this application, it streams the file of books into new entries in the catalog. Now is a great time for you to experiment with backpressure! Here are a few things to try:

- Have the librarian take more time adding a card entry. Instead of sending a `LibAck` message right away, use the technique you learned in chapter 4 to schedule the acknowledgement message after a short delay.
- The librarian takes time researching requests from customers. Start up a few instances of the customer application and send some requests while the librarian is busy adding new card entries.

As you explore Akka Streams, you'll discover that they can go beyond simple linear flows that consist of a source, flows, and a sink. Streams can be assembled into graphs that have multiple inputs or outputs at each stage. Table 7.1 defines some terms you may encounter that describe different stream processing stages.

Table 7.1 Akka Streams processing stages may be categorized based on the number of inputs and outputs.

Type	Inputs	Outputs
Source	*	1
Sink	1	*
Flow	1	1
Fan-In	multiple	1
Fan-Out	1	multiple
BidiFlow	multiple	multiple

* External to the stream, such as a file connector

7.4 Introducing Reactive Streams

So far in this chapter, you've learned about backpressure as a reactive technique and applied it to Akka's Streams library. Akka Streams is built on backpressure with actor-based underpinnings. Other streams could be built on different frameworks but still support backpressure. *Reactive Streams* is "an initiative to provide a standard for asynchronous stream processing with non-blocking back pressure" (from www.reactive-streams.org). In other words, it's a distillation of the core features that a reactive implementation needs to provide. Reactive Streams provides a common language that allows different reactive implementations to interoperate.

Akka isn't the only implementation. Most notably, Reactive Streams is incorporated into Java 9 through Java Enhancement Proposal JEP-266. Spring Framework version 5 incorporates Reactive Streams through Project Reactor (https://projectreactor.io). Other implementations include RxJava, which is part of the ReactiveX project (https://reactivex.io), Ratpack (https://ratpack.io), and Eclipse Vert.x (http://vertx.io). More implementations are appearing regularly. Reactive Streams includes a Technology Compatibility Kit (TCK) to help validate new implementations as they appear.

Reactive Streams should be viewed as APIs for providers. If you've settled on using a single toolkit such as Akka for your entire application, you don't use it directly. If you want to get two reactive systems to interoperate, and those systems don't already have a connector, consider using Reactive Streams to connect them.

The entire Reactive Streams API consists of four small interfaces:

- *Publisher*—The provider of a stream of elements
- *Subscriber*—The consumer of a stream of elements
- *Subscription*—The interface used for a subscriber to signal a publisher
- *Processor*—A processing stage that obeys the contracts of both publisher and subscriber

NOTE   Reactive Streams doesn't have any dependencies on Akka. Implementations don't have to be based on the actor model at all.

7.4.1 *Creating a Reactive Stream*

Creating a Reactive Stream between two providers is easy. All you need is a reference to a `Publisher` from one provider and a `Subscriber` from the other. The heavy lifting is performed by the provider's implementations of the interface (figure 7.6):

1 The application calls the `subscribe` method on the `Publisher`, passing a reference to the `Subscriber`.
2 The `Publisher` creates a `Subscription`.
3 The `Publisher` calls the `onSubscribe` method on the `Subscriber`, passing a reference to the newly created `Subscription`.

At this point, the `Subscriber` uses the `Subscription` to start sending asynchronous signals back to the `Publisher`.

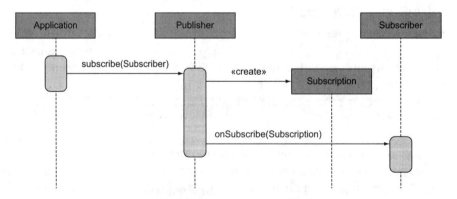

Figure 7.6   The application initializes a reactive stream by calling the publisher with a reference to the subscriber. The publisher creates a subscription and passes it to the subscriber.

WARNING   Reactive Streams doesn't allow the same `Subscriber` to have multiple `Subscriptions` to the same `Publisher`. Calling `Publisher` `.subscribe` more than once for the same `Subscriber` may produce exceptions or unpredictable behavior.

7.4.2   Consuming the Reactive Stream

The `Subscriber` has two signals that it can send back to the `Publisher`; it can request messages or cancel the subscription. No messages flow until the subscriber starts the flow with the first call to request messages.

The `Publisher` keeps calling the `Subscriber`'s `onNext` method with new messages until it has sent as many as requested. If the `Publisher` runs out of messages or if an error occurs, the `Publisher` signals the `Subscriber` by using `onComplete` or `onError`, respectively (figure 7.7).

The `Subscriber` can request that the `Publisher` stop sending messages by canceling the `Subscription`. In that event, the publisher is required to stop sending messages eventually, but it may not stop immediately.

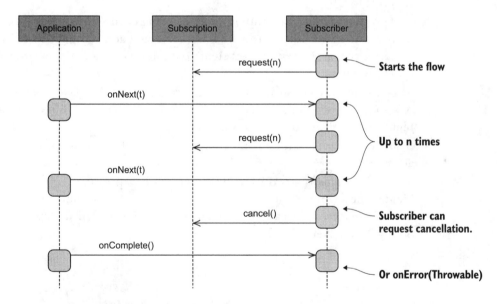

Figure 7.7   The publisher can end a stream by calling onComplete or onError. The subscriber can asynchronously request the publisher to end the stream by calling cancel.

TIP   The default mailbox in Akka is unbounded, but several of the other implementations are bounded. If you're integrating with a Reactive Streams implementation, be sure not to request more messages than your application's inbox can hold. Otherwise, you could be subject to the overflowing-buffer conditions discussed at the beginning of this chapter.

7.4.3   *Building applications with streaming*

It seems that the software world is heading to streaming. You find streams in Apache Spark, Storm, Samza, Apex, Flink, Kafka, and more. If you stop and reflect for a moment, you realize that the move to streaming is a consequence of software that better reflects the real world, because the real world has a lot of asynchronous events. No matter how many incoming messages a system can handle at the same time, a few too many events might arrive and spoil the fun. In the real world, the solution is to slow the influx to something that the system can handle. Reactive streaming brings the same solution to software by telling the source to slow down so the application can catch up. This chapter showed you how to do that. In the next chapter, you put this knowledge to use with two types of messages that often arrive in a stream: commands and events.

Summary

- Bursts of message traffic can overflow into unexpected parts of your system. Overflowing buffers damage resiliency because the system relies on lower levels to recover.
- Backpressure defends your application by telling clients how many messages it's prepared to handle. Backpressure is implemented according to the same reactive principles as the rest of the system, so it's nonblocking, message-driven, and asynchronous.
- Akka Streams are constructed from processing stages. A typical stream consists of a source, some flows, and a sink. The Scala DSL is a rich library for assembling commonly needed processing stages.
- A stream of events can be converted to messages that can be processed by an actor.
- Reactive Streams is an API for implementing backpressure. You can use it to identify messaging frameworks with backpressure support and to create more portable reactive applications. Implementations include Akka Streams, Java 9, Spring 5, and .Net.

CQRS and Event Sourcing

8

This chapter covers

- The basics of Command Query Responsibility Segregation
- CQRS in reactive systems
- Commands and queries
- CQRS and Event Sourcing combined

As you've seen in the previous chapters, the reactive paradigm is a powerful way to think about distributed computing. In this chapter, we build on that foundation by exploring two design patterns introduced in chapter 1: Command Query Responsibility Segregation (CQRS) and Event Sourcing (ES). We should note, however, that although these techniques work in concert and are a natural fit for reactive programming, they're by no means the only way to design a reactive system.

To achieve our goal of exploring these two design patterns, we look at a common type of application: the database-driven application, which is the foundation of many, if not most, systems built today. We explore the challenges in building these types of applications in a distributed environment and show you how, through the reactive paradigm, you can use CQRS/ES to overcome these challenges.

181

First, we need to state what we mean by *database-driven application*. The term can mean many things to many people, but at its root is a simple meaning: a software application that takes in and persists data and provides a means to retrieve that data.

After discussing the driving factors toward CQRS/ES, we explain the concepts and alternatives to a typical monolithic, database-driven application. We look beyond the theoretical notion of reactive applications being message-driven and ground that concept in a reality that uses CQRS commands and Event Sourcing events as actual messages.

8.1   Driving factors toward CQRS/ES

The relational database management system (RDBMS), traditionally in the form of a Structured Query Language (SQL) database, has directly affected how applications are built. Frameworks such as Java Enterprise Edition (Java EE), Spring, and Visual Studio made SQL the foundational norm for system development as we entered the age of affordable and more agile computing. Before SQL, mainframe systems were the central computing areas of business, and users were limited to using dumb terminals, reports, and so on. SQL databases offered an accessible, easy-to-use storage model; programmers quickly became dependent on the capabilities they offered and even built systems around them. The growing number of desktop PCs led to a growing number of systems built against these databases, and the creation of systems free from rigid management information systems fiefdoms was great for computing overall. Unfortunately, traditional solutions have clear limitations, preventing application distribution and usually resulting in monolithic designs such as *ACID transactions*. We discuss ACID transactions, the pitfalls of relational databases, and CRUD in the following sections.

8.1.1   ACID transactions

Typically, monolithic applications allow database transactions across domain boundaries. In this world, it's perfectly possible for a transaction to guarantee that a customer was added to a customer table before an order was added to an order table; we were able to make these separate table writes all at once because all of the data resided in the same database. These transactions are typically referred to as *ACID transactions*,[1] which have the following properties:

- *Atomicity* allows multiple actions to be performed as a single unit. Atomicity is the basis of transactions in which an update to a customer address can take place in the same unit of work as creating an order for that customer.
- *Consistency* means strong consistency, as all changes to data are seen by all processes at the same time and in the same order. This is also a characteristic of transactions and is so expensive that processes dependent on this type of consistency, such as traditional database-driven applications (usually, monolithic), can't distribute.

---

[1]   https://msdn.microsoft.com/en-us/library/aa480356.aspx

- *Isolation* provides safety against other concurrent transactions. Isolation dictates how data in the act of change behaves when read by other processes. Lower isolation levels provide greater concurrent access to data but a greater chance of concurrent side effects on the data (reads on stale data). Higher isolation levels yield more purity on reads but are more expensive and come with the risk of processes blocking other processes, or, worse, deadlocks, when two or more writes block each other indefinitely.
- *Durability* means that transactions, once committed, survive power outages or hardware failures.

A reactive application is capable of being distributed. It's impossible to have ACID transactions across distributed systems because the data is located across geographic, network, or hardware boundaries. There's no such thing as an ACID transaction across these types of boundaries, so unfortunately, you need to cut the cord of traditional RDBMS dependence. Distributed systems can't be ACID-compliant.

We say *traditional RDBMS* because some relational databases, such as PostgreSQL, have evolved and overcome relational limitations, with features such as object relational storage and asynchronous replication allowing distribution.

8.1.2 *Traditional RDBMS lack of sharding*

These RDBMS-based systems don't shard. *Sharding* is a way of spreading your data by using some shard key. You can use sharding to intelligently co-locate data and also to distribute that data. Sharding provides horizontal scaling across machine hardware and geographical boundaries; therefore, it allows elasticity and distribution of data. An example of sharding is a photo-sharing application that uses a user's unique ID as the shard key. All the user's photos are stored in the same area of the database. Without the ability to shard, a traditional RDBMS is reduced to throwing more hardware and storage at the problem for the same physical database, which is called *vertical scaling*, and you can scale only so far with interconnected hardware. *Horizontal scaling* is scaling across geographical or machine boundaries. Sharding is a way of achieving distribution and paves the way for dividing systems in terms of CQRS.

8.1.3 *CRUD*

As we discuss in chapter 1, Create, Read, Update, Delete (CRUD) is the in-place modification of a piece of data in a single location. With CRUD, all updates are destructive, losing all sense of the previous state of the data, including deletions, which are the most radical updates of all. With CRUD, valuable data is constantly lost. There's no concept of state transition—the current state of any object is all you get. A completed order, for example, is just that. All notions of the new order, fulfilled order, in-process order, and so on are lost. No history exists of the behavior of any given order, making it impossible to trace how it got from point A to point Z. CRUD isn't easily distributable, in that the domain is mutable. Any distributed entity could be changed anywhere at any time, and it's difficult to know the single source of truth.

With CRUD, you always have a single source of truth; all other references to the CRUD entity are made by copy or reference only.

Far and away the most common use of CRUD is in a relational database. In creating the database structure, follow widely accepted best practices so that you have no redundant data, and allow relationships through the use of primary and foreign keys. A foreign key, for example, is a customer table associated with a concrete, associated table of orders and joined by a foreign key field on customer in the orders table. The CRUD model can't scale because of the interdependency of the data constructs, which are bound together. *If the only way you can distribute is to distribute the entire thing, you haven't distributed anything.* The table structures follow the patterns of what you think your business objects will look like, usually through the use of hierarchical relationships. Then you attempt to layer on top an object-oriented domain structure to tie everything together. Although this approach is the foundation of many an application, the implied costs can be painful. Sometimes, CRUD is perfectly fine for simple applications. We'll use a contacts system as an example of such a simple system. This application to maintain contacts has no additional views, just the attributes of the contact as stored in the database. Furthermore, the contact has no relationships to any other domain, or, ideally, few other domains, and is effectively stand-alone. You should understand that it's easy to build this type of application, and if the simplicity of the system warrants it, using this type of application is perfectly fine. In most of the real work applications we've seen, however, CRUD isn't enough or is incorrect. You need another solution and a way to do away with all this pain. For those systems, apply CQRS, usually in combination with Event Sourcing.

8.2   CQRS origins: command, queries, and two distinct paths

Although many people are only now familiarizing themselves with CQRS, it has been around since early 2008. It was crafted by Greg Young, an independent consultant and entrepreneur. As Young puts it, "CQRS is simply the creation of two objects where there was previously only one. The separation occurs based upon whether the methods are a Command or a Query. This definition is the same used by Meyer in Command and Query Separation: a command is any method that mutates state and a query is any method that returns a value."

The single object you're used to is divided in two (queries and commands), and the two objects have distinct paths. A real-life example is the creation of an order, which is done against an order command object or module. The viewing of open orders would be against an order query module.

As its name portrays, CQRS is about commands, queries, and their segregation. We talk about these concepts in detail throughout this chapter, but in this section, we focus on segregation.

Because CQRS combines so nicely with Event Sourcing, we usually refer to the systems that we build with this model as CQRS/ES.

Unfortunately, the word *segregation* (the *S* in *CQRS*) often has a negative connotation, as it does when applied to human relations. When used in the context of reactive systems, however, segregation is a focal point for resilience. The dictionary defines *segregation* as "the action or state of setting someone or something apart from other people or things." This setting apart empowers CQRS/ES as a reactive pattern. Segregation in essence isolates each side of a CQRS/ES system, providing fault tolerance to the system as a whole. If one side goes down, complete system failure doesn't result, because one side is isolated from the other. This pattern is commonly referred to as *bulkheading*.

Bulkheading originated in the shipping industry, as shown in figure 8.1, in which bulkheads are watertight compartments designed to isolate punctures in the hull. Figure 8.1 (drawn by a famous New York City artist) has four bulkheads. If a bulkhead is compromised, the ship can remain afloat.

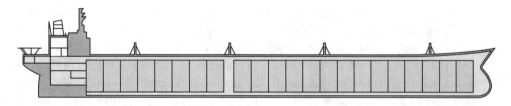

Figure 8.1   The SS *Not Titanic*. Bulkheaded compartments ensure that damage of one or more bulkheads doesn't take down the ship.

As the figure shows, if a bulkhead is compromised, water is prevented from flowing into another bulkhead, limiting the scope of failure. For the ship to sink, total failure, multiple bulkheads would have to fail.

The bulkheading pattern in CQRS can be demonstrated by a failure on the query (domain side) that precludes making any changes in an area of your domain. Because you've implemented the command side, all the data necessary to read the last known state of the domain is still available, and clients of that data are unaffected in terms of reads. We discuss bulkheading as it applies to CQRS later in this section.

Another aspect of segregation optimizes data writing versus reading. Rather than using a single pipeline to process writes (commands) and reads (queries), as in a monolithic CRUD application), CQRS implements two distinct paths: commands and queries, thereby achieving a measure of bulkheading.

This division shadows the Single Responsibility Principle (SRP), which states that every context (service, class, function, and so on) should have only one reason to change—in essence, a single responsibility. The single responsibility of the command side is to accept commands and mutate the domain within; the single responsibility of the query side is to provide views on various domains and processes to make client consumption of that query data as simple as possible. Through segregating and focusing on a single goal for each path, you can refine writes and reads independently. Also, you have bulkheading in that the command side functions independently of the query side, and any failures on one side don't directly affect the responsiveness of the other side.

Many applications have significant imbalances between reads and writes. Systems such as high-volume trading or energy may have a staggering number of writes in terms of trades or energy readings but much less viewing of that data, or at least the data is aggregated before it's read. The query side typically requires complex business logic in the form of *aggregate projections,* which are views on the domain(s) that usually don't look quite like the domain itself. An example is a view that includes customer information in detail, as well as order history and a list of sales contacts. The command side wants to persist. A single model encapsulating both tasks does neither well.

In figure 8.2, you see four CQRS command modules representing the sales, customer, inventory, and billing domains. Each domain is purpose-built to concentrate only on its narrow area of focus, with little concern about the other modules or how the data will be queried. The domain concerns are neatly modeled in each of the command modules; the Order to Cash query module handles all the heavy lifting required for presentation, which includes joining and pivoting the data to fit the client's needs. The Order to Cash query module is a first-class citizen in CQRS and exists solely to accumulate and return data across all the command modules.

In figure 8.2, you see that reads (queries) and writes (commands) follow their own discrete paths, independent of each other in real time, meaning that there's no connection between read and write data during reads and writes. Keep in mind that an asynchronous relationship exists between the command and query sides and the constant syncing up over time from the command to the query sides. The query data is

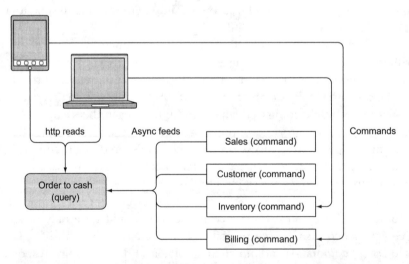

Figure 8.2 Two distinct paths: purpose-built domain and query modules focusing on a single duty

always waiting to serve the clients in the last known state, offering the highest performance and simplicity in terms of reads. The query store exists for the sole purpose of serving the clients; it may be built atop multiple domains or data feeds. Clients may use the read data to construct commands on the domains (command sides). Those commands are always sent to a single command side and may result in a change to the query side, but in an eventually consistent, asynchronous manner.

Figure 8.3 shows how bulkheading applies to a CQRS system.

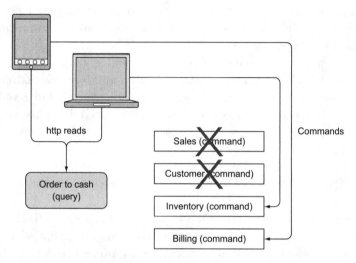

Figure 8.3   The natural bulkheading of CQRS. Two command modules are unavailable, but the rest of the system remains functional.

In figure 8.3, you see that the sales and customer command systems have gone down or become unavailable. The natural bulkheading that CQRS provides allows users full access to the data necessary to populate displays and issue commands, but those commands will fail against the systems that are down. You could queue up commands somewhere so that they don't fail, but this attempt is of little value, because the commands have no effect until the failed systems become available once again. A better design would be something like a redundant system to mitigate these situations. The main point is that the possibility of failure always exists; the best thing you can do is contain that failure in the best way possible.

8.3   *The C in CQRS*

The *command* side, sometimes called the write side, is about more than commands. It represents the domain only. Theoretically, the command side is never meant to be read directly.[2] The command side is tuned for high-throughput writes and may have

---

[2] Recent technologies such as Akka persistence allow in-memory domain state to provide simple and performant reads of the domain, but the lion's share of reads is left to the query side.

specific database and/or middleware selections for this purpose, differing from the query sides. In this chapter, we show CQRS with Event Sourcing, which is the most valuable pattern in our experience, but there's nothing to stop you from using CQRS alone when read and write separation is a requirement.

8.3.1   *What is a command?*

Before we define a command, review our definition of *message* from chapter 1: an immutable data structure used to communicate across service boundaries. One of the principal attributes of a reactive system is that it's message-driven. One type of message that allows message-driveness is a command. Commands are sent from clients or services to various other CQRS services.

A *command* is a request to do something, and that something usually is a request to change state. A command is imperative. Although it's authoritative in nature, it's a desire to have a system take an action, and as such, it may be rejected due to validation errors. Commands follow verb–noun format, in which the verb is the action requested and the noun is the recipient of that action. Following are two typical commands:

```
CreateOrder(...)
AddOrderLine(...)
```

8.3.2   *Rejection*

Rejection is an important concept in a CQRS system, but it can be confusing in dealing with the notion of a command. Because commands are authoritative in nature, acceptance is often assumed, because a command is an imperative delivered by the authority. As we mentioned earlier in this chapter, in the context of CQRS, a command is more a request than an order, so the recipient is at liberty to reject it. Rejection generally is the result of some form of business-rule violation or attribute-validation failure. An example is the rejection of a `CreateOrder` command. This request might be rejected because the sender doesn't have the proper credentials to create orders or has an overdrawn credit line, for example.

As we discuss in chapter 4, the command handler on the command side is also an anticorruption layer on its associated domain. Another interesting aspect of a command is its structure, in that it may contain multiple attributes requiring validation. This structure presents an intriguing question: When rejection occurs, is one error at a time or a list of errors reported back to the sender? We explore the answer to this in section 8.3.7. Command validation comes with a cost in terms of performance, so it isn't used sometimes, as in cases of high-volume trading.

8.3.3   *Atomicity*

There seems to be overwhelming buy-in on the microservice paradigm, in large part because of the popularity of the Reactive Manifesto. The microservice paradigm dictates building many services, each doing a few focused things, which implies atomicity. *Atomicity* means that each service solves a particular problem without knowledge of or concern about the internal workings of other services around it. This philosophy falls in comfortably with the Reactive Manifesto, so much so that it could easily be the fifth pillar.

Atomicity allows solutions to smaller problems. The smaller the problem and the larger the isolation of that problem, the easier it is to solve. Try to avoid cross-cutting concerns in your service code. If an external concern or edge case tries to work into your service, find a way to handle such cases elegantly and in a nonspecific way. Consider a service that applies discounts for books. One business case applies a greater discount if the book is bought in a store rather than online. Rather than add the ability to track whether any particular book was bought in a store, you could support this functionality in a more abstract manner, such as by adding a discount attribute that's not coupled to the external functionality that caused the discount—only the result. This sort of abstract design leads to a more open core behavior in your service and leads to less coupling.

8.3.4 *Jack of all trades, master of none*

Everyone is familiar with the saying "jack of all trades, master of none," which refers to a person who has a broad variety of skills but isn't particularly proficient in any skill. In many ways, this adage is apropos for CRUD-based solutions. In chapter 1, we explored a monolithic shopping cart example comprised of several services. Digging deeper into that design by looking at an individual service, you see why this design is a jack and not a master (figure 8.4).

In figure 8.4, all things related to orders are in a single monolithic application for the sake of transactionality, built with the traditional RDBMS techniques, resulting in subsystems being tied at the hip because they interact in some way. This application won't scale, and if one piece breaks, everything is broken.

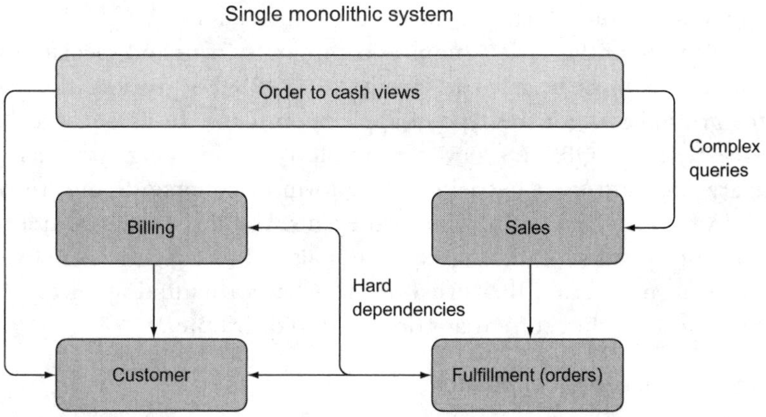

Single monolithic system

| Order to cash views |

Complex queries

| Billing | | Sales |

Hard dependencies

| Customer | | Fulfillment (orders) |

Figure 8.4 Detailed view of a monolithic order service; domains with hard dependencies on other domains in the same application instance

Within the order's functionality in figure 8.4 is a single domain aggregate representing `Orders`. Against this object, you action the three command behaviors (create, update, and delete) and the query behavior (read). The problem is that domain aggregates are designed to represent current state and aren't particularly conducive to data projections (queries). Usually, when projecting data, you need some form of aggregation, as you want to see more than the order on the screen. As a result, you have to rely on building data access object (DAO) projections off the aggregate, which in turn require dynamic querying based on underlying SQL joins. This design is messy at best and becomes a continual point of refactoring for query optimization. In the end, you're trying to use the aggregate for more than its design supports.

8.3.5 *Lack of behavior*

A major, costly area of pain in typical monolithic applications (typically, CRUD-based) is the absence of data needed to derive intent. We discuss this topic in detail in chapter 1, but it's important to review this topic, which is an area in which CQRS/ES shines. With CRUD, you have four behaviors: create, read, update, and delete. These behaviors are summary in nature, designed to modify current state models; they lack the historical deltas required for capturing purpose. This loss of intention has a significant effect on the value of business data, as you're unable to determine user motive, which is paramount to understanding the user base. In using CRUD models, you effectively throw away massive amounts of data.

To better understand your users' needs, you must be able to create a profile of their use habits so that you can accurately anticipate their future requirements. Creating this profile requires a detailed view of the actions that led up to a particular decision made by a user. Data capture at this level allows you to not only predict users' future needs, but also answer questions that haven't yet been asked (see chapter 1). Additionally, you can aggregate these results across your entire user base to discover all kinds of patterns related to the context of your system. In essence, this approach provides the bounty from which you can do Big Data analysis.

Building a system of this variety requires component focus and specialization. Your system components must be masters, not jacks. CQRS/ES provides the philosophy and lays the groundwork for this type of application focus. To demonstrate the focus and specialization of CQRS/ES, devise a simple order tracking system. Define the domain aggregates and their behavior in the form of commands, and record those behaviors (if valid) in the form of historical events. You'll see that you not only have access to the current state of the aggregate, but also can derive the state for any time in the past up to now. From this structure, you have a natural audit log, can infer motive, and have an architecture that's designed to distribute.

8.3.6 *Order example: the order commands*

This section looks at a familiar construct called an order. You've seen it before, which theoretically makes it easier to grasp what's different in CQRS. If you want a more interesting domain, look at the flight domain in chapter 5 or read later chapters.

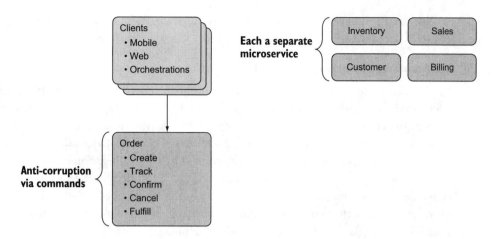

Figure 8.5   The new order domain, separated from other domains

An order domain would look something like figure 8.5.

You see the order domain as a separate and atomic service. The only way to inter-act is via commands sent to the service by HTTP, but any other transport protocol can do the job. How does the order service interact with the other services in the top-right part of the figure? They also receive commands and also emit meaningful business events. These events may consume services that trigger their own events.

The order commands functionally mutate the order, but technically, no object mutation occurs, because immutable objects are first-class citizens of a reactive appli-cation. The commands should be as granular as possible, because the events derived from those commands are the building blocks of the event-driven nature of your applications. The `ChangeOrder` command, for example, would result in an `Order-Changed` event. This event provides no business insight into what happened to the order, so any other system that consumes order events must consume every `Order-Changed` event and interrogate it to determine whether the change of the order is of interest.

A better, more-expressive option is to break the events down as `OrderShipping-AddressChanged`, `OrderTotalChanged`, and so on. The commands appear as follows:

- `CreateOrder()`
- `ChangeBillingAddress()`
- `ChangeShippingAddress()`
- `PlaceOrder()`

As we discuss in chapter 5 (which covers domain-driven design), `Order` is the aggre-gate root and contains `OrderLine` entities. All access to the order lines is through the root: `Order`.

Now that you have the idea of commands in place, the next section looks at a clean way to ensure that those commands are valid.

8.3.7   *Nonbreaking command validation*

Nonbreaking validation is important to the responsiveness and usability of any microservice. Microservices that accept commands should validate those commands as an anticorruption layer and not allow pollution of the domain within. At the same time, you should embrace and expect failure; the clients of domains may not fully understand the ins and outs of the commands they're sending. You can return a positive acknowledgment that the command is accepted and do your best to process it and generate resultant events, or you can create a convenient set of failed validations. The client can inspect these validations, make the repairs, and send the commands again. This technique is especially valuable when teams are working in parallel, microservices are evolving, and quick code fixes can be made to speed integration. It's easier to deal with an in-your-face command failure than to try to read another team's documentation as its domain evolves.

We don't break, not ever, because we're building a reactive-responsive application. Not breaking means guarding against nulls, empty strings, and numericals versus text, as well as more complex structures that you can validate against a known set of valid values.

The example in listing 8.1 uses the Scalactic library. Implementation details may vary, but the contract is the important thing. Using REST over HTTP, you can express the contract for a command response as a 400-bad request containing a JavaScript Object Notation (JSON) list of the failed validations or a 204-accepted response, meaning that the command is considered valid and the system will make its best effort to process that command. This listing shows how you might implement some validation on an imaginary `Order` domain object.

Listing 8.1   Order validation

```
trait ValidationFailure {
  def message: String
}

case class InvalidId(message: String) extends ValidationFailure
case class InvalidCustomerId(message: String) extends ValidationFailure
case class InvalidOrderType(message: String) extends ValidationFailure
case class InvalidDate(message: String) extends ValidationFailure
case class InvalidOrderLine(message: String) extends ValidationFailure
case class InvalidOrderLines(message: String) extends ValidationFailure

object OrderType {                        ◁──┐ A structure you can validate
                                             │ order type against
  type OrderType = String

  val Phone = new OrderType("phone")
```

```
    val Web = new OrderType("web")
    val Promo = new OrderType("promo")
    val OrderTypes: List[OrderType] = List(Phone, Web, Promo)
}

import org.scalactic._
import Accumulation._
import OrderType._

case class OrderLine(
  itemId: String,
  quantity: Int
)

case class Order private[Order] (          ◄─────┐   The domain aggregate
  id: String,                                    │   for Order
  customerId: String,
  date: Long,
  orderType: OrderType,
  orderLines: List[OrderLine]
)

object Order {

  def apply(customerId: String, date: Long, orderType: OrderType, orderLines:
    List[OrderLine]): Order Or Every[ValidationFailure] =
    withGood(
      validateCustomerId(customerId),
      validateDate(date),
      validateOrderType(orderType),
      validateOrderLines(orderLines)
    ) { (cid, dt, ot, ols) => Order(UUID.randomUUID.toString, cid, dt, ot,
    ols) }

  private def validateId(id: String):       ◄─────┐   The default constructor is private, so you
    String or Every[ValidationFailure] =           │   can ensure proper validation upon creation
    if (id !=null && !id.isEmpty)                      by using apply in the companion object.
      Good(id)                                         All validations are performed and result
    else                                               in a call to the order's default constructor
      Bad(One(InvalidId(id)))                          (thereby creating the order and returning
                                                       it) or a collection of the failures.

  private def validateDate(date: Long): Long Or Every[ValidationFailure] =
    if (date > 0)
      Good(date)
    else
      Bad(One(InvalidDate(date)))

  private def validateCustomerId(customerId: String): String or
    Every[ValidationFailure] =
    if (customerId !=null && !customerId.isEmpty)
      Good(customerId)
    else
      Bad(One(InvalidCustomerId(customerId)))

  private def validateDate(date: Long): Long Or Every[ValidationFailure] =
    if (date > 0)
```

```
        Good(date)
      else
        Bad(One(InvalidDate(date)))


    private def validateOrderType(orderType: OrderType): OrderType Or
      Every[ValidationFailure] =
      if (OrderTypes.contains(orderType))
        Good(orderType)
      else
        Bad(One(InvalidOrderType(orderType)))

    private def validateOrderLines(orderLines: List[OrderLine]):
      List[OrderLine] Or Every[ValidationFailure] =
      if (!orderLines.isEmpty)
        Good(orderLines)
      else
        Bad(One(InvalidOrderLines(orderLines.mkString)))
}
```

> **Each validation may be made as elaborate as necessary. These validations are simple.**

Using the code in listing 8.1, you can try constructing an order a couple of times, once with valid attributes and again with a couple of invalid ones, as seen in the following listing.

Listing 8.2   Order validation demonstration

```
scala>
import com.example._
println(Order("cust1", 1434931200000L, OrderType.Phone,
    List(OrderLine("item1", 1))));
Good(Order(14bad175-0fd9-4710-aa5b-
    c75006dc1246,cust1,1434931200000,phone,List(OrderLine(item1,1))))
```

> **As you can see, the order is created successfully.**

```
scala>
import com.example._
println(Order("cust1", 1434931200000L, OrderType.Phone,
    List(OrderLine("item1", 1))));
Bad(Many(InvalidCustomerId(), InvalidOrderType(crazy order)))
```

> **The order is not created and the two validations are returned.**

Listing 8.2 shows embracing failure as a natural course of business via nonbreaking validation. It shows that clients are imperfect and that invalid data is expected but not allowed to pollute the domain. Instead, the code returns the validations cleanly to the client so that it may change its call properly.

8.3.8   Conflict resolution

Now that you have a means to break down and distribute your applications in terms of queries and commands, you need to pay attention to a small price to be paid, which is data consistency. To understand the problem, consider the following example. An aircraft at 5,000 feet of altitude is issued a command by the tower to reduce that altitude by 2,000 feet. Then that same aircraft is issued that same command by arrivals, which last understood the aircraft's altitude to be 5,000 feet. This sort of behavior could easily cause a catastrophe. To guard against this situation, include an expected aggregate version in each command. Only commands that match the expected version of the current aggregate version are processed. The problem is that an action (command) may be taking place on a domain aggregate based on a stale assumption about that aggregate. With a distributed application, special attention must be paid to aggregate versions. A version is established each time any part of the aggregate state is changed and that change results in one or more events being persisted to the data store, which may be called the event store on the command side. Each command is atomic from start to finish, meaning that if another command comes in, it's handled only after the previous one has mutated (changed) the aggregate state.

In the next section, we show you how to view all this wonderful domain data, now carved up into independent and atomic services, by using the query side (the Q in CQRS).

8.4 The Q in CQRS

In this section, we show you how to address the impedance mismatch between the read data and the domain data in which it derives. The asynchronous nature of updating the query data provides a clean separation from the sources of the data, with no interruption of any runtime behaviors on the command or query side. But there's a small price: this design is subject to inconsistency, in that there's always some delay between the current state of the domain(s) and the query stores that depend on them. The guarantee is that if all activity stopped in a series of connected CQRS systems, all data would eventually look the same, becoming *eventually consistent*. These stores are sometimes called *projections* of the domain. With CQRS alone, as opposed to CQRS with Event Sourcing, you don't prescribe how the changes to the command side affect any given query sides.

8.4.1 Impedance mismatch

When it comes to servicing clients of your systems, one of the first challenges you run into is object-relational impedance mismatch. Figure 8.6 should be easy for non-engineers to follow. Hook up a small hose to a large one, and when the water flowing from the source meets the greater resistance (impedance, in this case) of the smaller hose, water is forced back and lost via leakage farther upstream. In the figure, the leakage is in the large hose's connection to the faucet. The queries you need to view the data

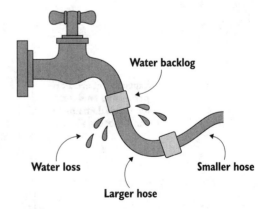

Figure 8.6 Impedance mismatch in water flow. A large hose feeds into a small one, resulting in undesired water flow in the opposite direction and water loss.

usually are a different shape from the data associated with the domain, which is also an impedance mismatch.

The term *impedance mismatch* comes from the electrical-engineering term *impedance matching*. In electronic-circuit design, *impedance* is the opposition to the flow of energy from a given source. The idea is that as one component provides energy to another, the first component's output has the same impedance as the second component's input. As a result, the maximum transfer of power is achieved when the impedance of both circuits is the same.

This impedance mismatch, when it occurs between read and write concerns, can be a significant challenge in standard CRUD relational applications. Object-oriented domain models that employ CRUD rely on techniques that encapsulate and hide underlying properties and objects. The problem results in CRUD semantics, requiring object relational mapping (ORM), which must expose the underlying content to transform to a relational model, thus violating the encapsulation law of object-oriented programming (OOP). Although this problem isn't the end of the world, it cripples your ability to distribute.

Figure 8.7 shows an impedance mismatch in software.

Using figure 8.7 as a reference, suppose that you want to view the entire order status to get an overall picture of the order, who sold it, what was bought, what was shipped, what cash was collected, and so on. Because the domains are nicely broken apart, even to the point of being separate services, this Order to Cash view doesn't exist—certainly not as a first-class citizen—within the diagram. The order status must be built on client demand by querying across all the necessary domains, which is an expensive operation that's hard to keep tuned, let alone scale. What's clearly missing

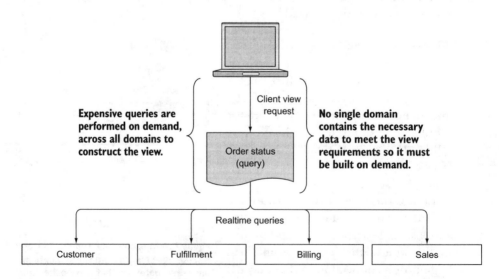

Figure 8.7   Impedance mismatch in software

is a query as a first-class citizen. This scenario demonstrates an impedance mismatch between the reality of the domains and the way that the clients desire to view them. As a large hose overwhelms a small one, trying to cobble together a client presentation in real time is problematic, leading not to water loss, but to loss in performance, risk, and errors.

8.4.2 What is a query?

A CQRS *query* is any read on a domain or a combination of domains. The associated domain data is considered to be a projection of the domain. A *projection* is a sort of picture of the domain state at a point in time and is eventually consistent with the events in which it's derived. The domain on the command side is rarely read directly but used to build up current state that clients can read quickly. In CQRS queries, no calculations are performed on reads; the data is always there, waiting to be read and indexed according to the client's needs. Storage is cheap, so different client data requirements mean multiple projections, avoiding antipatterns such as the additions of secondary keys, or, worse, table scans to search within projections. Query projections can be as simple as the latest state of any domain or as complex as data from different domains. Figure 8.8 shows the Order to Cash scenario, which also serves as a nice example of a query side.

In figure 8.8, you see the independent command sides of sales, customer, inventory, and billing asynchronously feeding the Order to Cash query module. By the time a client makes a call to view Order to Cash, all the data is built and waiting.

Now look at a simple projection of employee event data, assuming that the command side is using Event Sourcing (which we discuss in the next section). For this example, it's enough to understand that the example has no single representation of

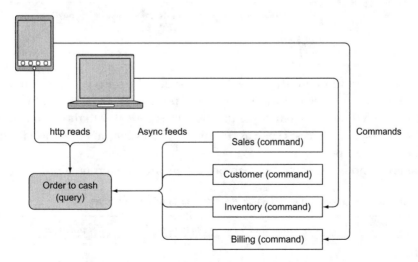

Figure 8.8   Order to Cash query side, constantly fed command-side events to build itself

an employee, but several events that tell the story of that employee from start to finish. In this story, an employee has been hired, had his pay grade changed, and was terminated. The example uses a *query projection*, which is a static view on the employee to show his current state at any given time. The domain doesn't represent the current state of the employee; it shows a series of events occurring on that employee over time. Suppose that human resources required a view that shows all nonterminated (active) employees. Use JSON to express the contents of the event data for ease of reading. The reason is that different events of a single domain are usually written to the same event log/table, so that each one has a different footprint, and these differently formatted events don't lend themselves to tabular presentation.

Table 8.1 shows events occurring on a single employee over time.

Table 8.1   Events that have occurred on the employee aggregate

1	`EmployeeHired({"id":"user1","firstName":"Sean",` `"lastName":"Walsh","payGrade":1,"version":0})`
2	`EmployeeNameChanged({"id":"user1","lastName":"Steven","version":1})`
3	`EmployeePayGradeChanged({"id":"user1","payGrade":2,"version":2})`
4	`EmployeeTerminated({"id":"terminationDate":"20150624","version":3})`

The read projection of this employee is indexed on the employee's ID and contains all employees, although this example illustrates only one.

After the third event, `EmployeePayGradeChanged`, the projection appears as shown in table 8.2.

Table 8.2   The read projection of the employee *before* the termination occurs

ID	lastName	firstName	payGrade
user1	Steven	Sean	2

After all events through `EmployeeTerminated`, the query projection is empty because this user no longer exists in the eyes of the consumer. Note that the event logs still exist, even though the employee functionally is gone due to the termination. This data is valuable for use cases such as rehiring as well as for data retention for employment compliance purposes.

Table 8.3 shows the employee read projection after the termination.

Table 8.3   The read projection of the employee *after* the termination occurs

ID	lastName	firstName	payGrade
...crickets			

Because this query is constantly being updated in the background, data is always hot, ready and waiting to be read. This asynchronous building of the read data in the background does away with much of the pain of impedance mismatch. In the next section, we review that pain.

8.4.3 *Dynamic queries not needed*

In CQRS queries, data is aggregated asynchronously and is always ready and waiting. The difference in user experience is sometimes staggering with the reduced latency of the CQRS approach; the screens render in the blink of an eye. What you see is what you get. No magic happens at query time. The data is a certain size and shape in the database, and that size and shape are exactly what the client receives, although it's marshaled to JSON and so on. This distinct design of the read side makes it easy to support, track down anomalies, and debug applications without digging through and debugging code.

Because we're beating CRUD to death in this chapter, we'll give it one last kick in the teeth. In the world of CRUD, queries become expensive to run and maintain, and sometimes require constant tuning. In the old, monolithic world, it's common for clients to request aggregated domain data—domain data mashed up across multiple domain contexts. Attempting to get at this data at runtime is ridiculous; we know because we've done it, and it was a significant source of problems. This pattern requires presentation to domain tier adapters that make multiple calls to the back end domain to create aggregated data transfer objects (DTOs). Another pattern is to make SQL/NoSQL requests to the database directly from the presentation tier, bypassing the domain. If you design your systems this way, they're closely coupled and can't be distributed.

8.4.4 *Relational versus NoSQL*

Most of us have used relational (SQL) databases at some point in our careers, and those databases have worked well. You can use SQL for Event Sourcing as well as the CQRS query side, but the concrete column model (in which every column and its type is known at design time and enumerated in a table) is inflexible compared with NoSQL. NoSQL allows the storage of documents containing any number of attributes that need not be known at design time, making the construction of CQRS/ES systems much faster and more agile than the construction of relational models containing strict sets of table fields. With NoSQL, you can serialize an object and its varying fields to a table. The table may also contain multiple types of objects of differing sizes and shapes, making it easy to store all the events of a domain type. With SQL, you have to know the columns ahead of time and constantly maintain migration scripts when your event or read stores change over time—lots of overhead that you can avoid by using any of the excellent open source NoSQL solutions available today.

So far in this chapter, you've learned about the distinct paths of CQRS and seen the distinct nature of the command and query sides. How they relate is where Event Sourcing is a natural fit and sits atop CQRS nicely, as we discuss in the next section.

8.5   Event Sourcing

Event sourcing makes the source of all domain behavior the accumulation of the events that have taken place on that domain. No order is sitting in any database as part of the domain. The state of the order at any time is the accumulated playback of the events. It's possible to use Event Sourcing independently of CQRS, although the two are complementary, as commands can result in events. We've seen large clients in which the adoption of the message-driven architecture is too ponderous, given the legacy systems and infrastructure; sometimes, compromises must be made. In this chapter, we concentrate on the CQRS/ES combination.

8.5.1   What is an event?

An *event* represents something meaningful in the domain that has occurred and is usually in the past tense, such as `OrderCreated` or `OrderLineAdded`. Events are immutable in that they represent something that happened at a particular point in time and are *persistent*, meaning that they're stored in an event log such as a distributable database like Apache Cassandra. At any point in time, it's possible to witness the state of the domain by the ordered accumulation of the events through that point in time. These events even appear with deletes, which are also additive, like any other event. A delete doesn't occur as it would in CRUD; the event states that the domain object no longer exists at that point in time. Events are a cornerstone of being message-driven and are a great way to provide meaningful communication among microservices. Because it's possible to have a large number of events on some domains, increasing the amount of time it takes to replay the events to derive current state, there's the concept of the snapshot. We talk more later about replay and in-memory state as well as projections.

As you see in figure 8.9, an *order* is a sum of its events over time.

A single order is the sum of its events.

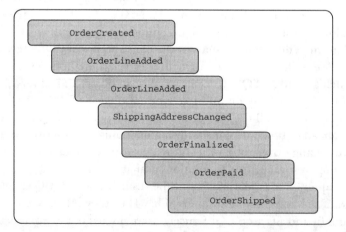

Figure 8.9   The events over time *are* the order.

Event Sourcing for the win!

In spring 2014, many technical dignitaries presented at the PhillyETE conference. On that occasion, we went to dinner with a group including people from Typesafe and Dr. Roland Kuhn, head of the Akka team. Greg Young walked in, still wearing his name tag, so we had the pleasure of meeting him and joining in some discussions.

We talked about CQRS and Akka, and about how we implemented command sourcing for some of our microservices. He blasted us for that practice for several reasons, most notably use cases involving one-time-only actions associated with commands such as a credit card transaction that would never be repeated with the playback of events. At this point, Roland and I challenged Greg, and by the end of the conversation, Roland and the Akka team decided to remove virtually all references to command sourcing from Akka Persistence documentation and to embrace Event Sourcing only. Pretty cool!

SNAPSHOTS

If you have a domain with millions of events, materializing state on that domain is non-performant; the answer is snapshotting. *Snapshotting*, which involves separate storage from the event log, is the periodic saving of the state of the entire domain. *Replay* is the full or partial rebuilding of state based on event history. On replay, the snapshot is the first thing retrieved; all events that occurred after the snapshot are replayed atop it.

Consider an energy-industry example. Various energy readings come into a domain representing a large industrial battery. Each second, a reading comes in for charge and discharge kilowatts. The state of the battery includes its kilowatt hour capacity. These events add and subtract from that state. Every day, a snapshot is saved to the database so that all events need not be replayed.

REPLAY AND IN-MEMORY STATE

Replay is ordered retrieval of the snapshots and events stored in their storage mechanisms. Implementing replay is as easy as doing a read of the latest snapshot from one table, querying all the events that have taken place since the snapshot, and having the domain object apply those events one by one. Akka persistence has an elegant solution to this problem, as replay and snapshotting are built in. You model the domain, such as an order, as a persistent actor. When the actor is instantiated, Akka persistence automatically sends the snapshot and all the appropriate events to the actor as messages. From there, materializing the current state is a simple matter of building up private state within the actor from those messages. This state functions as a projection of the order and may be queried on in a performant, distributed manner.

Replay is an important aspect of Event Sourcing, in that there are no guarantees that all produced events will be received and successfully processed for every consumer. No true reliable messaging exists among so many moving parts—hence, the need for replay to rebuild application state when in doubt.

Another valuable application of replay is seeding data. Microservices normally can't be guaranteed to have the same up and down time as the services with which they interact. Seeding provides the ability to catch up on all the events a service missed upon coming back online, as well as when the new service is spun up for the first time in an environment. Replay to the rescue!

8.5.2   *It's all about behavior*

With Event Sourcing, events mimic real life, and no behavior is lost. At some future point, it's possible to answer questions that the business hasn't even yet asked. Events capture the true in-sequence behavior in the domain that map to real life. When you look at the concept of CRUD, you see a nonbusiness set of operations: create, read, update, delete. These operations aren't meaningful behavior; fortunately, you can leave them behind in favor of explicitly expressing your domain via events.

8.5.3   *Life beyond distributed transactions*

What are you going to do without trusty ACID transactions, in which an update to an order could contain an update to a customer as a single unit? These transactions have been convenient to use to ensure multiple operations, using ORMs and paying a high penalty in terms of distribution. It turns out that these cross-boundary transactions aren't necessary most of the time. You should carefully think through service-level agreements (SLAs) in the rare cases in which ordered transactions must occur as a single unit. In most cases, you can rely on eventual consistency across microservice boundaries in place of traditional transactions. Too often, strong consistency is the default in application design. When consistency is your go-to choice, you're choosing it over availability, making this default expensive. Making this choice is like putting your hands up in the bank in case it gets robbed.

In situations that require stronger consistency, you can employ the Saga Pattern (discussed in chapter 5). This pattern is implemented with the Process Manager Pattern in Akka. With this pattern, it's possible to perform a sequence of commands or other messages across different contexts in the form of an orchestration. The pattern is a state machine, so each state has recovery logic in case of failure.

8.5.4   *The order example*

In this section, you model your domain as a CQRS/ES command side by using an Akka persistent actor. You see how to ensure consistency of the order domain by using versioning, as well as examples of modeling the domain state, commands, and events.

Because domain state is a function of events occurring over time, it's usually necessary to model the most current state of the domain exclusive of any consistency scheme (the guaranteed latest state.) You can approach this model by using a distributed database such as Cassandra and by using a *read projection*, which is a picture of the current state stored in the database. That state, however, is eventually consistent and doesn't include the most current state guarantee.

To attain the most guaranteed view of current state, use Akka persistence to model your domain. When you use a single persistent actor in an actor cluster to represent a single domain object, that actor may contain the current state and can be the single point of access to that domain object. When you use actors in this way, you get caching for free because the actor can contain mutable internal variable(s) that it updates upon each new or replayed event. This mutable state is acceptable because it's completely internal to the actor, and, therefore, thread-safe. The materialization of state inside the actor allows in-memory reads of that current domain state that may be used in orchestrations across domain objects. These actor implementations are also singletons (there is only ever one in the running system for any given aggregate), so there is no danger of contention while the aggregate is making a decision during command processing.

In the following listing, you see how to model state by using an Akka persistent actor. The code illustrates state management of an order aggregate modeled as a persistent actor.

Listing 8.3 Persistent order actor

```
package com.example

import java.util.UUID
import akka.persistence.PersistentActor
import org.scalactic._
import Accumulation._
import OrderType._

object OrderActor {
 object OrderType {
   type OrderType = String
   val Phone = new OrderType("phone")
   val Web = new OrderType("web")
   val Promo = new OrderType("promo")
   val OrderTypes: List[OrderType] = List(Phone, Web, Promo)
 }

 case object CommandAccepted

 case class ExpectedVersionMismatch(expected: Long, actual: Long)

 case class CreateOrder(
   id: UUID,
   customerId: String,
   date: Long,
   orderType: OrderType,
   orderLines: List[OrderLine])

// The add order line command.
 case class AddOrderLine(
   id: UUID,
   orderLine: OrderLine,
   expectedVersion: Long)

 case class OrderCreated(
  id: UUID,
```

Companion object for the order actor for neat encapsulation

A simple acknowledgment object signifying that command is accepted

The create and add order line commands

Any command must specify the last known version of the order.

The order created and order line added events

```
          customerId: String,
          date: Long,
          orderType: OrderType,
          orderLines: List[OrderLine],
          version: Long)

        case class OrderLineAdded(
          id: UUID,
          orderLine: OrderLine,
          version: Long)
      }

      class OrderActor extends PersistentActor {
```

This actor has a single instance in the cluster.

```
        import OrderActor._

        override def persistenceId: String = self.path.parent.name + "-" +
            self.path.name
```

The internal state of the actor, changed each time a command is processed

```
        private case class OrderState(
          id: UUID = null,
          customerId: String = null,
          date: Long = -1L,
          orderType: OrderType = null,
          orderLines: List[OrderLine] = Nil, version: Long = -1L)

        private var state = OrderState()
```

The receive to use when the order hasn't been created, which would result in the initial state of the order

```
        def create: Receive = {
          case CreateOrder(id, customerId, date, orderType, orderLines) =>
            val validations = withGood(
              validateCustomerId(customerId),
              validateDate(date),
              validateOrderType(orderType),
              validateOrderLines(orderLines)
            ) { (cid, d, ot, ol) => OrderCreated(UUID.randomUUID(), cid, d, ot, ol,
        0L) }
            sender ! validations.fold(
              event => {
                sender ! CommandAccepted
                persist(event) { e =>
                  state = OrderState(event.id, event.customerId, event.date,
        event.orderType, event.orderLines, 0L)
                  context.system.eventStream.publish(e)
                  context.become(created)
                }
              },
              bad =>
                sender ! bad
            )
        }
```

With successful validation, you can store the event and perform any side-affecting logic, such as emitting the event to interested parties via the event stream, transitioning to the new command handler, and updating the state.

The created handler handles commands other than creation. This line illustrates the add order.

```
        def created: Receive = {
          case AddOrderLine(id, orderLine, expectedVersion) =>
            if (expectedVersion != state.version)
```

```
              sender ! ExpectedVersionMismatch(expectedVersion, state.version)
          else {
            val validations = withGood(
              validateOrderLines(state.orderLines :+ orderLine)
            ) { (ol) => OrderLineAdded(id, orderLine, state.version + 1) }
            .fold(
              event => {
                persist(OrderLineAdded(id, orderLine, state.version + 1)) { e =>
                  state = state.copy(orderLines = state.orderLines :+
        e.orderLine, version = state.version + 1)
                  context.system.eventStream.publish(e)
                }
              },
              bad => sender ! bad
            )
        }
    }

  override def receiveCommand = create

  override def receiveRecover: Receive = {
    case CreateOrder(id, customerId, date, orderType, orderLines) =>
      state = OrderState(id, customerId, date, orderType, orderLines, 0L)
      context.become(created)
    case AddOrderLine(id, orderLine, expectedVersion)            =>
      state = state.copy(orderLines = state.orderLines :+ orderLine, version =
      state.version + 1)
  }

  def validateCustomerId(customerId: String): String Or
      Every[ValidationFailure] =
    if (Option(customerId).exists(_.trim.nonEmpty))
      Good(customerId)
    else
      Bad(One(InvalidCustomerId(customerId)))

  private def validateDate(date: Long): Long Or Every[ValidationFailure] =
    if (date > 0)
      Good(date)
    else
      Bad(One(InvalidDate(date.toString)))

  private def validateOrderType(orderType: OrderType): OrderType Or
      Every[ValidationFailure] =
    if (OrderTypes.contains(orderType))
      Good(orderType)
    else
      Bad(One(InvalidOrderType(orderType)))

  private def validateOrderLines(orderLines: List[OrderLine]): List[OrderLine]
      Or Every[ValidationFailure] =
    if (!orderLines.isEmpty)
      Good(orderLines)
    else
      Bad(One(InvalidOrderLines(orderLines.mkString)))
}
```

Sets the initial command handler to the create partial function, the first state of the aggregate

receiveRecover builds up state from the events that took place in the past. There's no need to validate. Recovery is executed when the actor is instantiated by the cluster.

As you can see, Akka persistence provides an elegant way to handle all aspects of CQRS/ES domain design, including clean and nonbreaking validation and uncompromising data consistency. Next we look at consistency concerns that exist in the new world of CQRS/ES.

8.5.5   *Consistency revisited*

With the disconnect that exists between the query and command sides, which are now separate concerns, both query and command sides are message-driven and eventually consistent using events. Consistency becomes an important aspect to consider. Consistency describes the guarantees of how distributed data is propagated across distributed systems and prescribes the manner in which data is seen across partition boundaries. The three types of consistency used in computing are *strong consistency, eventual consistency,* and *causal consistency,* and we talk about them in the following sections.

STRONG CONSISTENCY

Strong consistency guarantees that all data is seen across all partitions, at the same time, and in the same sequence. Strong consistency is expensive and prevents you from distributing your applications. Surprisingly enough, strong consistency has been the go-to method of consistency in system development for some time. When you use database transactions with ORMs such as Hibernate, you get this level of consistency, but in most cases, no requirements dictate a need for this consistency. Think through any use of strong consistency carefully, because the only way to support this level of consistency is with close coupling of the related systems, which can lead to a monolith. We recommend that you never use strong consistency across distributed boundaries; the cost is too high.

EVENTUAL CONSISTENCY

Eventual consistency is cheap and easy to implement, and you should strive to make it your consistency mode of choice. With this method, your data eventually becomes consistent across partitions, but the timing and ordering aren't guaranteed. Make eventual consistency your first and (we hope) only consistency model. The typical flow of eventual consistency is for the CQRS command side to emit an event by using some bus, such as Akka cluster. On the read side of another microservice is an event listener actor that subscribes to that event over the Akka event stream. Upon receipt of any such message, that actor determines how the message affects the read projection(s) that it oversees and mutates those projections accordingly to match the latest state of the domain(s).

CAUSAL CONSISTENCY

Causal consistency is the second-most-expensive consistency model, and you should avoid it whenever possible, although you're likely to run into use cases that require it. Causal consistency guarantees that all partitions see the same data in the same sequence but not at the same point in time. Think of causal consistency as being an orchestration across your microservices/domains. In the next example, we show you an excellent pattern for this purpose, Process Manager.

8.5.6 *Retry patterns (reference reactive design patterns)*

In a distributed, reactive application, it's difficult and most likely impossible to have 100% reliable messaging, but you can do your best to make messaging as reliable as possible by using durable messaging (Kafka or RabbitMQ) or the delivery semantics in Akka cluster.

Akka messaging semantics allow you to retry message delivery between actors until the message is known to be delivered to the recipient. The following list describes these semantics:

- *At-least-once* is the least expensive retry method, requiring the sending side to maintain storage of outstanding messages. With at-least-once, the sender always tries to redeliver a message until a confirmation of receipt is received from the recipient. With this method, it's possible to deliver a message more than once, because the sender may be receiving but having difficulty sending the confirmation response.
- *Exactly-once* is the more expensive means of messaging, requiring storage on the sending and receiving sides. With exactly-once, a message is retried until it's received, and the recipient is guaranteed to process it only once.

Always use at-least-once if you can.

In the next section, we discuss command sourcing versus Event Sourcing.

8.5.7 *Command sourcing versus Event Sourcing*

Command sourcing is logging commands as the source of record rather than the events, and *Event Sourcing* is logging the events. Command sourcing creates a problem in that commands don't always result in a change of domain state and are rejected. Why would you want to have a rejected command as a central part of the domain? It doesn't make much sense unless you have a clear requirement to do so for audit purposes, and in such a case, the events should be logged as the source of record as well.

Another problem with command sourcing is that replay is an important part of CQRS/ES. Commands may trigger side effects such as a one-time credit card transaction, whereas the events occur after that logic and may be used to replay and rebuild domain state without any side effects. Replay of commands is complex and problematic, and should be avoided. Stick to Event Sourcing if you can.

Summary

- CQRS allows an easy way to be nonmonolithic, as reads are separated from writes, typically as separate applications.
- CQRS provides an easy way to bulkhead applications.

- Relational databases typically don't scale, due to transactionality.
- Event Sourcing provides a nice basis to be message-driven and ensures that no historical behavior is lost.
- Akka provides an elegant CQRS and Event Sourcing solution out of the box.
- Think carefully about your consistency models, and always lean toward the less-expensive option of eventual consistency.

A reactive interface

Now that you've seen how to build a focused microservice containing CQRS command or query functionality, how do you get at it? How does a client use these shiny new reactive applications? Now you need an interface for your service to allow its rubber to meet the road. The service interface (or API) is the way for clients as well as other services to interact with that particular service. In this chapter, we show you how to create a service interface using the most common reactive tools and standards. This chapter also shows you how to add a RESTful interface to your services and shows some basics such as authentication, logging, and bootstrapping.

9.1   *What is a reactive interface?*

The reactive interface is treated as the outer layer of the service, and the overwhelming go-to interface of choice these days is representational state transfer (REST) over HTTP. REST is a lightweight interface, typically using JavaScript Object Notation (JSON) as the payload of choice. Extensible Markup Language (XML) is sometimes used as well, but it's considered to be more verbose. This chapter focuses on servicing RESTful clients such as UIs and doesn't cover streaming as an interface. But streaming is becoming more common as a way to connect services and systems, and the subject can easily fill an entire book.

In the following two sections, we cover the API layer and the headless API.

9.1.1   *The API layer*

Reactive applications are reactive on all levels, including the API layer. The interface should be nonblocking and responsive. As it sits on a reactive, CQRS service, its command-side interface is whizzy fast, because the incoming commands are accepted in real time by the service and responded to immediately. The query side is equally fast; because reads of query data require no manipulation or joins, the data is returned immediately.

Though we concentrate on RESTful APIs in this chapter, you can sometimes get away with serialized object communication between services, especially when those services are running on the same Akka cluster. If you can use this type of communication, go for it, and eliminate the overhead of JSON marshaling in favor of friendly case classes.

9.1.2   *The headless API*

Headless API describes the need for every service to contain its own interface. Figure 9.1 shows a couple of services containing headless APIs. It's important for each service to be deployed and scaled independently, each having its own interface to the outside world. This interface provides access to the specific functionality of the service, but doesn't prescribe how the service data should be displayed or consumed. The separation of the consumption of the service from how the service data will be used is made possible by a headless API.

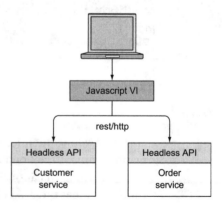

Figure 9.1   Customer and order services with headless APIs

In the past, you may have built applications that included a graphical user interface (GUI or UI). The UI design was closely coupled to the business logic implementations and in many cases contained embedded business logic. A headless API presents a specific area of functionality as an interface, such as REST, and leaves the business of UI presentation to the UI designers and coders, using JavaScript libraries such as Angular.js and Backbone.js. An example way of the past is a monolithic application that serves up all pages by using Java Server Pages (JSP), Java Server Faces (JSF), or some other back end UI mechanism from within the application itself. The headless API decouples the UI from the application, which frees front end developers to provide a pleasurable and interactive experience for users without regard to solving business problems. Likewise, the API layer—the application—has no concern about or interest in how its raw data is presented. The UI developers address the available service APIs to build the best, most responsive displays. The back end provides a lightweight RESTful interface, as shown in figure 9.2.

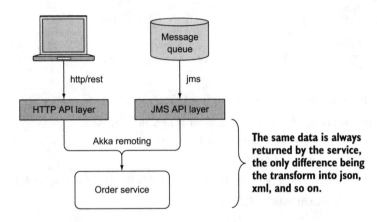

Figure 9.2 Incoming requests are converted to and from HTTP and JMS.

As you can see, the microservices have a distinct RESTful interface available for any consumer, such as the JavaScript client depicted in the figure. In the next section, we discuss REST and JSON in more detail, including how the interface typically appears.

You should look at RESTful or any other API as a layer that sits atop your service logic and functions as a dumb adapter to that service. It should be simple to pick one service interface, perhaps using message queuing instead of HTTP, with no difference in how that service performs its duty. Therefore, it's of the utmost importance not to include any business logic in the API layers. Transform incoming requests to requests that the service layer understands, such as a message to a service actor using a case class as the payload. The response from the service is likewise transformed back to the API protocol (`http/rest/json`) before the ultimate response to the client.

9.2 *Expressive RESTful interfaces*

REST and JSON have become the protocols of overwhelming choice for service interfaces using HTTP. REST gained popularity over Simple Object Access Protocol

(SOAP) and XML. SOAP is verbose and complex, and XML is quite verbose. REST and JSON offer a simpler and easier to use solution. SOAP was anything but simple and required a strict interface described with XML, contained in schema documents, to access a service. REST is much simpler. If there's an available RESTful service and you know how to call it, have at it. The payload within the JSON is free-form and may contain whatever attributes the server desires, which results in a great deal of flexibility.

The following sections illustrate the differences between the older use of XML and JSON, which is more commonly used today. These sections also show you how to create the most descriptive and intuitive interfaces with REST and JSON.

9.2.1   *JSON vs XML*

An example of a JSON payload for getting an order looks like this:

```
{"orderId": "12345", "status": "Shipped", "items": [{"itemId": 321, "name":
    "sink"}, {"itemId": 987, "name": "faucet"}, {"itemId": 756, "name":
    "drain"}]}
```

The JSON is readable once one understands a few concepts:

- Any object, such as `order` or `item`, is wrapped in braces.
- Collections of objects are wrapped in brackets.
- All attribute names are wrapped in quotes.
- Attribute values are wrapped in quotes for strings but not for numeric values.

Now compare the JSON with its XML counterpart:

```
<order><id>12345</id><status>Shipped</status><items><orderItem><itemId>321</
    itemId><name>sink</name></orderItem><orderItem><itemId>987</
    itemId><name>faucet</name></orderItem><orderItem><itemId>756</
    itemId><name>drain</name></orderItem></items></order>
```

You can see that the XML is a bit boilerplate and hard to read, whereas if you have a decent grasp of JSON, you can easily understand the JSON snippet. Imagine how unwieldy a complex data structure in XML can become.

HTTP headers are used in both requests and responses, describing the payload type as well as other metadata. When using JSON, you must set the `"Content-Type"` header to a value of `"application/json"`.

9.2.2   *Expressive RESTful interface URLs*

A good API in any language clearly expresses the intent and capabilities of any given call against the API. HTTP has been around for a while; it prescribes clear verbs and response codes for any given call, which you can use to standardize your RESTful APIs as much as possible. Following are the verbs you'll use most frequently:

- *POST*—A POST signifies that something new is being created. For something like adding a new customer order, use a post.

- *PUT*—A PUT means that you want to do an in-place modification of something that already exists, such as changing an order ship date.
- *GET*—A GET is a simple read of one or more things, such as orders. A get can contain query parameters (/orders?id=order1) or URL parts (/orders/order1). The latter URL style is preferred.
- *DELETE*—Use a DELETE when you want to delete something, such as a single order.

When you issue commands to command side services, use POST. CQRS applications use only POST or GET.

The response codes are important and should be used consistently for common purposes. These codes include

- *200/Ok*—Usually returned for successful gets.
- *201/Created*—The result of a successful post or put.
- *202/Accepted*—Signifies that the request will be processed, but doesn't guarantee the outcome. This code is used for the command side to accept commands and make a best effort to process those commands.
- *400/BadRequest*—Signifies that the URL is incorrect or a POST or PUT contained malformed or incorrect data. Use this code for returning failed command validations along with the JSON formatted reason(s).
- *401/Unauthorized*—Signifies that you don't have access to the URL.
- *404/NotFound*—Signifies that the GET resulted in no returned data found on the server.
- *500/InternalServerError*—The least friendly sort of response, which should be avoided if possible. As is the nature of reactive and all other applications, however, things sometimes fail.

9.2.3 Location

In practice, for create, read, update, and delete web applications, the URL for POST, PUT, and DELETE is the same; the only difference is the verb used in that URL. The best practice is to return the "Location" HTTP header upon a successful post. The value of that header is the URL representing the entity created for the client to access later. For an order, the header would look like this:

```
"Location": "/orders/order1"
```

The client would have knowledge of the server and would append the location to the server HTTP address. Returning only the relative URL as above is the best practice; the instance of the service needn't necessarily have knowledge of the host name or IP address leading to it, which could change at any time.

Now that you're familiar with the best and most expressive use of REST, look at some reactive RESTful library choices that are available.

9.3   *Choosing your reactive API library*

A great many Scala and Java libraries are available to serve up your RESTful HTTP services. In this section, we talk about the most likely candidates: Play, Akka HTTP, and Lagom. Lagom is new but appears to be the go-to framework for RESTful applications working together in a clustered environment; it firmly embraces CQRS and Event Sourcing in an opinionated fashion.

Lagom

Lagom is much more than a RESTful framework; it's a combination of everything we discuss in this book. *Lagom* is a Swedish word that means *not too big or too small*, which is a nod to how you should use domain-driven design to size a microservice. Lagom is an abstraction over Akka and Play that includes CQRS, Event Sourcing, Kafka as a messaging backplane, and Apache Cassandra as the default database. Any and all of these things may be overridden by other choices, but we believe that Lagom is the easiest way to build fully decoupled, reactive, and collaborative microservices that result in lower-cost manpower, maintenance, and hardware.

It isn't fair to compare Lagom with something like Spring, which is designed to build simple services that work independently. The problem is that distributed microservices need a well-understood way to provide a system of collaborative microservices. Designing these services to work together without being coupled is a tricky proposition that Lagom covers well. The unfortunate truth is that building systems that scale isn't as simple as building a system for a few users. Lagom provides the guard rails and abstractions that make this difficult task much easier.

9.3.1   *Play*

The Play open source framework (https://www.playframework.com) is mature and has powered many an enterprise at high levels of scale. We've had great success using Play in high-scale, high-throughput environments. For a large diet and wellness client, using a load balanced set of four instances of Play services, we migrated massive user data into the new generation of services by using Play backed by a Cassandra cluster, and saw around 12,000 POST requests per second. Not bad!

Play offers a slightly opinionated way of building a complete, production-ready service. Play takes away the hassle of inventing your own wheels for application layout, logging, configuration, localization, and health monitoring. Play is usually used to build stateless applications, containing any number of Play instances backed by a large database. In this scenario, the application state is contained in the database and must be read *before* being acted on. When the application nodes are stateless, the state is then contained in the database and this has implications for causal consistency concerns (when atomic ordered operations must be performed on the domain). Think through your use cases carefully before going stateless. You can use Play coupled with Akka Cluster to get atomic, in-memory state in the middle tier, but this method

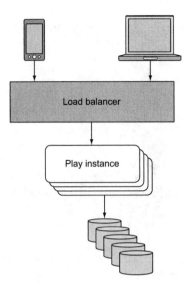

Figure 9.3   Play runtime footprint

requires some work, and you're probably better off using Lagom for such efforts. Lagom's applications are all clustered and take advantage of persistent actors to represent domain aggregate singletons. Figure 9.3 shows the typical Play application layout.

In the figure, the architecture is simple, with a load balancer handing off requests across all the Play instances. Each instance is backed by a large database cluster, such as Cassandra.

9.3.2   *Opinionation*

This topic deserves its own section. As software craftsmen at startups where we built new things, we shied away from opinionated frameworks as a rule to gain the utmost flexibility in choosing every aspect of our stack. We were building a complex Internet of Things (IoT) energy application and believe that our views were warranted for that time and place. Unfortunately, we were also building a framework instead of simply concentrating on our business cases. It's always better to use a framework to perform the technical heavy lifting, especially with the complexities of distributed applications.

The opinionated nature of Play (and, for that matter, Lagom) is good for most teams. With a less-opinionated library such as Akka HTTP, teams might build the same kinds of services in different ways.

9.3.3   *Application structure*

Play dictates a default folder layout. It's not recommended in most cases to change that default layout, because it's nice for a developer with Play experience to join a team and instantly recognize the project structure, which reduces onboarding headaches. The application structure is shown in figure 9.4.

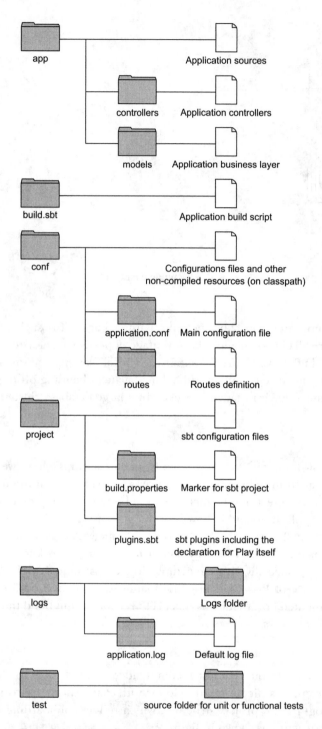

app   Application sources

controllers   Application controllers

models   Application business layer

build.sbt   Application build script

conf   Configurations files and other
                             non-compiled resources (on classpath)

application.conf   Main configuration file

routes   Routes definition

project   sbt configuration files

build.properties   Marker for sbt project

plugins.sbt   sbt plugins including the
                declaration for Play itself

logs   Logs folder

application.log   Default log file

test   source folder for unit or functional tests

Figure 9.4   Play application structure

Play has folder structures other than the ones shown in this figure, but they deal mostly with UI presentation, and you're not interested in serving up a UI as part of your service, only a headless API. This struture is the one you're most likely to use.

9.3.4 *A simple route*

The first thing you need to do to create any route is define your route in the routes file inside the conf folder. In this section, you build a simple route to handle an HTTP client's request to get all customer orders. The routes file appears as shown in the following listing.

Listing 9.1 Get-orders routes file

```
# Routes
# This file defines all application routes (Higher priority routes first)
# ~~~~
GET     /orders controllers.OrderController.getOrders
```

> You specify the URL that will handle the request to get all orders, /orders. Then you specify the controller and controller function to handle the request.

You can also define a URL parameter by using a colon followed by a descriptive name. These parameters are strings by default. To consume them as another type, such as int, you would specify the type to the right, such as getOrders(customerId: Int). Play does the mapping automatically.

Listing 9.2 shows an OrderController, but what is this madness? You're doing top-down design, so create that next layer: the controller. Controllers live in the controllers package. The order controller appears as shown in the following listing.

Listing 9.2 OrderController

```
package controllers

import java.util.UUID
import javax.inject._

import akka.pattern.ask
import play.api.mvc._
import models._
import akka.actor.ActorRef
import akka.util.Timeout
import play.api.libs.json.Json
import services.OrderService.GetOrders

import scala.concurrent.ExecutionContext
import scala.concurrent.duration._

class OrderController @Inject() (orderService: ActorRef)(implicit ec:
    ExecutionContext) extends Controller {

  implicit val timeout: Timeout = Timeout(5.seconds)
```

> The timeout is used against the ask (?) of the actor for the customer orders. This timeout may also be configured in application configuration.

This function maps to the routes file for get-orders. The customer UUID is automatically dealt with, and the argument is unmarshaled to the UUID by Play.

When using Play JSON, you must minimally create this implicit write so that Play knows how to output to JSON. This code is the most common and simplest way, but complex JSON output is also supported.

```
implicit def orderFormat = Json.format[Order]

def getOrders = Action.async { _ =>
  (orderService ? GetOrders)
    .mapTo[Seq[Order]]
    .map(res => Ok(Json.toJson(res)))
}
}
```

The implicit request object is passed in here, but you aren't using it, so ignore it for the get.

The compiler knows that there is a JSON marshaler in scope for that return type. The sequence of orders is returned and wrapped in the HTTP ok (202).

The ask of the actor isn't type-safe, so you must specify what response type is expected so that the response can be transformed.

9.3.5   Nonblocking service interfaces

The API should be nonblocking from start to finish, meaning that the only open socket/handle is held by the client. All service, database, and (heaven forbid) real-time service calls are done with nonblocking futures, whereas the results are processed asynchronously and when complete. *Futures* are scheduled computations that are to be carried out at some point, depending on resource availability. The computations that deal with the results of those futures are parked until the future has done its work. All threads associated with creating the future and dealing with the result are freed until the future gets access to the CPU and associated resources to complete its computation. Upon completion, the callback logic is allocated thread(s) to reactively complete their tasks by using the future results. A finite number of threads is available to your processes, and keeping those threads available allows your computing resources to scale to the maximum before you have to add hardware.

> **WEB SOCKETS**   It's possible to be completely nonblocking from the client using web socket technology to achieve callbacks from the UI to the back end. In practice, we've seen very little use of web sockets, although it would make for a more reactive experience for the UI; typically, the client blocks until the response is received.

The client (mobile device, PC, and so on) blocking is of much less concern than blocking at the server level, as the blocking will occur only on that device, which affects only that user. You may remember from chapter 1 that the Universal Scalability Law dictates that blocking of any kind will affect scale and make your application less reactive. If you're blocking, you can add hardware only to a point, and when you hit that point, any further hardware shows diminishing returns and reduces scale.

Now we'll show you nonblocking in practice, using order creation as an example. The client sends you a new order in JSON format. The service validates the `Create-Order` command and issues the command to the order service, where you stop and println an `OrderCreated` event. (Later in this chapter, you might see an order persistent actor instantiated as well as the persistence of the `OrderCreated` event to the database.) The following listing shows the simple order domain represented in a Scala package object.

Listing 9.3   Order domain objects

```scala
case class OrderLine(
  itemId: UUID,
  quantity: Int)

case class Order(
  id: UUID,
  customerId: UUID,
  orderLines: Seq[OrderLine])
```

The following listing shows the order service.

Listing 9.4   Order service

```scala
object OrderService {
  case object GetOrders

  case class CreateOrder(ustomerId: UUID, orderLines: Seq[OrderLine])
  case class OrderCreated(order: Order, timestamp: Long)
}

class OrderService extends Actor {

  val fakeOrders = Seq(
    Order(UUID.randomUUID(), UUID.randomUUID(),
      Seq(OrderLine(UUID.randomUUID(), 9))),          // The data returned is
      Order(UUID.randomUUID(), UUID.randomUUID(),     // dummy test data.
      Seq(OrderLine(UUID.randomUUID(), 3)))
  )

  override def receive = {
    case GetOrders          => sender ! fakeOrders   // The fake orders are
    case CreateOrder(order) =>                        // returned to the message
                                                      // sender on GetOrders.
      println(s"generating event: ${OrderCreated(newOrder(cid, lines), new
      Date().getTime)}")
  }
  // Upon receiving the CreateOrder command,
  // simulate the OrderCreated event in a println.
  def newOrder(customerId: UUID, orderLines: Seq[OrderLine]): Order =
    Order(UUID.randomUUID(), customerId, orderLines)  // Helper function to
}                                                     // create an order,
                                                      // generating a unique ID
```

The following listing shows the play routes file tying the URL to the controller function.

> **Listing 9.5   Play routes file**

```
GET     /orders controllers.OrderController.getOrders
POST    /orders controllers.OrderController.createOrder
```
Specify the routes you handle and map them to your controller functions.

Finally, the following listing shows the fully implemented order controller with JSON marshaling.

> **Listing 9.6   OrderController**

Play responds automatically with configured error response upon timeouts in communicating with the order service (such as InternalError).

```
class OrderController @Inject() (orderService: ActorRef)(implicit ec:
    ExecutionContext) extends Controller {

  implicit val timeout: Timeout = Timeout(5.seconds)

  implicit def orderLineFormat = Json.format[OrderLine]
  implicit def orderFormat = Json.format[Order]
  implicit def createOrderFormat = Json.format[CreateOrder]

  def getOrders = Action.async { _ =>
    (orderService ? GetOrders)
      .mapTo[Seq[Order]]
      .map(res => Ok(Json.toJson(res)))
  }

  def createOrder: Action[JsValue] = Action.async(parse.json) { request =>
    request.body.asOpt[CreateOrder].foreach { o =>
      orderService ! o
    }

    Future.successful(Accepted)
  }
}
```

These formats enable automatic marshaling and unmarshaling to JSON.

Return all orders asynchronously and wrap in Ok response the 200 HTTP code.

Create order attempts to extract the CreateOrder command and optimistically respond with Accepted. You can do more things, such as validation and a possible response with BadRequest, but we're keeping the listing simple.

You can see that building fully featured, reactive, and RESTful applications is quite simple with Play. In the next section, we look at Akka HTTP.

9.4   *Akka HTTP: a simple CQRS-esque service*

Another RESTful toolkit is a bit different from and more functional than Play. Akka HTTP is also a Lightbend open source product but comes from a different origin. Created by the spray.io team and labeled Spray, it was purchased by Lightbend and rewritten by the Akka team to better fit the overall Akka framework. Whereas Play is expressive, with strict definitions of routes that in turn point to functions to handle all URLs, Akka HTTP treats a service interface as being more of a chain of functions. A particular route is a function chain, but separate routes may be defined atomically, according to their areas of interest, and then themselves chained at the top level of the application. In figure 9.5, the step 1 and 2 routes are concatenated in step 3.

With Akka HTTP, gone are the opinionated ways of the Play framework; you're free to create your REST-based microservice in any way you see fit. The

```
1.   Val myGetRoute =
       path("hello") {
         get{
           ...
         }
     }

2.   Val myPostRoute =
       path("hello") {
         post{
           ...
         }
     }

3.   ... and at runtime startup
     val my Routes=myGetRoute-myPostRoute
```

Figure 9.5   Akka HTTP route modularity

use of either of these RESTful toolkits depends on the capabilities of the team as well as personal preference. Like Play, Akka HTTP includes a runtime and can act as a container, or you may use the container of your choice and use it as a library.

In this section, you dive into a complete web service using Akka HTTP and CQRS/ES semantics. You stop short of implementing any persistence or true service behavior, which is beyond the scope of this chapter, but you use a CQRS command for demonstration purposes. Following is a simple order domain. Note the use of Java UUIDs for unique domain identifiers; you'll see a lot of them. The order and its order lines may appear to be unfriendly, with these cryptic identifiers for customer, item, and order ID, but these are true domain objects that exist solely to satisfy the command and event behavior. Views may be modeled on the CQRS query sides that can present orders with other friendly attributes such as customer name and address.

The order service is an actor that receives CQRS commands as its message interface. In the real world, this service would use persistent actors to represent the orders, and the events would be persisted to an event store (database). Listing 9.7 shows the order service implemented as a simple Akka actor with a companion object containing its `CreateOrder` command as well as the `OrderCreated` event. The order service has the same behavior as the earlier Play example in listing 9.5.

Listing 9.7   OrderService

```
object OrderService {
  case object GetOrders

  case class CreateOrder(ustomerId: UUID, orderLines: Seq[OrderLine])
  case class OrderCreated(order: Order, timestamp: Long)
}
```

```scala
class OrderService extends Actor {

  val fakeOrders = Seq(
    Order(UUID.randomUUID(), UUID.randomUUID(),
      Seq(OrderLine(UUID.randomUUID(), 9))),
    Order(UUID.randomUUID(), UUID.randomUUID(),
      Seq(OrderLine(UUID.randomUUID(), 3)))
  )

  override def receive = {
    case GetOrders            => sender ! fakeOrders
    case CreateOrder(order) =>
      println(s"generating event: ${OrderCreated(newOrder(cid, lines), new
      Date().getTime)}")
  }

  def newOrder(customerId: UUID, orderLines: Seq[OrderLine]): Order =
    Order(UUID.randomUUID(), customerId, orderLines)

}
```

At this point, we show the HTTP interface for the service implemented in Akka HTTP. The trait contains only the logic it needs to satisfy the interface and interact with the service layer. The trait specifies the resources it needs, implemented by the wrapping implementation—in this case, the runtime object. You'll notice that this route handles only URLs prefixed with /order. The get and post are implemented inside that block. The post assumes that the JSON entity will be a new order and deserializes it as such. Also in the post, the preferred CQRS command semantics are to accept the command and return the status code reflecting receipt of the command only. Then the Create-Order command is invoked on the order service. There are no guarantees that the order will be accepted. In practice, you would validate the order first and possibly return failed validations with a bad-request status, but we're keeping the following listing simple.

Listing 9.8   OrdersRoute

```scala
trait OrdersRoute extends SprayJsonSupport with AskSupport {

  def orderService: ActorRef
  implicit def ec: ExecutionContext
  implicit def timeout: Timeout

  implicit val DateFormat = new RootJsonFormat[java.util.UUID] {
    lazy val format = new java.text.SimpleDateFormat()
    def read(jsValue: JsValue): java.util.UUID =
    UUID.fromString(jsValue.compactPrint.replace("\"", ""))
    def write(uuid: java.util.UUID) = JsString(uuid.toString)
  }

  implicit val orderLineFormat = jsonFormat2(OrderLine)
  implicit val orderFormat = jsonFormat3(Order)
```

State your resource needs of the order service, execution context, and timeout, which will be implemented in the bootstrapping in the next section.

Define the JSON format for the UUIDs, which is a bit tricky.

```
implicit val newOrderFormat = jsonFormat2(NewOrder)

val ordersRoute =
  path("orders") {
    get {
      complete((orderService ? GetOrders).mapTo[Seq[Order]])
    } ~
    post {
      entity(as[NewOrder]) { newOrder =>
        orderService ! CreateOrder(newOrder.customerId,
newOrder.orderLines)
        complete((StatusCodes.Accepted, "order accepted"))
      }
    }
  }
}
```

The rest of the order is quite simple in terms of the JSON protocol.

The path directive results in any URL to /orders being handled in the inner get or post routes.

The get of all orders is implemented as an ask to the service actor. The ask assumes that the service will respond to sender with a sequence of orders. Akka HTTP uses the Spray-JSON marshaling of the order and presents it as a JSON collection.

In the next section, we show you how to wrap up everything in a runtime and then start and run the application. We provide concrete implementations of all the abstract requirements in the trait, the order service, timeout, and execution context. This runtime object runs in an SBT terminal until any key is pressed. This technique is borrowed from the Akka documentation and is as elegant a way to stop the process as any. You point your route to the orders route set up in the trait you extended. This is a nice way of building composable routes that are concatenated at runtime. The result is a clean, modular design of your individual routes. See the following listing.

Listing 9.9   OrderWebService

```
object OrderWebService extends OrdersRoute {

  implicit val system = ActorSystem("order-system")
  override implicit val ec: ExecutionContext = system.dispatcher
  override implicit val timeout = Timeout(5.seconds)
  override val orderService = system.actorOf(Props(new OrderService))

  def main(args: Array[String]) {

    implicit val materializer = ActorMaterializer()

    val route = ordersRoute

    val bindingFuture = Http().bindAndHandle(route, "localhost", 8080)

    println(s"Serving from http://localhost:8080/\nPress any key to kill...")
    StdIn.readLine()
    bindingFuture
      .flatMap(_.unbind()) // trigger unbinding from the port
      .onComplete(_ => system.terminate()) // and shutdown when done
  }
}
```

Sets up a reactive stream flow on your actor for backpressure against faster or slower consumers

The host and port are bound to the HTTP process and run.

The sample code for this chapter includes everything above and does indeed run. We used postman to test it, and here are the payloads to play with, which use the URL http://localhost:8080/orders:

- The get route has no body. Be sure to set the `Content-Type` HTTP header to `application/json`.
- The post route can use the following JSON payload. Notice that the client provides only the customer and order lines; the `orderId` is generated by the service and results in a full order:

```
{
  "customerId": "e9adbed8-dae1-4d5b-92f0-2f056d3e4195",
  "orderLines": [
    {
      "itemId": "050dea2d-448b-4ae6-a128-a1d381e396d2",
      "quantity": 9
    }
  ]
}
```

As you can see, Akka HTTP is functional and can be as concise or spaghetti-like as you choose to make it. To make it as concise as possible, we recommend that you associate any single route with a specific CQRS command or query side.

Next, consider Lagom for your RESTful service needs.

9.5 *Lagom: the order example*

Lagom is a complete open source solution that builds not only web interfaces, but also fully reactive, scalable applications. Lagom was built in response to the widespread migration of monolithic applications to microservices and to support large scale. Lagom is also a solution to the difficulty of properly designing fully reactive application stacks and as such is highly opinionated. In Lagom's view (and indeed our own view), CQRS and Event Sourcing are the best ways to build these systems at scale. Lagom takes the opinionation even further by providing Cassandra database and Kafka messaging support for ease of development by default, embracing them as great choices for storage and distributed pubsub of events. Distributed pubsub is a great way for services to interact in a loose, coupled manner. Publishers of events need not know the subscribers and subscribers need not know where the events are coming from. Lagom is built atop years of reliability baked into Play and Akka, but provides abstractions to make the difficult less difficult. Like Play, Lagom allows code hot-swapping right in your IDE, so there are no costly compile/deploys between code changes. Even with the goal of making reactive applications as easy as possible, these applications aren't easy or simple. The fact is that the way you need to build applications today, supporting a sea of data due to the IoT is vastly different from the way you built things even 10 years ago. Systems are now more complex because of the amount of users and data, and that complexity is growing at a monumental pace.

NOTE In this chapter, we focus only on Lagom's RESTful capabilities. You can view the complete capabilities at http://www.lagomframework.com.

Lagom is yet another way to define your RESTful interfaces, with the controllers describing the routes they handle. Everything is in one place, and you don't have to keep two things in sync as you do in Play, with its routes file. The following listing illustrates the differences.

Listing 9.10 Lagom OrderService

```
class OrderService extends Service {
  val fakeOrders = Seq(
    Order(UUID.randomUUID(), UUID.randomUUID(),
      Seq(OrderLine(UUID.randomUUID(), 9))),
    Order(UUID.randomUUID(), UUID.randomUUID(),
      Seq(OrderLine(UUID.randomUUID(), 3)))       Again, return a fake collection
  )                                            ◁— of orders from this service.

  implicit val orderLineFormat: Format[OrderLine] = Json.format    ◁─┐
  implicit val orderFormat: Format[Order] = Json.format
                                                    These implicit formats
  def getOrders: ServiceCall[NotUsed, Seq[Order]] =   enable Lagom to marshal
    ServiceCall { _ =>                                  the order to JSON.
      Future.successful(fakeOrders)
    }
                                         The function call to back the
  override def descriptor = {         ◁— route returns the fake orders.
    named("orders").withCalls(
      restCall(Method.GET, "/orders/get-orders", getOrders)
    ).withAutoAcl(true)
  }                              ◁─┐
                                   The descriptor says what URLs you handle
}                                  and how they map to your functions.
```

You can see that even though Lagom is a complete framework that's capable of complex, distributed capabilities, the web-service aspect is simple and compact.

9.6 *Play vs Akka HTTP vs Lagom*

As you saw in the preceding listings, Akka HTTP is all code and no magic, which provides a great overall picture of an entire HTTP service. Indeed, the code in listing 9.10 is contained in a single file. It's easy to see the entire thing in a bird's-eye view, and there's less mystery in Akka HTTP than in Play, which does some of its magic at compilation and runtime by bringing routes and marshalers together. Akka HTTP demands more developer expertise but provides great flexibility. The choice comes down to the expertise and risk tolerance of your team and/or the system you're building. Lagom is sort of a hybrid as an entire web service, and its descriptor is in one file, but it feels more like Play than Akka HTTP does.

Play is a framework. The advantage of Play is that it makes standardizing your applications easier in terms of patterns and external libraries. This advantage is important in the following situations:

- You have a large team and not enough oversight or code review.
- Turnover and hiring top talent are issues.

In an environment like this one, it may be hard for more aggressive developers to swallow the entire drink. They may want to swap out pieces of the framework in favor of what may be new, cool, or even better. Pressure may be applied on those developers, resulting in stagnation of the code dependencies, which may lead to turnover.

Lagom is a framework, but an opinionated one that prescribes not only how best to build your headless API, but also how to build a distributed microservice by using CQRS and Event Sourcing. If you want to build individual microservices as part of a cohesive collection of microservices adhering to the standards explained elsewhere in this book, we urge you to look at Lagom.

Table 9.1 illustrates the differences among these frameworks. You'll notice that it covers the overall features rather than only the RESTful ones.

Table 9.1   Comparing Akka HTTP, Lagom, and Play

Feature	Akka HTTP	Lagom	Play
Functional design	Yes	No	No
Self-contained	Yes	Yes	No-need routes file
CQRS	Yes-no guardrails	Yes	No
Event Sourcing	Yes-no guardrails	Yes	No
Default Kafka integration	No	Yes	No
Default Cassandra Integration	No	Yes	No
Stateful domain	Yes	Yes	No

Summary

- RESTful interfaces are a clean, common way to have a headless API for your services.
- HTTP paired with JSON provides an expressive means of accessing your services, as well as describing their capabilities.
- The three top choices for serving up reactive, RESTful applications are Play, Akka HTTP, and Lagom.
- RESTful interfaces interact with the CQRS command side in terms of responses and validation presentation.
- Lagom is an opinionated framework for building systems of cooperative microservices using domain-driven design, CQRS, and Event Sourcing.

Production readiness 10

If you've read this far into the book, congratulations! You know how to design an application that's responsive, elastic, resilient, and message-driven. The next step is ensuring that those reactive design properties turn into real behavior when the application enters the turbulent world of a production system.

In the past, the gap between development and operations has been vast, sometimes with disastrous results. The modern answer is DevOps, which aims to close that gap with a combination of cultural change, integrated tooling, and automation. Covering the whole scope of DevOps is far beyond the scope of this book, but most of what applies to DevOps in general applies to reactive applications as well.

In this chapter, we look at some areas in which reactive applications differ in operation from other architectures, and we suggest a few things that you, as a developer, can do to make those applications easier to manage in production.

227

As is so often the case in modern development, we start with testing.

10.1   *Testing a reactive application*

Actors are message-driven, so the one thing you know about every actor is that it receives messages. It might even react to a message at some time in the future—maybe. That's not much of a basis for writing tests, is it?

Recognizing common patterns of actor behavior makes designing tests easier. When you've identified the behavior that needs to be tested, you can apply corresponding patterns for testing. The Akka `TestKit` can help with common patterns.

10.1.1   *Identifying test patterns*

Actors that react to receiving a message by causing some side effect, such as writing to a database, may be tested synchronously by passing them a message and observing the result on the external object. One approach is to instantiate the actor and call the `receive` method directly. That approach omits initialization steps, which can be difficult to get right and can lead to an erroneous test. Instead, as shown in figure 10.1, create a `TestActorRef` for the actor being tested and the details will be handled for you. The test case sends a message to the actor being tested, much as in the final application. After the message is sent, the test case uses assertions on the external object to verify that the test produced the expected result.

A similar situation arises when the actor reacts to a message by changing some internal state, as shown in figure 10.2. As with the side-effecting case just described, the solution is to create the actor by using a `TestActorRef`. Again, the test case sends a synchronous message to the actor. The difference is that the test case needs access to

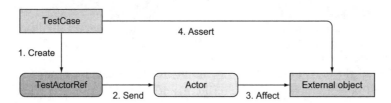

Figure 10.1   Actors with external side effects can be tested with traditional assertions on the affected object.

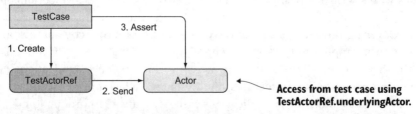

Figure 10.2   If the expected reaction is to change internal state, the assertion can obtain a reference to the underlying actor.

the actor too, rather than just an `ActorRef`. The underlying actor is available as a property of the `TestActorRef`. The test case uses assertions on the underlying actor to confirm that the internal state changed as expected.

An actor that returns a `Future` by using the *ask* pattern also can be tested by means of a `TestActorRef`, as shown in figure 10.3. Because this test is synchronous, the ask is executed on the same thread as the test case, and the `Future` is completed immediately. The test case can use `Future.get` and check assertions on the result.

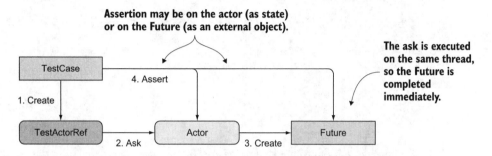

Figure 10.3   A TestActorRef can test the ask pattern by inspecting the completed Future it returns.

10.1.2 *Testing concurrent behavior*

All the previous cases use a `TestActorRef` to test the actor synchronously. It would be better to perform tests asynchronously, however, by sending a message to the actor and having it produce another message. Asynchronous tests can use the Akka `TestKit`.

Asynchronous request-reply is a common pattern in actor systems. An actor receives a message, and the sender expects a reply. Often, the sender is another actor, but for testing, the sender can be the test case itself. Do this by extending `TestKit` with the `ImplicitSender` trait, as shown in Figure 10.4. The `TestKit` expects an actor system to be passed to the constructor and uses the actor system to execute the actor asynchronously. The `ImplicitSender` trait ensures that replies from the actor are sent back to the test case.

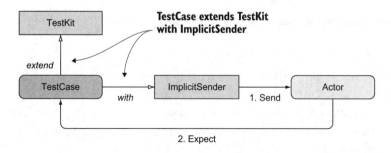

Figure 10.4   Use the TestKit to specify an expected reply.

Because the actor is executing asynchronously, time becomes a factor in the tests. The `TestKit` can enforce expectations for how quickly or how slowly the actor responds; it even allows for a scaling factor to account for the speed of the test server.

Cleaning up after a test

When a test specification extends `TestKit`, it passes an `ActorSystem` to the constructor. Be sure to shut down that `ActorSystem` at the end of the test, like this:

```
import akka.actor.ActorSystem
import akka.testkit.TestKit
import org.scalatest.{BeforeAndAfterAll, Matchers, WordSpecLike}

class TestMyActor extends TestKit(ActorSystem("TestSystem"))
  with WordSpecLike with Matchers with BeforeAndAfterAll {

  override def afterAll {
    TestKit.shutdownActorSystem(system)
  }
}
```

If the actor system isn't shut down, the test actors continue running and eventually consume all the system resources.

If the receiving actor reacts by sending messages to other actors rather than replying only to the sender, consider using two instances of `TestProbe` to stand in for the sending and receiving actors, as shown in figure 10.5. This class extends `TestKit`, allowing it to send, receive, and reply to messages and to create assertions about the messages it receives.

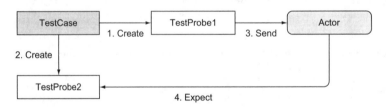

Figure 10.5   Use TestProbes in place of multiple ActorRefs.

Finally, integration testing may require having multiple complete actor systems exchanging messages. Each `TestProbe` accepts an `ActorSystem` as a constructor parameter, so one approach is to execute the two actor systems in the same Java virtual machine (JVM). If this approach isn't sufficient, and you need multiple JVMs, consult the latest documentation for `akka-multi-node-testkit`.

10.2 Securing the application

Any time one system connects to another, you must consider undesired communication as well as desired. Securing an application involves much more than just enabling HTTPS and calling it done; the process starts with knowing how to identify the threats.

In the past, security was often treated as an afterthought. More recently, well-publicized breaches have increased the focus on securing applications. The principles that apply to securing reactive applications are no different from those for securing traditional applications. The key is to take a disciplined approach to managing the threats and their corresponding mitigations.

In this section, you learn about the STRIDE approach, and you see how to use boundary services and HTTPS to counter some of the threats you identify.

10.2.1 Taking threats in STRIDE

When security professionals evaluate an application, they often use a threat-classification scheme called STRIDE. This system was developed by Microsoft, and not surprisingly, the name is an acronym for different threat categories:

- *Spoofing identity*—Performing an action by using another user's identity
- *Tampering with data*—Changing data as it's being processed or after it's stored
- *Repudiation*—Denying that a user has performed some action
- *Information disclosure*—Accessing information without proper authorization
- *Denial of service*—Preventing a system from servicing valid requests
- *Elevation of privilege*—Gaining access to more-powerful operations than intended

It's important to be systematic. Examine each interface in the system, and for each interface, ask questions about all six components of STRIDE. Keep track of your work. Figure 10.6 shows examples of threats.

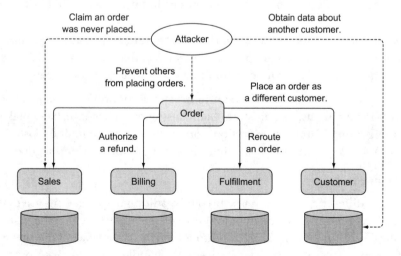

Figure 10.6 Use the STRIDE model to identify and categorize threats to the application.

TIP   The free Microsoft Threat Modeling Tool is a great way to develop and manage a threat model. It provides a drawing tool to model the data flow of the application, generate a STRIDE-based threat model of the data flow, analyze the threats, and track their corresponding mitigations. You can download the tool from https://www.microsoft.com/en-us/download/details.aspx?id =49168. Although the tool can be used to model threats to any application on any operating system, the 2016 version of the tool is available only for Windows.

Here are a few sample questions to get you started:

- *How do internal actors know that they're receiving messages from a trusted sender?* If an attacker finds a way to send messages directly to a service that's intended for internal use, checks that are supposed to have been performed by the sender can be bypassed. At minimum, this situation opens the application to data tampering, repudiation, and information-disclosure threats.
- *How do actors know that they're sending a message to a trusted receiver?* If an actor always sends a reply to the original sender, information disclosure is a risk because the sender address may be forged.
- *Are AJAX and WebSocket connections secured as well as the initial HTTPS request for the page?* One way to mount an identity-spoofing attack is to authenticate as one user and then change the username passed in subsequent requests. Potential solutions include not passing the username in the request, which could require maintaining session state on the server, and including a cryptographic signature with the data in the request to detect tampering with that data.
- *What limits resource consumption?* Suppose that the application starts a new actor for every new user. An attacker could exhaust all the memory by pretending to be many users at the same time, denying service to legitimate users. The elastic properties of a reactive system allow it to scale horizontally. Automatic scaling can fend off an attack but also could result in an expensive bill at the end of the month.
- *Can internal services be bypassed entirely?* This threat is especially important if the application uses a NoSQL persistence service that has an HTTP interface. Direct access to a data store can admit nearly any category of threat.

It's easier to attack a system directly than indirectly, so network access is a common theme across many threats. Administrative and customer-service interfaces make especially tempting targets. In the next section, you see a few ways to limit exposure to the outside world. (Making your job easier and the attacker's job harder is a good thing.)

10.2.2 *Barbarians at the gate*

Two important differences between reactive and traditional applications are that reactive applications tend to have many microservices and that they may be distributed across multiple servers, which translates into a large attack surface. One way to mitigate that threat is to create gateway services that handle requests from outside the

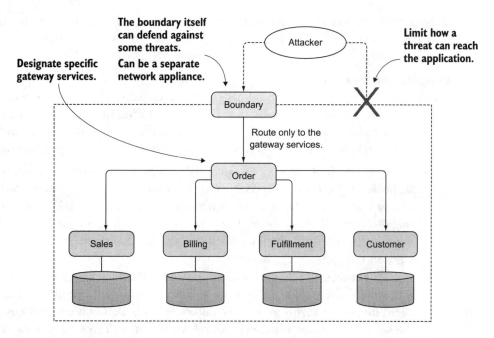

Figure 10.7 Allowing client access only to a few gateway services reduces the attack surface.

system and then ensure that other pathways into the system are blocked at the network level. Figure 10.7 shows this approach applied to the system described in the preceding section.

You have many ways to create a boundary that prevents traffic from reaching unauthorized endpoints, including the following:

- Preventing services on a private subnet from being reached directly via the internet
- Using a virtual private network (VPN) to encrypt and validate all communications among system components
- Using a firewall to monitor and block messages into the system

Each approach has advantages and disadvantages, and each can be used alone or in conjunction with others. What these approaches have in common is that they put the protected components in a common *threat zone*—a group of components that share a set of threats and defenses and that have a consistent level of trust in one another.

10.2.3 Adding HTTPS

HTTPS establishes Transport Level Security (TLS) on HTTP messages, which means that messages are encrypted between the two endpoints, so a client can communicate safely with a server. But which server? That question also can be answered by HTTPS, using a cryptographic certificate that's sent back to the client for verification. Modern browsers handle that verification automatically. Based on that information, a browser can be sure that it's connected to the intended server.

EVALUATING THE BENEFIT OF HTTPS

HTTPS also has the capability to validate in the reverse direction, so a client can present a certificate back to the server too. That form of identification is rarely used on the internet today. Instead, applications rely on means such as usernames and passwords. If you evaluate HTTPS in terms of the STRIDE threat model, you find that

- HTTPS in front of boundary services defends against threats that occur in transit between the client (browser) and the application. It does little to defend against compromised clients, though it has some benefit in conjunction with setting the secure flag in cookies. Consider this approach to be primarily a component of defending against identity spoofing, data tampering, and information-disclosure threats.
- HTTPS between services is useful to assure clients that they're communicating with valid services *if* they check the certificate. If it's important to validate the client too, client certificates are required. HTTPS used between services within the same threat zone is usually redundant. When HTTPS is used across threat-zone boundaries, the considerations are like those for boundary services.

Using HTTPS limits options for components such as load balancers, because the HTTP headers aren't visible to the intermediate nodes. Most often, HTTPS makes sense on the boundary between a browser and an application, but not for communication between servers within the application.

TERMINATING HTTPS

The point where an HTTPS connection is received and decrypted is called the *termination* of the connection. In the past, this function has been so computationally expensive that it often was left to dedicated hardware to perform Secure Sockets Layer (SSL) acceleration. This approach is seldom necessary with modern processors, but it still makes sense to isolate the termination from other functions. Often, the termination function is combined with load balancing. Following are some other approaches:

- Akka-HTTP can be configured for HTTPS.
- Play Framework provides a flexible web-facing front end.
- HAProxy or Nginx can be used as a load balancer and for termination.

The SSL configuration module used by Akka HTTP was originally part of the WS module from the Play Framework, so the first two options have a lot in common.

Now that the application is well tested and secure, it's well on the way to production readiness. Nothing ever seems to go that smoothly, of course. Sometimes, things go wrong, and you need to check application logs to discover what happened.

10.3 Logging actors

Logging is obviously message-driven. You might expect that nothing needs to be done to fit logging directly into a reactive system, but that's not true. The reason is that logging implementations often do the one thing that an actor shouldn't if it can possibly avoid doing so: perform synchronous I/O. In the most common logging packages, the decision about whether a message is logged synchronously or asynchronously doesn't come from the logger. Instead, that decision is made by the component, often called an `Appender`, that writes the message. `Appenders` usually are configured at runtime, which means that application code has no choice in the matter. A small change in log configuration can have a huge impact on performance.

This situation happens because logging libraries are designed to be simple and to work for any application; they don't assume that a sophisticated message-passing system is built into the application. In a reactive system, sophisticated message passing is exactly what you have available. The solution is to use this feature, and the next design choice is how to integrate it into the actors. Akka has that covered for you!

10.3.1 Stackable logs

Logging is a *cross-cutting concern*, which means that it's needed by many components that otherwise have little or nothing to do with one another. One way to approach these concerns is to use a *stackable trait*—a design pattern used to compose the functions of two different classes. You stack the logging function on top of another actor. Akka provides a stackable log in the form of `ActorLogging`, as shown in the following listing.

Listing 10.1 Stacking the ActorLogging trait on an actor

```
import akka.actor.{Actor, ActorLogging}

class SimpleLogging extends Actor with ActorLogging {

  override def receive = {
    case msg => log.info("Received {}", msg)
  }
}
```

> Stack ActorLogging to get a log that's integrated into Akka messaging.

> The methods of log are similar to those of other logging packages.

Stacking `ActorLogging` produces a `LoggingAdapter` that implements common functions such as `error`, `warn`, `info`, and `debug`. The implementations don't evaluate the parameters or perform string interpolation unless the log is enabled, so it isn't necessary to wrap these calls in the `isDebugEnabled` functions of some packages.

WARNING The log is intended for use within the actor, where thread safety isn't a problem. Be careful not to pass a reference outside the scope of the actor's thread, such as by referencing it in a `Future`.

The `LoggingAdapter` sends all log messages to an Akka *event bus*—an internal publish-and-subscribe system that's used to pass many of the built-in notifications that you've seen previously, such as actor life-cycle events, dead-letter notifications, and unhandled message errors.

Akka logging is intended to pass events to some other logging package that you select and configure.

10.3.2 Configuring the log system

Logging is configured through properties in application.conf. The default simply logs to stdout. For production, much more control is needed. The preferred configuration is a combination of *Simple Logging Façade for Java (SLF4J)* (http://www.slf4j.org) combined with *logback* (http://logback.qos.ch).

As shown in figure 10.8, filtering is applied to log events before they're published to the event bus, and the remainder of the logging is handled by the log event subscriber. You want the filtering to happen before a log event reaches the Akka event bus; otherwise, the production system could be clogged with debug messages that haven't yet been filtered. The approach Akka uses is to provide a `LoggingFilter` interface and an implementation, `Slf4jLoggingFilter`, that uses the SLF4J back end configuration rather than invent one of its own.

When the log event is published to the event bus, it can be read by a logger. The provided `Slf4jLogger` can be configured with logback as normal. If the application is being deployed to a containerized environment such as Docker, it's preferable to use the logback `ConsoleAppender` rather than the default stdout because it provides more control over filter configuration.

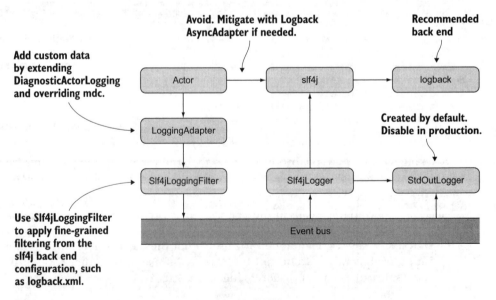

Figure 10.8 Akka integrates with logging through SLF4J.

Integration includes setting configuration parameters for the log system. The following listing shows a few of the values that you can set; more are available in the Akka documentation.

Listing 10.2 Log configuration in application.conf

```
akka {
  loggers = ["akka.event.slf4j.Slf4jLogger"]      ◄──┐
  loglevel = "DEBUG"
  logging-filter = "akka.event.slf4j.Slf4jLoggingFilter"      ◄──
  log-config-on-start = on
  log-dead-letters = 10
  log-dead-letters-during-shutdown = on
  actor {
    debug {
      lifecycle = on
      autoreceive = on
      receive = on
      unhandled = on
    }
  }
}
```

> **Recommended in place of the default StdOutLogger**

> **Consider filtering to only INFO or even higher in production.**

> **Refer to Akka documentation for auxiliary logging parameters.**

> **Activates additional filter based on the back end logging package**

> **Logs common actor events and messages**

TIP If the situation requires calling the logging package directly, such as a third-party JAR that has logging built in, be sure to configure an intermediate stage such as the logback `AsyncAppender` to prevent blocking I/O.

Sometimes, it's helpful to log every user message received by an actor. You can implement that type of logging easily by wrapping the receive function in the `Logging-Receive` trait, as shown in the following listing.

Listing 10.3 Logging every message received by an actor

```
import akka.actor.Actor
import akka.event.LoggingReceive

class WrappedLogging extends Actor {

  override def receive = LoggingReceive {      ◄──
    case _ => {}      ◄──
  }
}
```

> **Add LoggingReceive to log every message received by an actor, which also requires akka.actor.debug.receive = on to be configured in application.conf.**

> **Application Receive logic is within the LoggingReceive block.**

When something goes wrong in a monolithic application, you can often figure out what happened by analyzing the log messages associated with a single request. The same is true for a reactive application. The difference is that in a reactive application, the log messages associated with a single request may span many microservices. A few log options are related to remote messaging, but stitching logs together across many

JVMs to form a trace is difficult to do from scratch. Instead, consider using a dedicated system to collect and manage distributed trace events.

10.4   *Tracing messages*

Akka doesn't have tracing covered for you, but several solutions are available, so it isn't necessary to build something from scratch. Both of the monitoring tools described in section 10.5 include tracing modules that are specific to Akka. But because a dedicated tracing solution is designed to be general-purpose, it can cover both actor and nonactor system components.

Conceptually, tracing is simple. The systems that process messages generate trace events whenever a message is sent or received. Then the events are sent to a common collector, where they're correlated and queries can be run, as shown in figure 10.9. The result of a naïve implementation would be an immediate tripling of the number of messages being sent. You have the actual message, which is larger because of the tracing information that must be added, one trace message from the sender when a message is sent, and another from the receiver when a message is received. Two thirds of the traffic in the system would be sent to the single collector. This concentration of traffic wouldn't scale well, and it would scale even worse if you wanted to trace messages between actors within the same actor system in addition to messages that flow between systems. A tracing library can take care of managing the messages to the collector for you. Understanding a few basic strategies and selecting a tracing library such as one of the implementations described in the next section are enough to get you started.

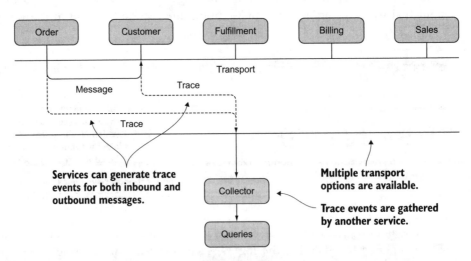

Figure 10.9   Tracing requires instrumentation on the services, a transport layer, and a collector to accumulate the trace events. Review the options available in the tracing package you choose.

> ### Different kinds of tracing
> This section describes tracing events related to processing a single transaction across multiple application components. Tracing also can be used to describe the events that come from a single component over the course of many transactions. Examples of this type of low-level tracing are dtrace and ktrace.

You can reduce message volume by accumulating trace events and sending many events to the collector in a single trace message. You can best accomplish this task with dynamic tuning to strike a balance between the number of events sent at the same time and the latency between when an event occurs and when it's sent to the collector. A good tracing package handles these concerns for you.

Another strategy to reduce volume is to sample events rather than trace every message. The decision to trace a chain of messages may be random, based on a parameter passed with the initial event, or based on some other criterion. One approach is to make a decision at the time of the initial event and carry it through subsequent messages. Alternatively, the decision may be delayed until after data is collected but not yet written to persistent storage.

In addition to deciding which events to trace and how to collect them, you must identify the data to be used to correlate events. One approach is to use application data from the log messages, such as customer identifiers, product stock-keeping units (SKUs), invoice numbers, account numbers, and so on. That approach may suffice in a small test environment, but it falls apart quickly in production. The queries are too complex, and developers must add the right information to the logs at the right place and at the right message level. A debug message isn't helpful if production operates with debugging turned off!

Rather than rely on application-specific information, it's preferable to have a consistent strategy for labeling events. One widely adopted strategy is the Dapper pattern.

10.4.1 Collecting trace data with the Dapper pattern

In 2010, Google described the Dapper pattern in a paper titled "Dapper, a Large-Scale Distributed Systems Tracing Infrastructure." When an initial message is received from the outside world, it triggers a tree of additional messages. The initial message is assigned a *trace ID*. In figure 10.10, that unique identifier is assigned by the order service. Each subsequent message is assigned a unique *span ID*, which is passed along with the trace ID. In the example, the first message from the order service is assigned span ID s1, which is passed along with the trace ID to the billing service. When the billing service in turn sends a message to the invoicing service, that message is also assigned a unique span ID. The new span ID is passed along with the original trace ID and the span ID of the parent message. The same pattern is repeated for the message from the order service to the fulfillment service; it continues to the warehouse, packing, and

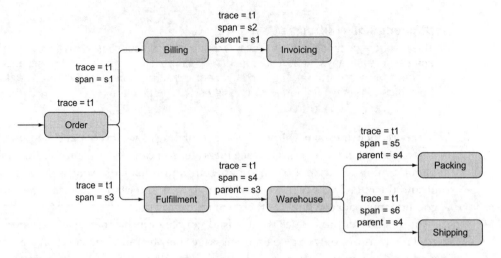

Figure 10.10 The original input is assigned a trace ID that's passed along with every resulting message. Each message is given a unique span ID, and the preceding (parent) span is also passed, if one exists.

shipping services. Using this data, you can construct the entire graph of messages triggered in response to a single initial message, and you can use the trace ID to correlate any message directly back to the original request without having to traverse each step along the way.

A minor weakness of the Dapper pattern is that it doesn't recognize when multiple messages come together to trigger a single outbound message. Figure 10.11 shows a simple case in which either of two messages in the "select carrier" actor could be considered to be the parent of an outbound message that contains the carrier selection. Normally, it's simplest to select the final message that arrives at the sending actor.

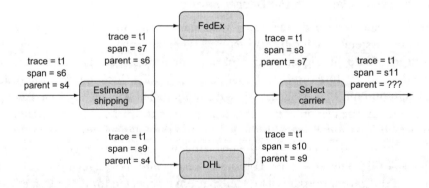

Figure 10.11 The Dapper pattern assumes that each message has a single parent span. When multiple messages are collected, the selection of which span to call "parent" may be arbitrary.

Several implementations are based on the ideas in the Dapper paper:

- *Dapper*—The original implementation by Google isn't open source at the time of writing, but the research paper that inspired many of the other efforts is available at http://research.google.com/pubs/pub36356.html.
- *Zipkin*—An open source implementation used by Twitter that draws heavily on the Dapper research paper, Zipkin (http://zipkin.io) offers some integration libraries supported by the OpenZipkin GitHub group and still more that are supported by the community. Zipkin is also interesting because it supports multiple transports, including HTTP, Kafka, and Scribe.
- *Jaeger*—A newer open source implementation from Uber that credits both the Dapper research paper and Zipkin as sources of inspiration (http://github .com/uber/jaeger).
- *Lightbend Telemetry*—A proprietary component of Lightbend Monitoring that integrates with Jaeger and Zipkin. Because it's embedded directly in Akka, it can provide instrumentation transparently as part of the configuration of the actors being monitored (https://developer.lightbend.com/docs/monitoring/ latest/extensions/opentracing.html).
- *Spring Cloud Sleuth*—An open source implementation specialized for Spring Cloud and featuring direct integration to Zipkin. Consider this implementation particularly in a mixed environment that includes both Spring and Akka components (http://cloud.spring.io/spring-cloud-sleuth).
- *Apache HTrace*—An open source implementation that as of this writing has Apache incubator status. It also has direct integration to Zipkin and features Java, C, and C++ libraries (http://htrace.incubator.apache.org).

Having multiple APIs available for tracing leads to the problem of having to choose one for your application. The task is further complicated by the features of the tracing system you choose, such as sampling, annotations, and different transports. Some libraries are available, but as of this writing, none has official support. Look at the existing instrumentations section of the documentation for the tracing system to find the latest developments.

10.4.2 Reducing dependencies with OpenTracing

OpenTracing (http://opentracing.io) addresses implementation dependence by providing standard instrumentation that can be configured with pluggable providers. OpenTracing was initiated by Ben Sigelman, who was also one of the authors of the Google Dapper research paper.

OpenTracing is based on a semantic model that's mapped idiomatically onto multiple programming languages. You use the language-specific OpenTracing API throughout your application and configure which tracing implementation will receive the data in just one place. Not every tracing implementation supports the complete set of languages, so you should consider all the components of your application in your choice of provider. Table 10.1 shows some of the combinations that are available.

Table 10.1   Most providers support the Java API but not a specialized Scala API. Check http://mng.bz/ Gvr3 for the latest support information.

Provider	Scala	Java	JavaScript	Go	Other
Zipkin		✓		✓	
Jaeger		✓	Node.js	✓	Python
AppDash				✓	
LightStep		✓	✓	✓	Python, Objective-C, PHP, Ruby, C++
Hawkular		✓			
Instana	✓	✓	Node.js		PHP, Ruby
SkyWalking		✓			

In OpenTracing, a span

- Begins a new global trace or joins an existing trace
- Has a name
- Has start and finish time stamps
- May have relationships to other spans, such as child of or follows from
- May have *tags*, which have a name and a primitive value such as a string, Boolean, or numeric value
- May have *log* items, which have a name and an arbitrary value

OpenTracing enables a span to identify multiple parent spans, which is a weakness of Dapper (discussed in the preceding section). But if the pluggable provider you use doesn't have that capability, only one parent is used.

Unless you're using Lightbend Telemetry you must do some integration with your actors, because Akka doesn't have built-in support for any of the OpenTracing providers.

10.4.3   *Integrating OpenTracing with Akka*

You've already learned that tracing involves the concept of a *span*, which is a chunk of processing that has its own trace measurements. In traditional systems, a span may be placed around a servlet receiving and responding to an HTTP request. An application might create additional child spans around a service call or database operation that happens during the course of processing the HTTP request.

In Akka, the most obvious place for a span is around an actor's `receive` function. Figure 10.12 shows that approach. As each message is received, you start a new span that continues for the duration of the receive processing. When your actor sends a message to another actor, it attaches context information about that span to the message. When

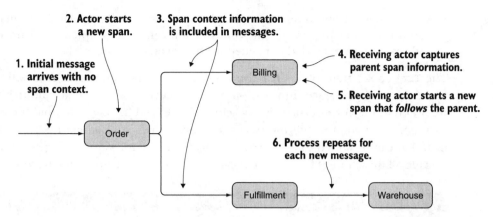

Figure 10.12 **Each actor starts a new span when it receives a message. If trace information about the sending span is found in the message, the new span records a reference to the parent.**

the receiving actor starts its span, it uses the context information to identify the sender as its *parent* span.

Before starting the integration, you need to add the OpenTracing API as a dependency in your build.sbt file. The examples in this section were created in version 0.31.0; add the following to libraryDependencies:

```
io.opentracing" % "opentracing-api" % "0.31.0"
```

Because the OpenTracing API is generalized for multiple languages and many design patterns, and is written in Java rather than Scala, the first step is creating a few adapters to fit better with Akka. The next section shows you an approach to building an adapter. After that, you use the adapter to instrument an example actor and configure an application with a tracer implementation.

BUILDING AN INTERFACE TO OPENTRACING

Each message carries the additional trace, span, and optional parent identifiers. In addition, metadata about each message sent or received by each actor needs to be collected and sent to the trace server. In a reactive system, the messages contain trace information, and the receive functions are instrumented to receive and manage the tracing spans. OpenTracing requires tracers to support two formats to carry the trace information: a binary format and a text-map format. For convenience and readability, choose a text map. The following listing shows a simple trait that can be mixed into message definitions.

Listing 10.4 Traceable messages with generic carrier information

```
trait Traceable {
  val trace: Map[String, String]
}
```
Trace information is carried in messages as an immutable Map.

> **NOTE** OpenTracing doesn't require the application to know what information is carried by the tracer. That information can be as simple as only trace and span IDs or extended as needed by the tracer.

The `Traceable` trait follows reactive conventions, so it's immutable. You will need a function to convert trace information from the current `Span` to an immutable `Map`. But where is the current span? Every actor being traced has a `var` to hold the current span and a function to tell the tracer to convert the span context information to a map that can be added to a `Traceable` message. The following listing shows how to provide all those things in a trait that can be added to any actor being traced.

Listing 10.5   Trait to hold the variable span and convert it to traceable representation

```
import io.opentracing.{Span, Tracer}
import io.opentracing.propagation.TextMap
import io.opentracing.propagation.Format.Builtin.TEXT_MAP
trait Spanned {

  val tracer: Tracer              ◁——  The tracer comes
                                        from the actor's Props.

  var span: Span = _              ◁——  The span state is
                                        a var, not a val.

  def trace(): Map[String, String] = {                              The span state is converted
    var kvs: List[(String, String)] = List.empty    ◁——             to a list of key-value pairs.
    tracer.inject(span.context(), TEXT_MAP, new TextMap() {  ◁——┐
      override def put(key: String, value: String): Unit =        The inject function is
        kvs = (key, value) :: kvs                                 supplied from the
                                                                  underlying tracer.

      override def iterator() =                        Injection doesn't need to
        throw new UnsupportedOperationException()      extract data from the message.
    })
    Map(kvs: _*)                   ◁——┐  Use the list of key-value pairs to
  }                                     create an immutable map that can
}                                       be included in a Traceable message.
```

Now that you have a way to hold a span and a way to add the span context information to an outbound message, the final piece you need is something to receive those messages and extract the span context.

As with logging, tracing is a cross-cutting concern, and stackable traits simplify implementation. `Receive` is just a type alias for `PartialFunction[Any, Unit]`, so a stackable version needs to override the `isDefinedAt` and `apply` functions. The `isDefinedAt` function just passes through to the `Receive` it's stacked on top of. The `apply` function

1 Extracts the span context from the incoming message
2 Starts a new span with a reference to the incoming span
3 Invokes the `apply` function on the underlying `Receive`
4 Finishes the span

Stackable tracing can be implemented as shown in the following listing.

```
import akka.actor.Actor.Receive

import io.opentracing.{SpanContext, Tracer}               Imports OpenTracing
import io.opentracing.propagation.Format.Builtin.TEXT_MAP  API components
import io.opentracing.References.FOLLOWS_FROM
import scala.util.{Failure, Success, Try}

class TracingReceive                          Require the wrapped Receive function
  (r: Receive, state: Spanned)                and the span state from the Actor.
  extends Receive {              Makes the trait stackable

  override def isDefinedAt(x: Any): Boolean =   Proxy isDefinedAt to the
    r.isDefinedAt(x)                            wrapped Receive function.

  override def apply(v1: Any): Unit = {         You can use the incoming message
    val operation: String = v1.getClass.getName  type as the operation name.

    val builder: Tracer.SpanBuilder =        Begins building
      state.tracer.buildSpan(operation)      the new span        Extracts the trace
                                                                 information from
    state.span = extract(v1) match {                            the incoming message
      case Success(ctx) =>
        builder.addReference(FOLLOWS_FROM, ctx).  Creates a reference to the
          startManual()                           sender, and starts the span
      case Failure(ex) =>
        builder.startManual()                       If no trace information
    }                                               was received, start a
    r(v1)                      Invokes the         new global span with
    state.span.finish()        wrapped Receive     no reference.
  }              Finishes     function
                 the span
  def extract(v1: Any): Try[SpanContext] = ???     The extract function
}                                                  is discussed next.
```

The extract function is implemented as a Try because it can fail in several ways, and you don't want the entire Receive to fail just because tracing information couldn't be extracted. If it fails, start a fresh global trace and continue. The extract can fail if the incoming message isn't Traceable, if the trace information is missing, or if the configured tracer is unable to read it. Other than error handling, the extract function is concerned mostly with converting mapping between Java and Scala collection data types, as shown in the following listing.

Listing 10.7   Extract decorator converts data types and handles errors

```
import io.opentracing.propagation.TextMap              The OpenTracing API uses
import java.util.{Iterator => JIterator, Map => JMap}  Java collections rather than
import scala.collection.JavaConverters._               their Scala counterparts.
```

```
def extract(v1: Any): Try[SpanContext] = v1 match {
  case m: Traceable =>
    if (m.trace.isEmpty) Failure(new NoSuchElementException("Empty trace"))
    else Try(state.tracer.extract(TEXT_MAP, new TextMap() {
      override def put(key: String, value: String): Unit =
    ➥ throw new UnsupportedOperationException()

      override def iterator(): JIterator[JMap.Entry[String, String]] =
        m.trace.asJava.entrySet().iterator()
    })) match {
      case Success(null) =>
    ➥ Failure(new NullPointerException
    ➥ ("Tracer.extract returned null"))
      case x => x
    }
  case _ =>
    Failure(new UnsupportedOperationException
    ➥ ("Untraceable message received"))
}
```

Extract function doesn't need to put data into the message.

Check whether the message can carry trace information.

OpenTracing extract may return null rather than throw an exception if no tracing data is found.

Otherwise, return the extracted trace information.

Signal messages that can't carry trace information.

Finally, an `apply` function in the companion object (see the following listing) makes stacking this trait more fluent, as you see in the next section.

Listing 10.8   The companion object

```
object TracingReceive {
  def apply(state: Spanned)(r: Receive): Receive =
    new TracingReceive(r, state)
}
```

Declare the Receive function as a second parameter list to make the trait easily stackable.

Now that you have a clean integration between Akka and OpenTracing, you can reap the benefits by instrumenting a few actors.

INSTRUMENTING AN ACTOR

Adding tracing to an actor is similar to adding logging. You include an appropriate library and add instrumentation around events that you want to trace. This example revisits the guidebook/tourist actor system from chapter 2. The source is available at http://mng.bz/oKwk. The first step is modifying messages to carry trace information by using the previously defined `Traceable` trait, as shown in the following listing.

Listing 10.9   Add traceability

```
object Guidebook {

  case class Inquiry(code: String)
  ➥ (val trace: Map[String, String])
  ➥ extends Traceable
}
```

Adds the trace information as a second parameter list

Labels the message as Traceable

TIP If a case class has multiple parameter lists, only the parameters in the first list are used to generate the `apply`, `unapply`, `equality` and other case class goodies. You can use multiple parameter lists to your advantage when adding trace information to messages. If you declare the trace information in the second parameter list, the rest of the actor can mostly ignore it.

Now that the guidebook message is `Traceable`, the next step is stacking `Tracing-Receive` on the existing `Receive` implementation. To prepare for that step, modify the `Guidebook` constructor to require a tracer. Next, add the `Spanned` trait to the actor so that it can keep track of the current span, and stack the trait. Finally, add a call to the `trace()` function as part of constructing `Guidance` messages. When you bring these steps together, the `Guidance` actor has the changes shown in the following listing.

Listing 10.10 Changes to the actor to support tracing

```
import java.util.{Currency, Locale}

import akka.actor.Actor
import Guidebook.Inquiry
import Tourist.Guidance
import io.opentracing.Tracer           ← The tracer is passed to
                                          the class constructor.
class Guidebook(val tracer: Tracer)  ←┘
⇒ extends Actor
⇒ with Spanned {                     ←┐ Adds span state
                                       │ to the actor
  def describe(locale: Locale) =
    s"""In ${locale.getDisplayCountry}, ${locale.getDisplayLanguage} is
    spoken and the currency is the
    ${Currency.getInstance(locale).getDisplayName}"""
                                          ┌ Stack TracingReceive on
  override def receive = TracingReceive(this){  ←┘ the receive function.
    case Inquiry(code) =>
      println(s"Actor ${self.path.name} responding to inquiry about $code")
      Locale.getAvailableLocales.filter(_.getCountry == code).
        foreach { locale =>
          sender ! Guidance(code, describe(locale))(trace())  ←┐ Adds the trace
        }                                                       │ information to
    }                                                           │ the message
  }
}
```

As you can see, the integration isn't too intrusive for the actor, especially when you consider how useful it can be to have a complete map of every message that passes through your application. Whether it makes sense to track *every* message is up to you. Some tracing systems allow you to be more selective, depending on the tracer that's configured into your application. We cover configuring a tracer in the next section.

CONFIGURING A TRACER IMPLEMENTATION

One nice aspect of OpenTracing is that the tracer configuration can be handled in one place, as part of application initialization. In an Akka-based system, configuring tracing means adding the tracer to the driver. Start by including the tracer library to build.sbt as a dependency. For this example, use the mock tracer that matches the tracing API version. Add the following to `libraryDependencies`:

```
io.opentracing" % "opentracing-mock" % "0.31.0"
```

The mock tracer itself is easy to configure, as shown in the following listing.

Listing 10.11 Instantiating the tracing implementation and updating Props

```
import akka.actor.{ActorRef, ActorSystem, Props}
import io.opentracing.Tracer                          Imports the OpenTracing API
import io.opentracing.mock.MockTracer                 and a mock implementation

object GuidebookMain extends App {
  val tracer: Tracer =
    new MockTracer(MockTracer.Propagator.TEXT_MAP)    Instantiates the tracer

  val system: ActorSystem = ActorSystem("BookSystem")

  val guideProps: Props = Props(classOf[Guidebook], tracer)   ◁——  Adds the tracer
                                                                    to the Props
  val guidebook: ActorRef =
    system.actorOf(guideProps, "guidebook")
}
```

You can complete the implementation by making similar changes in the `Guide-book.Inquiry` message and the `Tourist` actor. As in chapter 2, you can start the systems in separate JVMs by using

```
sbt "-Dakka.remote.netty.tcp.port=2553" "runMain GuidebookMain"
```

and

```
sbt "runMain TouristMain"
```

You should see messages exchanged exactly as before, but now they're being traced too! Because you used just a mock tracer for the example, the traces appear as additional console messages. When you've selected a tracing implementation, follow its instructions to replace the mock tracer with the real tracer. The changes should affect the `GuidebookMain` and `TouristMain` drivers, but not the actors themselves or the messages. The changes to the actors and messages are universal and should work unchanged with any tracer that supports the OpenTracing Java API.

Congratulations! You've just instrumented a reactive system to work with multiple tracing libraries.

Operating a complete tracing solution may be more than your application needs. Sometimes, you just want to discover which actors exchange messages with which other actors, and a full tracing solution is too heavy. For a lightweight solution to finding pathways among actors, consider the Spider pattern.

10.4.4 *Finding pathways with the Spider pattern*

Rather than provide a trace of every message, the Spider pattern simply identifies pathways through an actor system. As the system expands to many actors, that pattern is more useful than you might expect. Because the pattern is lightweight, it's well suited for tracking interactions that happen among actors within a single actor system. Those pathways can get quite complex!

In the Spider pattern, each actor keeps track of other actors that have

- Sent it messages
- Been sent messages
- Been created by it

Individual messages aren't traced, so it isn't necessary for them to carry unique identifiers. The message definitions within the application can remain unchanged. Instead, a new message is added to the application. As shown in Figure 10.13, the new message is a probe that tells each actor to collect all the connection information it has, pass it along to a collection actor, and forward the same probe to each of those actors so that they do the same thing. The initial probe is assigned a unique identifier that the actors use to ensure that they don't respond to the same probe more than once. The information is passed via the existing Akka transport.

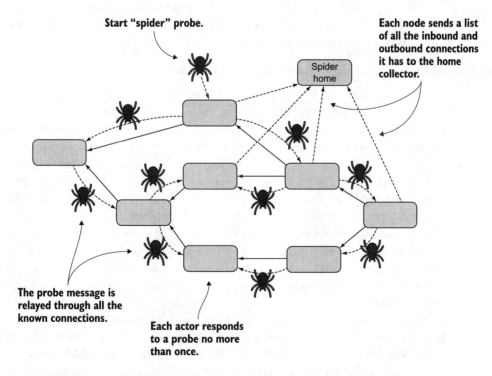

Figure 10.13 The Spider pattern is useful for finding connections among actors.

Implementing the Spider pattern requires the communicating actors to record the `ActorRefs` for the other actors. A drawback of this approach is that the `Actor` trait doesn't have an easy extension point to intercept messages, so the instrumentation may intrude into the actor code.

Raymond Roestenburg describes the Spider pattern in more detail in a blog post at http://letitcrash.com/post/30585282971/discovering-message-flows-in-actor-systems-with. The full post also describes ways in which this pattern can be extended to include diagnostic data, create a wiretap that copies all received messages, or perhaps kill slow actors.

Using the Spider pattern to kill slow actors requires knowing how fast the actor normally should perform, so that the pattern identifies unhealthy actors while leaving healthy actors to complete their tasks. Understanding the overall health of the application requires monitoring, which is the topic of the next section.

10.5   *Monitoring a reactive application*

If you add copious log messages to all the actors, turn on all the default logging, and configure the system to trace every message, you should be able to find bottlenecks where the application is slower than it needs to be. With all that instrumentation, the answer might well be that the logging itself is the bottleneck. At the other extreme, disabling the logging and tracing could make troubleshooting difficult or impossible.

There's no single correct way to get the right amount of monitoring, but some core metrics have proved to be useful. These are core metrics with Lightbend Monitoring and custom metrics with Kamon.

10.5.1 *Monitoring core metrics with Lightbend Monitoring*

In traditional systems, the emphasis is on monitoring indirect measures of system health, such as request threads, memory usage, and I/O operations. By contrast, the internals of an actor system focus on managing queues of work for actors to perform. The result is that monitoring focuses on counting things: number of actors, mailbox size, messages per minute, and the like. Figure 10.14 shows how counting is reflected in the default actor metrics displayed by the Lightbend Monitoring dashboard.

Reactive applications, particularly those that are based on strong domain-driven design, can use metrics that map more closely to the domain model. As you drill down from the dashboard into more detailed displays, Lightbend Monitoring shows metrics that are increasingly specialized to the actor system, such as how many actors of a type there are or the mailbox size for a group of actors that share a router. The Lightbend Telemetry component also features support for OpenTracing, as described in the preceding section.

Because actors and messages map to the domain model, you can ask real-world "Does this make sense?" questions about the metrics. If you have 50 percent more order actors than active customer orders, for example, that situation could be one to investigate. Likewise, if 1% of users appear to be clicking five times or more per second, that

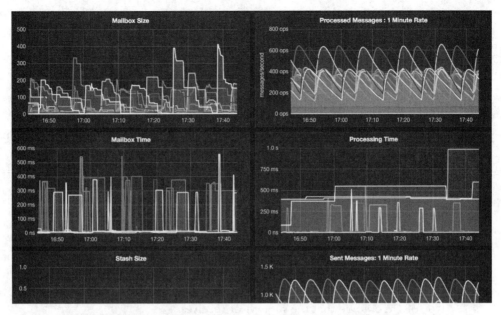

Figure 10.14   The Lightbend Monitoring dashboard emphasizes counts and rates.

statistic may indicate bot activity. The important thing is to remain curious about what the system is doing.

10.5.2   Creating a custom metric with Kamon

Kamon (www.kamon.io) is an open source tool for monitoring JVM applications. It integrates well with several popular toolkits for Reactive systems, including Akka, Spray, and Play Framework. It shines for its rich catalog of back end integrations. For simple development, you can use a back end that dumps metrics directly into application logs. In more advanced configurations, you can make a variety of choices. Because JMX is widely supported by commercial monitoring tools, you can use that back end as a bridge into enterprise systems as well.

Another benefit of Kamon is support for custom monitoring metrics. You can create instrumentation for exactly the measurement that's important. The down sides are that Kamon requires some development and that the documentation is sparse in places. Also, you need some familiarity with AspectJ, and the internals of Kamon use their own Akka and Spray configurations.

10.6   Handling failure

Distributed systems typically don't fail all at once. More often, individual services fail. One difficult design problem in a traditional architecture is deciding which component is responsible for recovery of which other components. Sometimes, the result is an endless stream of error messages in the log but no automated recovery. In an actor system, the answer is clear: every actor is a member of a supervision hierarchy and is responsible for all its child actors.

You really have only one recovery strategy: restart. Some basic design considerations are how much of the actor system to restart, how to prevent a large backlog of messages from accumulating during a restart, and how to ensure that data loss is zero or at least minimal.

Roland Kuhn has developed a more-advanced treatment of patterns for handling failure. He worked with Brian Hanafee and Jamie Allen to catalog them in *Reactive Design Patterns* (Manning Publications, https://livebook.manning.com/#!/book/kuhn/Chapter-1/).

10.6.1 *Deciding what to restart*

When a single child actor fails, the supervisor is notified through life cycle events and decides what to do. The most important decision is whether the failure handling should be applied just to the failing actor or to all the other supervised children as well. Within that strategy, the configuration can provide responses specific to each type of `Throwable` that the supervisor receives.

Often, the supervisor doesn't have enough information to make the best decision. If an actor experiences a networking error, for example, the error could be a transient problem affecting a single request, or it could be more pervasive. If the problem doesn't resolve itself right away, continually restarting a single actor or group of actors can exacerbate the problem. If multiple actor systems are using the same strategy, all of them may restart at the same time, and when the problem is cleared, it could lead to an immediate deluge of requests to the same service. One way to address this problem is to use a backoff strategy. In this strategy, the supervisor adds a delay before restarting. The length of delay increases randomly with each restart.

10.6.2 *Routing considerations*

An `ActorRef` survives a restart, so other actors continue sending messages, perhaps before the restarting actor is ready to process them. If an actor is going to take a long time to restart, you may want to suspend sending it new requests for some period, as shown in figure 10.15.

Keeping multiple remote routers apprised of the state of potentially multiple actors restarting can become very complex, especially considering that the network may have been the original source of the problem leading to the restart. Almost always, it's better to allow messages to continue to be queued during the restart or to use a local router with a pool strategy that takes workload into account, such as a `SmallestMailboxPool`.

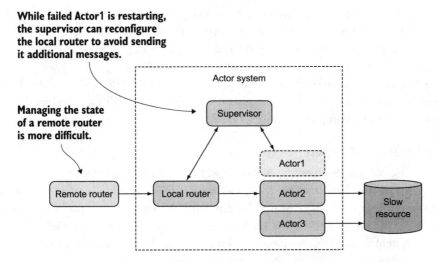

While failed Actor1 is restarting, the supervisor can reconfigure the local router to avoid sending it additional messages.

Managing the state of a remote router is more difficult.

Figure 10.15   It may be necessary to suspend sending messages to a redundant actor if recovery will take a long time.

10.6.3 *Recovering, to a point*

The amount of time allocated to getting the system running again is known as the *recovery time objective* and is one of two critical measurements for failure recovery, the other being the *recovery point objective*. The recovery point measures how much information, if any, was lost forever because of the failure (figure 10.16).

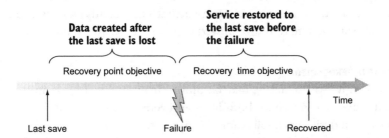

Figure 10.16   The recovery point objective measures how much data can be lost, and the recovery time objective measures how quickly the system is expected to recover to that point.

In a CQRS design such as you saw in chapter 8, the separation of recovery time and recovery point is made clear by the design itself. The command side is vulnerable to losing data from commands that hadn't yet executed when the actor failed. The query side can't lose any data, but building up a new cache can delay complete recovery.

In a traditional transactional database design, the recovery point is defined by the last successful commit to the database. If the commit boundaries don't correspond to handling a complete message, the database could be left in an inconsistent state that requires manual intervention to correct.

Recovering data that has been saved to disk is outside the scope of this book. For the most part, that discipline focuses on ensuring that writes are redundant so that failure of a single component doesn't lose data.

10.7   Deploying to a cloud

It's almost certain that your application will need to be packaged for deployment to some sort of cloud environment, such as Amazon Web Services (AWS) or Google App Engine. At the very least, it would be convenient to generate a package appropriate for the host operating system, such as deb or rpm packages for Debian/Red Hat Linux systems, msi for Windows, or dmg for OS/X. You can accomplish all those things and more by using the sbt native packager.

Packaging the application alone is no guarantee that the application will run successfully in every environment. It's very easy to create hidden dependencies on the runtime environment that constrain portability. One well-known approach to removing dependencies is the Twelve-Factor Application.

10.7.1   Isolating the factors

The *Twelve-Factor Application* concept, formalized by Adam Wiggins at www.12factor .net, describes a methodology for building applications that are easily manageable in a Platform as a Service (PaaS) environment. This approach was created based on Adam's experience with Heroku, but is equally applicable to other environments.

One factor is managing the code base so that each component is a separately deployable application. The deployment strategy can be further refined in a reactive application.

MANAGING CODE DEPENDENCIES

As a reactive design evolves, actors may be moved from one actor system to another. Sometimes, it makes sense to have both local and remote instances of the same actor available. In a well-designed application, it makes no difference to the actors how they're distributed. The deployment configuration can evolve as needed.

It would be inconvenient if the code base had to be refactored every time a deployment decision changed. At minimum, each actor system should be managed as a separate code base. Use that code base to contain the `main` function, extract environment variables, create the actor system, set up routers, start the initial actors, and perform any other housekeeping chores that would change if the deployment changed. Figure 10.17 shows the general idea.

The actors themselves can be packaged in whatever way makes sense for the domain model. In relatively small applications, it's convenient to define messages in

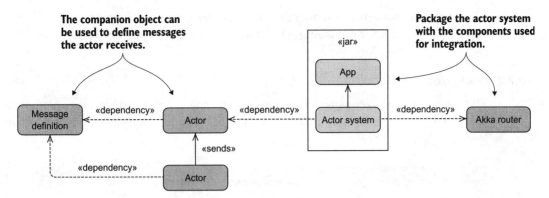

The companion object can be used to define messages the actor receives.

Package the actor system with the components used for integration.

Figure 10.17 Organize the application build components so that collaborating actors can be organized into the same actor system or different actor systems.

the companion object to the actor that receives them. As the system grows, that approach can create unwanted dependencies between the interface contracts and their corresponding implementation, at which point it makes sense to refactor them into separate traits.

Eventually, the application complexity may grow to the point that message serialization must be managed explicitly. Akka includes an extension point, `akka .serialization.Serializer`, that you can use to configure a serializer or inject a custom implementation. It even allows different serializers to be used for different classes, through the `akka.actor.serialization-bindings` configuration.

CONFIGURING WITH ENVIRONMENT VARIABLES

Akka's powerful configuration system allows you to configure many aspects of an application dynamically, without recompiling the code. Some aspects of configuration need to change in each deployment environment, however. Normally, development and production require different URLs for data storage, for example. It would be unwieldy and error-prone to keep separate application.conf files for each environment. Instead, those values should be provided by environment variables.

The syntax for referencing an environment variable within application.conf is straightforward, as shown in the following listing.

Listing 10.12 Instantiating the tracing implementation and updating Props

```
akka {
    enabled-transports = ["akka.remote.netty.tcp"]
    netty.tcp {
        hostname = ${?HOST}
        port = 2552
    }
}
```

The value of the $HOST environment variable will be substituted.

In a containerized environment such as Docker, use default ports and let the container handle port mapping.

When you have the environmental dependencies extracted from your application, the application is ready for packaging. One popular packaging option is Docker, as we discuss in the next section.

10.7.2 *Dockerizing actors*

The sbt native packager plugin makes it easy to build a Docker image for an application. Enable this plugin by adding it to the project/plugins.sbt file, as shown in the following listing.

> **Listing 10.13 project/plugins.sbt for the SBT Native Packager**

```
addSbtPlugin("com.typesafe.sbt" % "sbt-native-packager" % "1.3.4")
```

Next update build.sbt to enable the plugin, as shown in the following listing.

> **Listing 10.14 build.sbt updates for the SBT Native Packager**

```
name := "MyAppName"                                    ◁—  The name will be used as
                                                           the default container name
version := "1.0"                      ◁—                    for the Docker image.
                                         The version will be used
// ...additional directives              as the default container
                                         tag for the Docker image.
enablePlugins(JavaAppPackaging)   ◁—
                                    Enabling JavaAppPackaging automatically enables
                                    DockerPlugin and adds the archetype necessary for
                                    Akka to be packaged as a stand-alone application.
```

> **Setting the Docker tag**
>
> By default, the Docker tag is taken from the version property in build.sbt. If you prefer, you can override this value in build.sbt. To have images always tagged as the latest in Docker, for example, add the following line:
>
> ```
> version in Docker := "latest"
> ```

At this point, the command

```
sbt docker:stage
```

generates a Docker file and stages all the project dependencies in the target/docker/ stage directory. If a Docker server is running locally, use the command

```
sbt docker:publishLocal
```

to take the additional step of building the image. Verify that the procedure worked by using the docker command, as follows:

```
$ docker images
REPOSITORY        TAG        IMAGE ID        CREATED          SIZE
myappname         1.0        fe20268f78d9    6 seconds ago    662.9 MB
java              latest     861e95c114d6    2 weeks ago      643.2 MB
```

Many cloud providers can use Docker images. An easy way to get started is to install `docker-machine` and check the latest documentation for available drivers.

10.7.3 *Other packaging options*

If your application won't be run in a Docker container, other packaging options are available.

The Sbt Native Packager is built around format and archetype plugins. Format plugins describe how the application files are packaged for different target systems. In addition to the Docker format described in the preceding section, Native Packager includes formats for Windows, Linux (Debian and RPM), and Oracle's javapackager tool. Archetype plugins are concerned with application structure and scripting. The archetypes cover a wide variety of situations and are highly customizable to fit other situations.

Summary

- The Akka `TestKit` simplifies testing actor behavior. Some commonly used patterns can be combined to create necessary test conditions.
- Application security begins with a threat model that's used to analyze different ways in which the application may be attacked. The STRIDE system provides a systematic way to manage the threat model.
- Encrypted transports can limit the attack surface of an application.
- Logging is a side effect, just like any other I/O operation. Log messages should be treated the same way as any other message in a reactive application. Akka includes built-in support for message-based logging, using SLF4J and logback.
- Tracing involves instrumentation, a transport layer, a collector, and a query engine. OpenTracing provides an API for tracing, and other open source libraries integrate with OpenTracing.
- Kamon and Lightbend Monitoring provide monitoring metrics that are customized for Akka-based systems.
- Ability to recover from failure is measured by a recovery time objective and a recovery point objective. The recovery time objective measures how long it takes to become stable again. The recovery point objective measures how much data is lost.
- Dependencies on the environment should be factored out of the application and supplied by the runtime environment.
- The Sbt Native Packager can assemble an application for deployment to a cloud container service in Docker format and supports several other native package formats.

index